BOOTYFOOD

A DATE-BY-DATE, COURSE-BY-COURSE,
NIBBLE-BY-NIBBLE GUIDE TO CULTIVATING
LOVE AND PASSION THROUGH FOOD

BOOTYFOOD

JACQUI MALOUF

WITH LIZ GUMBINNER
PHOTOGRAPHS BY BEN FINK

BLOOMSBURY

Published by Bloomsbury, New York and London
Distributed to the trade by Holtzbrinck Publishers

Library of Congress Cataloging-in-Publication Data has been applied for.

ISBN 1-58234-263-6

First U.S. Edition 2004

10 9 8 7 6 5 4 3 2 1

Design by Elizabeth Van Itallie
Printed by C&C Offset Printing Company Ltd, China

FOR JIMMY AND KENNA, MY NEW FAMILY. I LOVE YOU.

CONTENTS

INTRODUCTION

BOOTY *n.* 1. A valuable prize, award, or gain. 2. *slang* Sexual intercourse.
FOOD *n.* Something that physically nourishes.
BOOTY FOOD *n.* Any food that causes weak knees, accelerated heartbeat, tingly body parts, and other symptoms traditionally associated with falling in love.

The parallels between food and sex (two of my favorite primal urges) have been drawn a million times. But interestingly enough, people rarely discuss the connection between food and relationships. Couples meet over food, they fall in love over food, and, if they're really naughty, they do stuff with whipped cream well after dessert time is over. "Our place" is more inclined to be a restaurant than a hardware store. "Our song" may be the one that was playing in the café on the very first date. And when couples break up, there are certain dishes laden with so much meaning, they never want to prepare them again.

Once you become aware of the monumental role that eating and cooking play in a romance, I guarantee you'll start having more fulfilling dining and dating experiences. Food can serve as a litmus test of relationship potential; if you've got culinary compatibility, your relationship is probably on the right track. Couples who cook together in the kitchen *cook* together in life.

For this reason, *Booty Food* is so much more than an aphrodisiac cookbook; it's about turning any food into an aphrodisiac.

Certainly there are plenty of yummy recipes on these pages involving oysters and caviar and the like, but I believe any food you're passionate about can get the proverbial juices flowing if shared with the right person under the right circumstances. Looking back through my own sordid past, I've realized that the most gratifying carnal encounters can equally start with a gourmet meal or with a fast-food burger on the side of the highway. (Don't tell the Rhode Island state troopers!) It just proves that it's not merely the food you eat that lends itself to adults-only activities, but the emotion that it invokes.

Fortunately, the world of sensual gourmet escapades is not limited to those with culinary-school diplomas. Whether your signature dish is coquilles St. Jacques or spaghetti and meatballs, prepare it with love, serve it on the good china, devour it by candlelight, and it could very well lead to one of those crazy, hold-onto-the-bedposts, all-night sessions that legends are made of. *Booty Food* isn't about being chained to the stove. (Wouldn't you rather be chained to the bed?) That's why you'll find plenty of time-savers and store-bought shortcuts to help you get over culinary performance anxiety or to allow you to realize your epicurean fantasies even more easily. Now, certainly not everyone eats the same way and not everyone loves the same way. Start this book at chapter 1, or open right to the section on naughty dessert activities. Make the breakfast recipes for dinner. Serve the first-date meal on your sixth date or make the party dishes for your in-laws—whatever turns you on. Although this book is overflowing with great suggestions, let it serve as a springboard for your imagination. Don't get too rigid with it. That could be the equivalent of holding up the *Kama Sutra* in bed, spending an hour turning the picture every which way to make sure you're doing "The Splitting of a Bamboo" right, and completely ruining the mood. What's the fun in that?

My only hope is that after spending some time with *Booty Food*, you are inspired to leave the office behind for a night, grab someone you love, and get busy on the kitchen counter.

Now go get some.

BOOTYFOOD

phase I
HEAT

Dating gets a bad rap. Married couples sigh to their single friends, *"We're so glad we don't have to go through* that *anymore."* You'd think they were referring to oral surgery and not the most electric and endearing part of many relationships. Although the search for a mate can be arduous at times, dating is great fun; so much fun, in fact, that it can become addictive. I'm sure you know the type who

S

never quite moves past the thrill of first and second dates (and first and only one-night stands). But when dating becomes courtship, things get really exciting. Just think of all the intoxicating firsts you're going to experience: the first awkward dinner followed by that first unforgettable kiss, the first homemade meal, the first sweaty make-out session. And, eventually, if things go your way, the first homemade breakfast. The deluge of romantic potential is an aphrodisiac in itself.

UP

first date eating

There are no recipes in this chapter because cooking isn't something you do on a first date—unless you want to sabotage it before it begins. So if you are fortunate enough to have already found a committed partner, skip this chapter. Then again, go ahead and read it. It just might remind you of how lucky you are.

THE MEET

There are entire books and countless magazine articles devoted to the topic of seeking out a potential mate, but here's my quick take on the subject.

Before you start stocking up on chocolate body paint, pushing the granny underwear to the back of the dresser drawer, or getting your kitchen in tip-top shape for erotic cooking adventures, there's one crucial thing you have to do: Get yourself a first date.

Conventional wisdom suggests that finding your soul mate, particularly once you hit thirty, ranges in difficulty from improbable to impossible. I beg to differ. People fall in love at eighteen and people fall in love at eighty. And sometimes, eighteen-year-olds fall in love with eighty-year-olds.

Whoever you are, wherever you live, and however many candles were on your last birthday cake, you are not going stumble upon the love of your life while moping around your living room watching Sally Jesse give makeovers to lucky ex-convicts.

You may be wondering, "Well, where the heck is he [or she]?" Chances are, the love of your life is out there somewhere, wondering the very same thing. Which means that out there (or oat there, as we Canadians say) is where you have to be too. Contrary to popular belief, there are plenty of ways to meet someone.

First, there's the much-maligned blind date. Some people just loooove being fixed up (I think there are two, actually), but it scares the bejesus out of me, both as the fixer and as the fixee. If you're going to allow friends to set you up, make sure they know you both pretty well. They should have your interests at heart and a good sense of what you're both looking for in a romantic partner. "Well, you're single and, uh . . . he's single" is not a good enough reason to accept a blind date with your friend's nice coworker from accounting.

The best blind-date advice I ever heard: You don't want to know too much about him before you meet, and he shouldn't know too much about you. If your well-intentioned yenta friend gushes that he kind of looks like George Clooney, there is no way in the world he can possibly live up to the image dancing around in your head. (Unless George has an identical twin that the world is not yet aware of, in which case I have first dibs.) Simply get any disclaimers out of the way—recently divorced, vertically challenged, lazy eye—and then trust your friend's judgment. The rest is up to chemistry or fate.

All skepticism aside, I know plenty of happily married couples who met on blind dates. As with tag sales, my motto is "You never know unless you go."

Which brings us to the 21st-century version of the blind date: the cyberdate. Using an Internet dating service is just like blind dating, and you don't have a friend to blame if the chick turns out to have a hump and not such a great personality after all.

Again, temper any high expectations you might have. People tend to be different on paper than they are in person. It's a lot like house hunting; everyone has fallen in love with a real estate listing at one time only to discover that the place is a pit. Which is not to say that everyone on the Internet lies—only most of them do. Hope for the best but expect the worst and you'll never be disappointed.

There's no accounting for chemistry. Which is why I have found that the best *meets* often happen in the flesh.

Bars, restaurants, nightclubs, and parties are tried-and-true locales for scoping out a long-term booty partner. But don't forget the post office, the modern-art museum, the supermarket, the dog run, the local bookstore, the airport gate, the commuter train, the save-the-caribou rally, the blaxploitation film festival; you never know where love may lurk.

If you want to take a more active role in your quest for booty on demand, volunteer for a cause that interests you or sign up for a course that sounds fun. It could be photography, screenwriting, politics, crop rotation in 14th-century Europe—it doesn't matter. You'll be assured that you share at least one common interest with your classmates, and one of your fellow mind-expansion seekers just may be The One. And leave it to me to suggest you investigate a wine-tasting seminar or a cooking course in your area. Your class will be filled with those who share your culinary passion or, perhaps, culinary ineptitude. At best, you'll come away with mad cooking skills and a partner with whom you can make beautiful pasta for decades to come. At worst, you get to eat your homework.

However you meet, soon enough it will be time for the first nerve-wracking date.

DINNER FOR TWO

Congratulations! You've made it this far, and that's no small feat. You're wearing an outfit you didn't just pick up off the closet floor, and you're armed with plenty of questions and friends' advice ("be interested not interesting," *yadda yadda* . . .). Plus, you have a lifeline standing by to ring your cell phone with a "family emergency" just in case.

So where are you going? Out to eat, of course.

Some people like to go to a movie or a play on a first date. I believe that this defeats the whole purpose of your rendezvous, which is to get to know each other better. You can't talk to each other in the theater, and if you do, you will completely annoy the audi-

table language

We're all familiar with body-language cues: crossing your arms, fiddling with your hair, touching your face. How about table language? Here's a completely unscientific but not too far-fetched look at the implications of your date's dining behavior:

- **Asks for dressing on the side** *Finicky in bed*
- **Orders meat rare** *Voracious in bed*
- **Orders extra-spicy** *Owns sex toys*
- **Orders chicken** *Prefers missionary position*
- **Sends food back** *Hard to please*

- **Doesn't like chocolate** *Doesn't like sex*
- **Orders oysters on the first date** *Premature ejaculator or will rush you down the aisle*
- **Orders caviar on the first date** *Overzealous; will stalk you*
- **Eats every course** *Can go for hours*
- **Flirts with the server** *Will sleep with your best friend*
- **Checks teeth/lipstick in knife** *Checks his or her hair during sex*
- **Finishes your food** *Steals the sheets*
- **Won't let you pay** *Wants to take care of you*
- **Stingy tipper** *Will buy you a Hershey's bar for Valentine's Day*
- **Orders coffee before you've finished eating** *Will please himself then instantly roll over*

SPINACH IN THE TEETH! SPINACH IN THE TEETH! It happens to everyone. Yes, even me. My advice? Mention it as if it's no big deal, then move on. If he or she catches it in the mirror before you point it out, your date will know you saw it and could remain mortified for the rest of the night. And that's not very conducive to a good-night kiss. But please, under no circumstances should you check your teeth in the knife. Even if you've eaten poppy seeds à la poppy seeds. That's like an instant "Don't call me, I'll call you" in my book.

ence. And with my luck, I will be among them. Besides, there's something a little disconcerting about sitting next to a stranger in the dark for two hours.

The ideal first date is a quiet dinner out together. Lunch is always an option, although there's not much sexual tension during the day and the lighting is never flattering.

I can't possibly evaluate a potential paramour until we've shared an entire meal together. I'm curious to see what he orders, how he orders it, and how he eats it. I want to know if he's rude to waiters or a lousy tipper—as a former waitress, these things matter to me and they can say a lot about a person. Is he a beer guy or a wine guy? Does he take sugar in his latte or reach for those evil little packets of chemicals? Does this sound like a lot of scrutiny for my suitor? Too bad. If you want some of this, baby, we're going to dinner.

Eating out together is a perfect way to examine whether this person will be worthy of a coveted spot on your speed dial. You're stuck together for an hour or more with nothing to do besides get to know each other better. As you chat, you'll certainly be making mental notes about the person across the table. And although I'm describing a man here, these questions hold true for both men and women:

➤ **CAN HE HOLD A CONVERSATION:** Is he charming and engaging? Does he talk at you or with you? Could you drive a double-wide truck through all the pregnant pauses? Is he getting a stiff neck from scanning the room whenever it's your turn to speak?

➤ **DOES HE HAVE A SENSE OF HUMOR:** Surveys indicate that this is the primary trait women look for in a man. (Surveys also indicate that people lie in surveys.) Is he more Jerry Seinfeld or Andrew Dice Clay? Are you laughing at his painfully funny anecdote about his first job interview, or are you wincing at his walrus impression, complete with straws up his nose?

➤ **IS HE INSECURE:** Is he trying too hard to impress you with his famous ex-girlfriend/Jaguar convertible/postgraduate degrees/future inheritance? Does he drop a dozen names of celebs in the first five minutes and refer to each of them as "a great friend of mine"? Does he start to turn purple when you mention that you may have, at one time in your life, gone on a date with a man before him?

➤ **DO YOU HAVE COMMON INTERESTS:** Would he rather spend a weekend spelunking in Vermont or shopping in Paris? Is he a cat person or a dog person? Which musicians get the most play on his CD changer? Does he like to cook or is he a SpaghettiOs kind of guy?

➤ **DOES HE HAVE BAGGAGE:** Does he unconsciously tear his napkin into shreds while describing his ex? Is it a cloth napkin?

ANYTHING BUT WHITE ZINFANDEL

Whether you're male or female, the ability to order wine well is a major turn-on. For me, a man who can deftly find his way around a wine list makes me think that he will be equally confident between the sheets. Choosing wine doesn't have to be intimidating. There are dozens of great wine books out there, and in a good restaurant the sommelier ("wine guy," for the uninitiated) will help you out if you just point him in a direction. If you don't know what kind you like, think about tastes you do like. Throw around words like *fruity* or *full* or *crisp* and you'll sound like you know what you're talking about. Let's say there are ten wines on the menu and you know none of them. Pick something between the second least expensive and the middle price range. It never fails. And don't worry too much about that outdated "white with poultry, red with meat." Drink what you like. I've had some highly memorable cheeseburger-Chardonnay experiences.

➤ IS HE EMOTIONALLY READY FOR A COMMITTED RELATIONSHIP: Does he spend an inordinate amount of time describing his sexual conquests? Does he think a wild kegger is the be-all and end-all on a Saturday night? Does he still believe it's his destiny to work ninety-hour weeks until he dies? Does he off-handedly refer to marriage as "an institutional evil created by man"?

➤ WOULD YOU SOONER HANG NAKED BY YOUR WRISTS IN TIMES SQUARE AT RUSH HOUR THAN ENDURE ANOTHER DATE WITH HIM: Sometimes, that's just how it goes. Better to find out now.

And, of course, you'll need to ask all these questions of yourself. This is a two-way evaluation. So be charming, be interested, be cool. A first date may be the last time you're both on your best behavior, so make the most of it.

Remember that when it comes to desperation, people have a fine-tuned olfactory sense; they can smell it like bloodhounds. Just relax and let the date run its course. And be happy! People who are happy with themselves attract other people who are happy with themselves. Together, they become very happy couples. This, in turn, makes sad, single people even more depressed. And thus, the cycle continues.

Good manners are key at all times, but especially during your first dinner together. You don't have to memorize Emily Post to adhere to the basic rules of etiquette. And I'm not talking about Rules rules. Just good, commonsense rules.

If you're a man, let your date walk to the table ahead of you. This is a big deal where I'm concerned. Allow her to sit with her back to the wall so she can see and be seen. Don't open your menu until she does, and let her order first. Good manners indicate that you're likely to be attentive to her away from the dining table—or on the dining table—as well. Behave in a way that would make your mom proud, but don't go overboard; a guy who orders for me without knowing my tastes raises an instant "control freak" flag. Just relax and have fun.

YOU ARE WHAT YOU ORDER

So far, your date is charming, witty, polite, and, gosh, aren't those green eyes just *dreamy?* Hey, you're not doing so badly yourself either. But the truth is, none of it may mean squat. The eating part is where the true connection begins.

As I mentioned before, I put a lot of stock in a first meal with a man. It's primal; the human race has two basic needs in order to survive—food and procreation. So why shouldn't one lead to the other? Food not only fuels our bodies, it fuels our passion. I'm pressed to recall even one romantic comedy where the sparks didn't fly over a shared meal.

Your menu selection definitely has implications. So think good and hard about what you order on your first date. I'm no herbivore; meat is my manna, and that could be a problem if I

a side of guatemala

Working in the restaurant industry you hear it all. My favorite has to be: "She'll have the fajitas [silent j pronounced] with a side of Guatemala." The Guatemalans might be mildly amused by this, but your date might not. Go ahead and point at the item if you're afraid to say it out loud. Or simply ask your server how to say it. Unless he's a complete snob or hoping for a smaller tip, he should enjoy playing the expert.

I'm no Berlitz instructor, but here are a few pronunciations of commonly butchered food words. Can't hurt; could help. Even I have a hard time with niçoise and dauphinoise, but when said correctly, foreign-food words can be a major turn-on (remember *A Fish Called Wanda?*)

On the other hand, words said with over-gusto can be off-putting and pretentious. You don't want to come off as Mr. I-Took-Italian-Classes. And please don't call a tomato a *tomahto* unless you're holding a British passport.

FRENCH:	Coq au Vin	coke oh *van*
	Crepes	kreps
	Croissants	kwah-*sahn*
		(not crass-*ant*!)
	Dauphinoise	doh-feen-*wahz*
	Fois Gras	fwah *grah*
	Niçoise	nee-*swahz*
	Paillard	pie-*yard*
	Steak au Poivre	steak oh pwav
	Ratatouille	*rat*-tat-*too*-ee
	Quiche	keesh
VEGGIES:	Radicchio	ra-*deek*-ee-oh
	Endive	*en*-dive, on-*deeve*
	Haricot Verts	*har*-ick-oh vayr
ITALIAN:	Bruschetta	brusk-*etta*
	Espresso	ess-*press*-oh
		(not *express*-oh!)
	Pancetta	pan-*chet*-uh
	Fettuccine	*fet*-uh-*chee*-nay
	Aglio y Olio	*ah*-lee-oh ee *oh*-lee-oh
	Osso Buco	*ah*-so *boo*-ko
	Carpaccio	car-*pahtch*-ee-oh

MEXICAN:	Quesadilla	*kess*-uh-*dee*-yah
	Guacamole	gwak-ah-*mole*-ee
	Fajitas	fa-*hee*-tahs
	Tortilla	tor-*tee*-yah
	Salsa verde	salsa *vayr*-day
	Mole	*mo*-lay
WINE:	Cabernet	cab-er-*nay*
	Merlot	mayr-low
	Pinot Grigio	pee-noh gree-jee-oh
	Pinot Noir	pee-noh nwar

FIRST DATE RED FLAGS

SHE SLIPS THE WAITER HER PHONE NUMBER WHILE YOU'RE PAYING THE BILL.

HE DECIDES THAT YOU OWE A LITTLE MORE TAX SINCE YOU HAD THE PIE.

HE STILL REFERS TO HIS EX-WIFE AS HIS WIFE.

SHE DESCRIBES HER FANTASY NUPTIALS, INCLUDING THE MOMENT WHERE YOU BOTH JUMP OUT OF THE PLANE.

HE REFUSES TO TAKE OFF THE HEADPHONES.

SHE STILL REFERS TO HER HIGH SCHOOL BOY-FRIEND AS "THE BASTARD."

SHE PICKS A FIGHT WITH A GUY A LOT BIGGER THAN YOU ARE.

HIS FRENCH ACCENT MYSTERIOUSLY DISAPPEARS BY DESSERT.

HIS WEDDING RING FALLS OUT OF HIS POCKET.

were dating a veggie guy. Everyone has his or her own dating deal-killers when it comes to food.

In general, guys dig chicks who eat. What is it about women who are nervous to eat in front of men? I'm scared to think of what goes on—or doesn't go on—in these women's bedrooms. Trust me, ladies. If you pick at your hold-the-cheese, hold-the-dressing salad, you're not going to come across as a woman who brings men to their knees on a regular basis. But a woman who's not afraid to pick up a rack of juicy spare ribs and lick them to the bone? Buckle up, guys. You're in for a wild ride.

You don't want to set yourself up for clumsy moments, either. Just this one time, you might want to avoid foods that take some dexterity to get from plate to mouth. Linguine, small bony birds, and onion soup can be dangerous; there's nothing more awkward than inadvertently flinging red sauce on your date's shirt or sending a Cornish game hen flying across the room.

GO FOODS VERSUS NO FOODS

Scrod isn't sexy. It just isn't. Even the word itself is the semantic equivalent of thinking about baseball during sex. Scrod is what I'd call a No food. A food that says "I have to be getting back to the convent now." The recipes you'll find in the ensuing chapters are Go foods, or foods that promote *It*. It. As in, "What do you mean, you two haven't done *It* in the kitchen yet?"

Now let's get the whole aphrodisiac thing out of the way, shall we? Yes, it has actually been proven that there are certain foods that can turn the nether regions into bionic wonders (see chart, pp. 16–17). But if oysters make you gag and Tater Tots get you going, then, by all means, Ore Ida is all righta by me. In fact, my personal aphrodisiacs are cheeseburgers, French fries, and a man holding a pair of tongs over a barbecue grill. It's a caveman thing: Man make fire for me. Man gooood. Of course I also love lobster, caviar, linguine with shrimp, and great wine, but it's more a matter of taste than folklore. My No foods? That's easy: scungilli, cockles, Brussels sprouts, rice cakes, sauce on the side, soy milk, and sparkling wine "product." Any guy who brings a bottle of I-Can't-Believe-it's-not-Champagne to my house should not expect to get his coat off, let alone the rest of his clothes.

Here's a tip for creating and ordering sexy food: Think of words you'd use to describe your romantic life—*hot, luscious, fiery, succulent, sinful, adventurous, steamy, gooey*. You should be able to use them to describe the foods you're eating together too. I don't really see scrod as fitting any of these descriptions.

Of course, if food alone were enough, you could very well have picked up any old cookbook and started living out your *9½ Weeks* fantasies on the linoleum floor. But we all know that that's not the case. How you prepare it, serve it, eat it, and the mood you create around it often have more significance than the actual food you're eating.

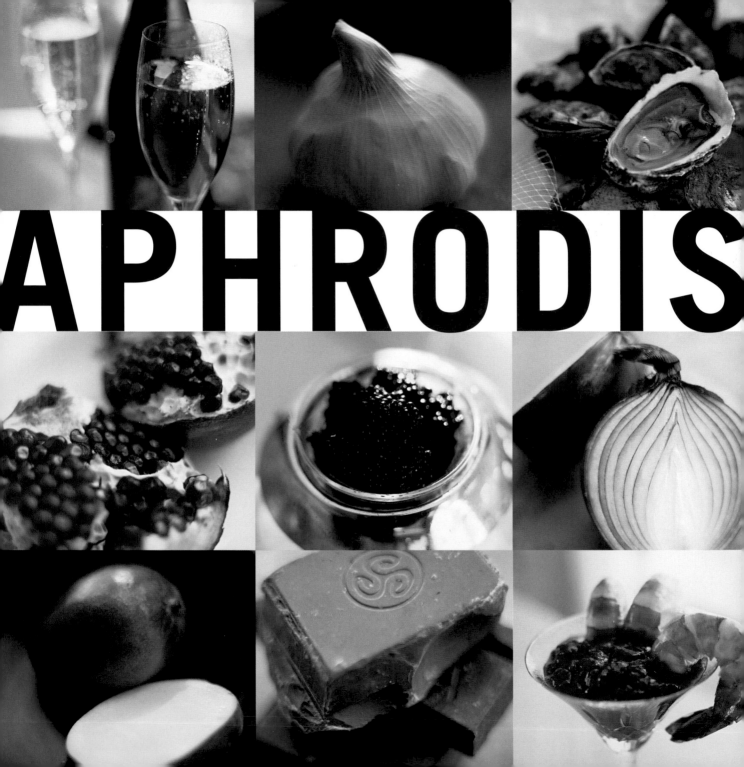

APHRODIS

The following is a partial list of foods reputed to get you all sweaty and tingly. As for the whole rhino-horn business, I'd skip it. Not only does it sound disgusting, but you're not going to feel very sexy knowing you've just contributed to the endangered species list.

herbs, spices, and seeds

BASIL. Known as "sister of Venus." Essential in both ancient love spells and a caprese salad.

CLOVES. Increases sexual appetite and, as a bonus, speeds up digestion.

GARLIC. Wards off the undead in bed too. Associated with strength and virility in European, Eastern, and Indian cultures.

GINGER. Early Indians suggested you mix it with honey and half-boiled eggs to ward off impotence.

GINSENG. The word literally means "man root." Ginseng is a mild stimulant and increases endurance in men.

MINT. Contains oils with a mildly aphrodisiac effect.

NUTMEG. Has similar chemical properties to mescaline. Believed to prevent premature ejaculation, although I can't vouch for this personally.

PINE NUTS. The Roman poet Ovid mentioned pignoli nuts in *The Art of Love*. Add them to garlicky pesto for a love potion disguised as linguine.

PUMPKIN SEEDS. Roast them on Halloween, dress up in your sexiest costume, and you and your lover may not reappear until Thanksgiving.

SAFFRON. The very expensive stamen from the crocus flower. It's reported to make erogenous zones all the more sensitive.

WALNUTS. The Latin name means "glans of Jupiter." Used in ancient Roman fertility rites, Wiccan marriage spells, and really good brownies.

fruits and vegetables

ARTICHOKES. The French insist upon the aphrodisiac qualities of artichokes, and they know a little something about love.

ASPARAGUS. Incredibly powerful, particularly for men. And delicious with hollandaise sauce.

BANANAS. A banana a day keeps the Viagra away.

BEANS. Lima beans, string beans, even baked beans. Beans were banned long ago in Catholic cultures because they were said to encourage lewd behavior. Horny nuns, baaadd.

CARROTS. Vitamin A isn't the only benefit, if you know what I mean.

FIGS. Greeks, Romans, and Indians don't agree on much, but they agree that figs will put you in the mood.

GRAPES. Associated with Dionysus, Greek god and patron saint of baby making. Fermented, they're even more powerful as wine.

MANGOES. Indians applied it as a paste to help strengthen their genitals, but just eating one will probably do.

MUSHROOMS. Just don't eat the poisonous ones. Death is *not* sexy.

ONIONS. Ancient Hindus and Greeks spoke of the stimulating properties of onions. And crying while you cut them gets you good sympathy points.

POMEGRANATES. Lebanese love fruit. Even the *Kama Sutra* says so.

POTATOES. Honeymoon in Boise, anyone?

SPINACH. Loaded with iron to give you the stamina that hot relationships require.

STRAWBERRIES. Sweet, succulent, and they fit perfectly between parted lips.

TRUFFLES. They even smell like sex.

seafood

ANCHOVIES. They get your love loins going. Just ask any Italian.

CAVIAR. More expensive than subscribing to the Spice Channel, but entirely worth it.

OYSTERS. The grand poobah of all aphrodisiacs. Casanova ate fifty a day.

SHRIMP. The slightly less potent stepsister of the oyster, for those "only once tonight, honey" kind of evenings.

sweets

CHOCOLATE. Believed to release the same chemical in the brain that's released during sex. Need I say more?

HONEY. Especially when consumed with a side order of you, honey.

LICORICE. The smell of black licorice alone supposedly increases blood flow to the sexual organs. The *Kama Sutra* describes several licorice recipes to promote sexual vigor.

MARZIPAN. Increases desire if eaten before lovemaking. Decreases desire if you get crumbs in bed.

VANILLA. A bubble bath scented with vanilla always gets me in the mood. Used in love spells by the modern-day tarot-card set.

beverages

CHAMPAGNE. The original glasses were designed to mirror the shape of Marie Antoinette's breasts.

COFFEE. Reputed to prolong erections and increase libido. Plus, your lover will never fall asleep on you.

COGNAC. The French drop in an egg yolk as an aphrodisiac, but I prefer it on its own; salmonella isn't sexy.

LIQUEURS. Particularly the green ones, like Benedictine and Chartreuse.

RUBY PORT. It does it for me, especially with anything chocolate.

TAWNY PORT. Supposedly powerful when blended with strawberries.

SO YOU THINK THIS PERSON IS WORTHY OF A SECOND DATE? PERHAPS EVEN A HOMEMADE NIBBLE OR TWO? THEN GET YOURSELF TO THE KITCHEN. DON'T WORRY . . . WE'RE TAKING THIS VERY SLOWLY. I'M NOT SOME WANTON COOKING WENCH, YOU KNOW.

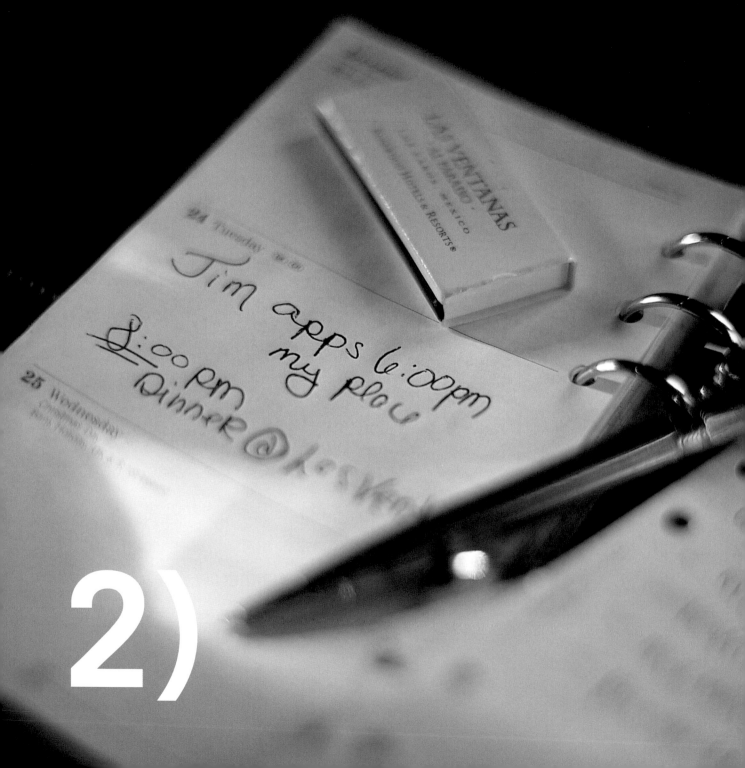

in for appetizers, out for dinner

WELCOME TO MY INNER SANCTUM

My honey cooked dinner for me on our second date. Although he's an avid home cook and it seemed like no big deal to him, it could have sent a different woman into commitment freak-out mode. A homemade meal is an intimate thing. Save it for when you want to get . . . well, more intimate. Unless of course you're sure that you're both wildly in love.

Provided your first date went smashingly, you'll want to up the ante on the next one and get to know each other a little bit better. How do cocktails and snacks at your house sound?

As an intermediary step, consider having your future love monkey *chez vous* for nibbles and cocktails before going out for dinner. Invite him or her over with time to spare before your reservation time.

First of all, clean your home. All of it. Guys with nasty bathrooms or kitchens skeeve me out. I don't care how nice the rest of the house is; if the bathtub is ringed with slimy stuff from the '70s, the first thing I think is *Well, we'll never be showering together.* This is the first time your date is seeing you in your natural habitat, and you want it to make as good a first impression as you did. This doesn't mean you should hide your pet tarantula or move the Barry Manilow CDs to a dresser drawer. It's important to let your date know who you really are. If he questions your *Wizard of Oz* commemorative-plate collection, don't stammer that you're holding them for your grandmother. He should know that they're your most prized possessions and that the Glinda plate is the first thing you'd save in a fire. He'll find out eventually anyway. If he doesn't like you for who you truly are, this relationship is not going to go very far. You can fight about where to display them when you two move in together.

However, there are some potential home-base embarrassments you can avoid. Remember, everyone snoops. Sometimes intentionally (your medicine cabinet—hide the Rogaine!), sometimes unintentionally (your refrigerator). Is there anything at all lurking in the icebox that could cast you in a less than flattering light? Moldy vegetables? Wine coolers? A leftover birthday cake that reads "I love you Pookie"?

I can forgive a bachelor-pad fridge stuffed with boil-in-a-bag dinners; I will assume the challenge of teaching him the errors of his ways. Conversely, when I notice the refrigerator door is lined with exotic mustards and imported jams, the crisper is chock-full of exotic lettuces, and the wine rack is home to some fabulous vintages, I get dizzy with the potential.

Just before your date arrives, get some tunes cranking on the CD player. Old R&B, Mozart, Tom Waits—whatever makes you comfortable. If you bonded over the Sex Pistols on your first date, then dust off the *God Save the Queen* CD and turn it up. There's no right or wrong music. If she's mentioned an affinity for Louis Prima, you'll score big if the strains of "Jump, Jive, an' Wail" welcome her through the door. This says to her, "Hey, I was listening to you." Trust me: Women are into guys who listen to them.

The only music I suggest you avoid is so-called groovy sex music; if I arrive at a guy's apartment for the first time and he hits the play button on Ravel's "Boléro," it screams loud and clear, "I'm only taking you to dinner so I can see you naked." *Booty Food* was created to help you find and nurture more meaningful relationships. One-Night Stand Food is a whole different subject and I'm not going to help you out there.

That said, when your date arrives, get a drink into his or her hands right away to help

TEQUILA, THE LIBIDO ENHANCER.
The legend of tequila is that it was formed by a lightning bolt sent down from the Aztec gods. Tequila can also inject electricity into your evening. It's different from other hard liquors in that it supposedly contains mildly hallucinogenic properties, which is undoubtedly the reason that after two shots of tequila, you're reasonably certain that you're the best dancer on the floor.

The proper way to do a tequila body shot: Sprinkle a bit of salt behind your partner's ear, down the neck, across the belly, or on any other spot that seems in need of a good licking. Place a wedge of lime in his or her mouth, rind side in. Lick the salt. Drink the shot. Bite the lime. Don't ruin the moment by launching into "Louie, Louie" afterward.

lubricate the lips and ease the anxiety. It is *not* intended to get you boinking like bunnies; there will be plenty of time for that later. Make sure to have both red and white wine on hand until you know your partner's preference. You can find a splendid Pinot Noir or Shiraz for less than $15. I'm a bit of a wine snob, but I'm not a red wine snob. In the warmer months, a chilled white Albarino from Spain always hits the spot. Don't feel you need to spend $600 on a vintage Bordeaux. Of course it would make me more inclined to wear my good underwear on the next date, but it's not essential.

And don't be stingy; open a new bottle. I don't want to be offered a previously uncorked bottle of Merlot. It would only leave me to imagine what buxom blonde helped to polish off the first four glasses.

If you're feeling more adventurous, mix a martini or whip up a pitcher of icy Pomegranate Margaritas. Make the effort, go a step beyond offering the lone skunky beer left over from last year's Super Bowl party, and I guarantee you'll get farther down the booty path.

DON'T GO ALL THE WAY ON A SECOND DATE

Drinks are essential before dinner, but it's nice to have something to nosh on as well. However, as I mentioned before, cooking for a partner is not something you want to delve into too quickly. Appetizers are a great way to start slow and still show off your culinary IQ. Great predinner nibbles whet the appetite for dinner and you. They're like a culinary tease: Your lips say no, but your Prosciutto-Wrapped Melon says, "Ummmm, maybe . . ."

Your gourmet flirtation needn't be complex. Put out some rich Kalamata olives or delicate cornichons—those sour little French pickles. (They always remind me of an illicit romp in the Jardin de Luxembourg a few years back.) Forgo the been-there Brie and try a delicious Explorateur or a creamy Vacherin with some fresh figs and grapes. Go to a gourmet shop and buy some prepared antipasti including sweet roasted eggplant, peppers, zucchini, artichoke hearts, and tender mozzarella. You can even serve basic nuts from a can (no, not beer nuts), provided you take them out of the can first.

Go a baby step further and try my recipe for a simple Caprese Salad, or wrap some salty prosciutto di Parma around luscious slices of ripe melon. Putting in just a hint of effort can really go a long way toward making a delicious impression. As an added benefit, food preparation helps to keep you from obsessing about the night ahead.

The following recipes are my favorite second-date appetizers because they're pretty hard to mess up, even when I'm suffering from the he's-going-to-be-here-in-an-hour-and-I-just-overplucked-one-eyebrow jitters.

SHORTCUT: You can purchase bottles of pomegranate juice in ethnic markets or health-food stores. Or, instead, use a couple of dashes of grenadine, which is made from pomegranates. Caution: Pomegranates are an age-old fertility inducer. Proceed at your own risk.

Pomegranate Margaritas

In Greek mythology, the beautiful Persephone was held in the underworld as Hades' love slave. After eating a pomegranate seed, she was doomed to remain there all winter long. With any luck, these frosty margaritas will help you hook your very own love slave for life. If you're not a pomegranate fan, just omit the puree and make classic margaritas.

1 pomegranate, seeded and juiced, or 4 ounces pomegranate juice (see shortcut)
Juice of 5 limes (about 5 ounces), reserving 1 small wedge to moisten glasses
Kosher salt for rims of glasses
3 ounces gold tequila
1 ounce orange-flavored liqueur, like Cointreau or Grand Marnier
1 teaspoon powdered sugar
Ice cubes
Pomegranate seeds for garnish

• Chill two long-stemmed glasses.

• Juice the pomegranate by rolling it under the heel of your hand, using enough pressure to soften the fruit. Carefully cut a 1-inch slit in the skin (if you do it under running water the juice won't splatter). Over a wide-mouthed glass, squeeze out as much juice as possible. Then split the fruit apart and remove the seeds, reserving about 2 tablespoons of intact seeds for garnish.

• Place the seeds in a 1-quart Ziploc bag, and press down on the seeds with the heel of your hand to extract the rest of the juice. Strain out the seeds. All together, you should have about ½ cup of pomegranate juice.

• Salt the rims of the glasses by rubbing the reserved lime wedge around them, then dipping them in kosher salt.

• Combine the pomegranate juice, tequila, liqueur, lime juice, sugar, and a handful of ice in a cocktail shaker, and shake vigorously until it's all frothy.

• Strain into glasses, and garnish with the reserved pomegranate seeds.

SERVES 2 / PREP TIME: 15 MINUTES

If you're still single,
the supermarket can be an excellent place to get to know other
gourmands. Especially the produce
aisle: All those ripe, juicy fruits and
vegetables are very sensual. To find
a cantaloupe that's ready to be
taken home and savored, just sniff
that melon, baby. She'll tell you
when she's ready with a sweet fragrance that comes right through the
rind. The melon should feel heavy
for its size, and slightly soft at the
blossom end (that green dot on
top). The netting pattern in the rind
should look consistent all the way
around, and you shouldn't feel any
soft spots or bruises. If the melon
looks as sunken as a sixty-year-old
rock star's face on a Sunday morning, move on to the next one.

Prosciutto-Wrapped Melon

Those Italians got it goin' on with this dish. Prosciutto is Italian ham, cured and thinly sliced.
The texture is soft and the salty quality plays beautifully against the sweet, juicy ripe melon.
You can find prosciutto di Parma—the mac daddy of Italian pork products—at a good butcher,
Italian market, or specialty-food shop. A little pricey, but your booty bambino is well worth it.

1 small ripe cantaloupe, cut into 8 wedges
¼ pound prosciutto di Parma, very thinly sliced
2 teaspoons extra-virgin olive oil
1 lime cut into wedges for garnish (optional)

• Rinse the melon, then cut in half and remove the seeds. Cut each half into 4 wedges and
then remove the flesh from the skin. Wrap overlapping prosciutto slices (about 2 slices)
around each wedge. Arrange on individual plates or a small platter.
• Drizzle with extra-virgin olive oil and garnish with lime.

SERVES 2 / PREP TIME: 10 MINUTES

Caprese Salad with Fresh Basil

Caprese salad just means mozzarella, tomato, and basil. Sounds schmancy, though, doesn't it? Use
fresh mozzarella; the softer and fresher, the better. I love mozzarella di bufala, made with buf-
falo milk. Make your own if you're Italian—or if you have nothing better to do than make
cheese. You can also substitute roasted red peppers for the tomatoes, or alternate red and yellow tomatoes to make the dish sweeter and even more beautiful.

1 pound fresh mozzarella, sliced into ¼-inch rounds
3 large ripe tomatoes, like beefsteak, sliced into ¼-inch rounds
15 to 20 fresh sweet basil leaves, rinsed and dried
3 to 4 tablespoons extra-virgin olive oil, for drizzling
A few drops balsamic vinegar (optional)
Kosher salt
Freshly ground black pepper
4 teaspoons rinsed and dried capers for garnish (optional)

• Arrange alternating slices of mozzarella and tomato on individual plates or on one platter.
Arrange in a straight line, a curved form, or a circle: They all work nicely.
• Insert whole basil leaves between the slices so they are just visible.
• Drizzle with extra-virgin olive oil and, if you wish, a few drops of balsamic vinegar.
• Sprinkle with salt and pepper, and garnish with capers.

SERVES 2 / PREP TIME: 10 MINUTES

SHOULD I ON THE FIRST DATE? THE GARLIC QUESTION. Garlic is not only a proven aphrodisiac, it increases stamina and virility, so, by all means, indulge! Just make sure that both of you do (and have some mints on hand for afterward). On the other hand, if it's going to make you self-conscious, forget it. The last thing you need on a first date is more anxiety.

Roasted Red Pepper Hummus

Hummus brings me back to my Lebanese roots and is far more impressive than serving sour cream mixed with onion-soup mix. The sweetness of the roasted red peppers makes this traditional recipe ever more tasty. If you're worried about garlic breath, you can use a little less than the recipe calls for. Serve with pita bread or sliced veggies and bring on the belly dancing!

1 large red bell pepper
1 can (14 ounces) chickpeas, drained, reserving ½ cup liquid
1½ tablespoons lemon juice
1½ tablespoons tahini
1½ large garlic cloves, peeled and crushed with pinch of salt
1 tablespoon extra-virgin olive oil
Kosher salt
Freshly ground black pepper
¼ teaspoon cayenne pepper
⅛ cup toasted sesame seeds, still hot from toasting

• Roast the red bell pepper directly over a gas burner, under a broiler, or on a grill. Turn frequently with tongs until it is blackened and the skin is blistered all over, about 10 to 12 minutes. Place the pepper in a loosely sealed paper bag or in a covered bowl to steam for 10 minutes to loosen the skin. When the pepper is cool enough to handle, rub the skin off with your fingers, a paper towel, or the backside of a paring knife. Slit the pepper open and remove the stems and seeds.

• Put the roasted pepper, chickpeas, lemon juice, tahini, crushed garlic, and extra-virgin olive oil in the bowl of a food processor, and puree until nearly smooth, pausing to scrape down the sides of the bowl. Moisten with some of the chickpea liquid and season with salt, pepper, and cayenne. Continue to process until smooth, and adjust seasoning if necessary. Transfer the hummus to a mixing bowl.

• Toast the sesame seeds over a medium-high flame in a frying pan, tossing constantly until golden brown. Add the hot sesame seeds to the hummus for an extra bit of flavor and crunch.

• Serve with crudités, toasted pita triangles, or tortilla chips.

MAKES 3 CUPS / PREP TIME: 15 MINUTES / COOK TIME: 15 MINUTES

CAVIAR
FOR
NEWBIES

If you're in serious wooing mode, then go for the mother lode for your date: caviar. Yes, it's expensive. It can set you back $50–100 an ounce, but for damn good reason. Careful, though, not everyone likes it and ordering it just because it's pricey is every bit as pretentious as showing up for your date in a shiny new midlife-crisis mobile. Money is an aphrodisiac, but only when wielded the right way.

Caviar is simply fish roe, or eggs, preserved with salt. Red salmon roe is often called caviar, but true caviar comes only from the sturgeon.

The three basic types of caviar:
- **BELUGA.** Yum, yum, and yum. Beluga is the largest berry with the mildest taste, and is widely accepted as the best. The 000 grade is the lightest gray in color and most delectable, while 0 is the darkest.
- **OSSETRA.** The smallest-grained type of caviar, medium-size berries. It's generally grayish, gray-green, or brown, and has a nice, nutty flavor. Makes a lovely garnish.
- **SEVRUGA.** The most intense flavor. It comes in colors from golden brown to green to bluish. It's the smallest type of sturgeon caviar, and runs about half the price of beluga.

Iranian caviar is delicious and can be more reasonably priced than Russian varieties. I recommend using Iranian or sevruga caviar in recipes. Beluga is best on its own; you don't need to dress it up, nor would you want to.

You'll know caviar is fresh if you can roll the berry on your tongue and it stays firm. If it bubbles or fizzes, then run! Run away! Caviar keeps for about two months in the refrigerator (although in my home it rarely lasts a day). Keep caviar in the coldest part of your fridge until fifteen minutes before serving. Then place the open tin on ice and serve with a nonreactive spoon, like bone, horn, or china. Set it out with little bowls filled with crème fraîche, diced onion, chopped hard-boiled egg (whites in a separate bowl from yolks), lemon wedges, and a little basket of toast points.

To eat, just spread some crème fraîche over the toast, add caviar and garnishes to your liking, and squeeze a bit of lemon over the top. Heaven.

Caviar goes quite nicely with champagne, icy vodka, and foreplay alike, although vodka is a bit more hip and less cliché than champagne. My favorite vodkas are Grey Goose, Belvedere, and Chopin—the gorgeous bottles alone are worthy of the tiny black gems, and the taste of the vodka helps to balance the salty bite.

Grilled Red Bliss Potatoes with Wasabi Crème Fraîche and Sevruga

This recipe is utterly delectable, with just a bit of wasabi powder blended into the crème fraîche to give it some bite. I recommend using sevruga or Iranian caviar here. Beluga would be a waste of money *and* the beluga; the spicy wasabi would blow out the delicate flavor. It's the same reason you don't make mimosas with Dom Perignon. Enjoy!

⅔ pound small Red Bliss potatoes
1½ tablespoons olive oil
Kosher salt
Freshly ground black pepper
1½ teaspoons wasabi powder
⅔ cup crème fraîche
50-gram tin (or 2-ounce jar) Iranian or sevruga caviar
Chives, chopped, for garnish

• Preheat a skillet on medium heat. (If you have a grill pan it will leave grill marks on the potatoes, which will make the presentation even more exquisite.)
• Wash the potatoes, leaving the skins on. Then slice them into bite-size rounds about ¼-inch thick. Use only the middle part of the potato with the widest circumference. You should have about 20 good slices.
• Brush potatoes on both sides with olive oil, and season with salt and pepper.
• Grill until light golden brown, about 10 to 15 minutes, then flip and grill the other side. Remove from heat and place on a paper towel to drain.
• Gently fold wasabi powder into the crème fraîche. Put the mixture in a squeeze bottle if you have one.
• Arrange the potato slices on a platter and squeeze or spoon about a teaspoon of wasabi crème fraîche on each slice. Garnish with ¼ teaspoon of caviar on each. Add a sprinkling of chives if desired, and prepare for your eyes to roll back in your head while you eat.

ENOUGH FOR 2 PEOPLE / PREP TIME: 10 MINUTES / COOK TIME: 15 TO 20 MINUTES

YOU MADE THE LAST RECIPE, DIDN'T YOU?
YOU WENT OUT AND GOT A TIN OF SEVRUGA
AND EVEN MADE THE LITTLE GRILL MARKS ON
THE POTATOES. YOUR DATE WAS CHARMED
AND YOUR STOCK WENT UP ABOUT 50 PER-
CENT. THEN YOU WENT ON TO DINNER, WHERE
THERE WAS SO MUCH ELECTRICITY BETWEEN
YOU, ALL THE OTHER COUPLES IN THE RESTAU-
RANT WENT HOME AND HAD FIGHTS BECAUSE
YOU MADE THEIR RELATIONSHIPS FEEL STALE
AND TIRESOME. SIGH. A PERFECT NIGHT. AND
NOW, A PERFECT MEAL. YOUR HOUSE. HOW
DOES 8 P.M. SOUND?

3)

starting slowly: the first home-cooked meal

There are no hard and fast rules about the right time to cook for a partner. Some people do it on the first date and some people do it weeks into the relationship. My rule of thumb (and other body parts): If you're fairly certain that the fluttery feelings are mutual, then go for it.

Cooking for someone, like sleeping with someone, isn't necessarily something you want to do right away. Both can lead to tremendous anxiety: What if she thinks I was terrible? What if I used up all my tricks the first time? What if his ex is better than I am?

CHECK YOUR EQUIPMENT

I wouldn't embark on a big cross-country road trip without a comfy sweatshirt, good tunes, a cell phone, my shades, and plenty of Pringles. (Mmmm . . . Pringles.) Not to mention someone I could share a confined space with comfortably for three thousand miles. Cooking is no different.

Before you can work your way toward a life of contentment, true love, and booty on demand, there are certain items you're going to need. The graduate course can be found in Phase III. The following are just the essentials:

IN THE KITCHEN:

➤ **A GAS STOVE.** I believe if I'm not cooking with gas, I might as well order in. I save the electricity for the bedroom. If gas isn't an option for you right now, don't sweat it; but if you can swing it, the result will be more booty.

➤ **AT LEAST THREE GOOD SHARP KNIVES.** A heavy nine- or ten-inch chef's knife, an eight-inch serrated knife for bread and tomatoes, and a three- to four-inch paring knife. If you want to get fancy with fish knives and cheese knives, you'd better eat your Wheaties; your dance card is going to be full.

➤ **HEAVY-BOTTOMED POTS AND PANS.** Like driving a sports car with manual transmission, you really feel you're cooking when you use the kind of pot a chef would use. For starters, you'll need one pot that's large enough for pasta or two small lobsters, small and medium-size saucepans, and a medium fry pan. Don't forget the lids.

➤ **CROCK POT OR ROASTING DISH.** Essential for cooking whole poultry, roasts, and baked casserole-type comfort foods. Le Creuset makes fabulously attractive ones in colors to match any kitchen.

➤ **CUTTING BOARD.** Gimme some wood, baby. If I'm cutting fish or chicken, I'll cover the board in plastic wrap or aluminum foil for salmonella-free cooking and easier clean up. Although plastic boards aren't as sexy, they are preferred by professionals. Plastic makes for easier clean up and is effortless to take care of; well-used wooden boards need to be treated monthly with mineral oil to keep from warping or cracking. Get yourself a couple of each.

➤ **AT LEAST ONE OVEN MITT AND A POT HOLDER.** People who wad up old T-shirts to take cookies out of the oven do not inspire lust, no matter how good the kitchen smells.

➤ **DISH TOWEL, FREE OF STAINS AND RIPS.** You're over twenty-one; go to Kmart and splurge on a new one.

➤ **ESSENTIAL GADGETS.** A whisk, a slotted spatula, a rubber spatula, a ladle, spring-loaded tongs (the French tickler of kitchen gadgets; I don't know why, I just love them), a well-worn wooden spoon, a slotted spoon, and a hand grater for Parmesan at the table.

➤ **A STAINLESS-STEEL COLANDER.** It has a plethora of uses, from draining pasta to holding yet-to-be-washed veggies to serving fresh fruit bedside. Large and small strainers are a nice bonus.

➤ **A GREAT PEPPER MILL.** Select a mill that allows you to adjust the grind from coarse to very fine. Toss out the pepper shaker or donate it to your local coffee shop.

➤ **A FOOD PROCESSOR.** Fact: People who own food processors are usually gainfully employed.

➤ **A GLASS BLENDER.** Plastic blenders are creepy; they're the polyester suits of the culinary world. You'll need a solid blender that can hold up through years of Pomegranate Margarita making.

➤ **A WINE RACK THAT HOLDS AT LEAST SIX BOTTLES.** Proper wine storage starts here. Bottles grouped haphazardly on a counter are only acceptable when you've had a party the night before.

➤ **A WINE PRESERVATION SYSTEM.** Vacu Vin is one of the least expensive. It pumps the air out of unfinished bottles (rare in my home) to ensure that you're not drinking vinegar the following night.

➤ **EMERGENCY BOTTLES OF WINE.** Minimum of one red and one chilled white. If you have the space, have two of each in expensive and moderate price ranges. Also, one bottle of champagne, chilled. As far as I'm concerned, this is as important as the fire extinguisher.

➤ **FIRE EXTINGUISHER.** The only purchase you never intend to use.

IT'S NOT THE SIZE, IT'S WHAT YOU DO WITH IT: SELECTING KNIVES

Don't buy your knives prepackaged in a boxed set. Go to a good kitchen store or department store and get help from someone who knows his stuff. Avoid knife stores staffed with recent parolees. To find the right knife for you, you have to pick it up. It won't bite. It should feel slightly heavy and evenly weighted in your hand. Compare it with a cheaper knife, and you'll feel the difference immediately. It's best to invest in a good hand-forged, high-carbon stainless-steel set, even if you can't afford all of them at once. And don't forget a sharpening steel. I like working with a ten-inch chef's knife, but many women can't handle a full ten inches. (Wink.) Eight inches can still get the job done quite nicely.

AT THE TABLE:

➤ **SERVICE FOR FOUR THAT MATCHES.** This means dishes *and* silverware; don't confuse shabby chic with shabby. Martha Stewart knows what she's talking about with the white plates. You want the food to be the star of the table, not the dishes.

➤ **NICE WINEGLASSES THAT MATCH.** Appropriate glassware is indicative of your evolution as a human being. Thin tumblers or juice glasses can be used for wine if you're feeling kind of Euro.

➤ **CLOTH NAPKINS OR NICE PAPER NAPKINS.** Repeat after me: "Paper towels stay in the kitchen. Toilet paper stays in the bathroom."

➤ **COFFEE MUGS.** Dainty little teacups have never inspired the phrase "Let's get busy." Invest in a matching set of coffee mugs; get rid of the mishmash of freebies from clients and lame Christmas gifts past.

➤ **CANDLES IN VARIOUS SIZES.** But don't go so over the top that your abode looks like Nosferatu's passion pit.

And make sure your refrigerator has been cleaned recently and defrosted at least once this year, whether or not you're dating. As a favor. To me.

A LOT OF WOW, A LITTLE EFFORT

So you've got the equipment and you've got a willing dining companion. It's time to make the first meal. Or is it? Before you come down with a case of culinary performance anxiety, your first meal needn't be Grilled Lamb Chops with Shaved-Truffle Gnocchi. Prepare something you're already comfortable making, or use one of the following recipes, which impress with minimal effort; Blue Cheese Arugula Salad is as easy to make as tossing iceberg lettuce with dressing from a bottle and ranks about ten times higher on the booty meter.

If you're already at ease in the kitchen, go all out on one dish, then exercise restraint and keep the rest of the meal simple. The first time the love of my life cooked for me, he made me a fabulous big-deal meal that you'll find in chapter 5. Thank God he *bought* the chocolate cake he served for dessert. If he had made that from scratch as well, I think it would have sent me running for the nearest cab. Cooking for someone is about showing you care. It is *not* a mastermind effort to smother someone until he has no choice but to promise to worship you and do your bidding. Like that tired cliché about buying the cow when you can have the milk for free, in the kitchen it's better to leave them begging for more too.

The setting you create is every bit as important as the food. When your date arrives, don't have golf on the TV. Don't have bras flung over the shower rod. Pick the right music, whatever that means for you. Dim the lights or pop in low-wattage soft pink bulbs, but err on the side of brighter rather than darker. You want your date thinking *Ooh . . . romantic*. Not *Ooh . . . bordello*. Set the table nicely with matching dishes, flatware, and glasses, but don't overdo it. A simple vase brimming with your date's favorite flowers and a couple of candles are more than enough. Hint: Save the silver for later (because if things go well, there will indeed be a later).

Make sure you're pretty much ready to go when your dinner companion arrives, then get a beverage into his or her hand right away. Don't ask for help washing the dishes afterward, since you want to make your date feel like the most valued guest who's ever set foot in your home. Although if he wants to help with any of the work, let him. Just don't go ballistic if he doesn't do things exactly the way you want them; if he pours water in the wineglasses it is not a sign of the apocalypse.

Now, I could talk the bark off a tree (as a friend once put it), but not everyone is comfortable making conversation. If you're nervous during dinner, simply babble about what's in front of you. Food not only gets relationships going, it can get the verbal repartee going too. Confess that the sight of Brussels sprouts sends you into a tizzy and compare culinary war stories. Describe the best cooking tip your grandma ever gave you. Explain how you discovered the wine you're serving on a trip through Tuscany—it may lead to a great travel discussion or a tasty anecdote about sneaking that illegal third bottle of Brunello through customs.

Any of these ideas are more interesting than talking about the weather and safer than revealing what religion you're hoping to raise your children. You'd be surprised how many great discussions spring forth from an offhanded remark about food. Although reminiscing about your whipped cream encounter at the office holiday party—not a good idea.

Good food—any good food—made well is Booty Food.

Before you embark on your culinary journey, I have just a few words of wisdom: Nobody's perfect. And certainly, nobody's perfect in the kitchen. Even Julia Child used to drop whole roasts on the floor. If culinary disaster makes an uninvited appearance, a good sense of humor can go a long way. Bonding over undercooked pasta is every bit as romantic as bonding over a perfect meal, and makes a more entertaining story for your best man to recount at your wedding.

Pan-Roasted Chicken with Rosemary-Lemon Butter

This is a four-thousand-year-old Booty Food recipe from the Greek isles, with a tart, lemony bite. Don't feel that making chicken is a cop-out; keep in mind that chefs are judged by how well they prepare a basic roasted chicken. A simple dish done well is far more impressive than a complex one done badly. Serve with a crisp Mediterranean white wine and start throwing plates.

NOTE: Chopping up a whole chicken is not my thing, but if you're not intimidated by it, it is cheaper. Otherwise, buy the parts fresh or frozen. This sauce is also superb with lamb. Prepare the same way, substituting beef stock for the chicken stock.

NOTE: Roasting the chicken whole is also an option, but be sure to finish cooking in the oven until the juices run clear.

1 (3-pound) chicken, cut into 8 pieces (leaving skin on and bones in)
3 ounces butter (¾ stick), softened
6 sprigs rosemary, about 4 inches each, 3 reserved for garnish
3 cloves garlic, minced
Kosher salt
Freshly ground black pepper
Juice of 2 lemons (about 6 tablespoons)
3 tablespoons extra-virgin olive oil
¼ cup white wine
⅛ cup chicken stock
1 lemon, thinly sliced into rounds for garnish

- Preheat the oven to 350 degrees.
- Wash and dry the chicken. Slightly separate the skin from the meat to make room for the lemon-herb butter.
- Place 3 tablespoons of the softened butter into a small bowl. Remove the leaves from 3 sprigs of rosemary and roughly chop them. Combine with garlic, salt, pepper, and half of the lemon juice, and blend into the butter.
- Spread most of the lemon-herb butter under the skin of all the chicken pieces. Rub the outside of the chicken with the remaining herb butter, and season with salt and pepper.
- Get your frying pan nice and hot, and heat the olive oil. Pan-roast the chicken, using tongs to turn the pieces so they brown evenly on all sides, about 10 to 12 minutes. Pour excess fat from the pan, and place it in the oven for 13 minutes, or until the juices run clear when the meat is pricked to the bone.
- While the chicken is roasting, prepare the sauce: Combine the white wine, chicken stock, and remaining lemon juice in a small saucepan, and simmer over low heat until the liquid is reduced by about half. Cover to keep warm.
- Arrange the chicken on a platter. Whisk the remaining butter into the sauce, and adjust seasonings. Pour over chicken, and garnish with the remaining rosemary sprigs and lemon slices.

SERVES 2 / PREP TIME: 15 MINUTES / COOK TIME: 30 MINUTES

**STARTING SLOWLY
DESSERTS** Home-baked goodies may be a little overwhelming to
your date at this stage. To end your
dinner on a sweet note, instead
buy a pint of gourmet ice cream,
some biscotti from a local bakery
and serve with fresh berries or fruit
compote. You'll look booty-worthy
without looking desperate.

Blue Cheese Arugula Salad with Honeyed Walnuts

The Brits call arugula "rocket." I call it rocket fuel. It's got a peppery hot edge to it, reminiscent of mustard greens or watercress, and it's readily available. Be sure to wash it well, though; it's a dirty little green. Use a good-quality blue cheese, like Cabrales, a Spanish variety with the *cojones* of a buff matador.

¼ **pound walnut halves**
4 **tablespoons honey**
½ **pound arugula, washed well and gently dried**
¼ **pound sharp blue cheese, like Cabrales, crumbled**
½ **cup Balsamic Vinaigrette (recipe to follow)**

- Preheat the oven to 300 degrees.
- Spread the walnuts on a cookie sheet and roast for 10 minutes. Check frequently to ensure that the nuts don't burn.
- Place the honey in a medium bowl. Remove the nuts from the oven, add to the honey, and toss to coat. Return the honeyed walnuts to the cookie sheet and place them back in the oven for 2 to 5 minutes.
- Remove, and cool until the honey crystallizes.
- When you are ready to eat, toss the arugula, Cabrales, and honeyed walnuts with as much balsamic dressing as you like. Serve immediately, as delicate lettuces like arugula can easily become soggy. Limp lettuce is bad for booty.
  NOTE: Humidity can affect the honey and prevent it from crystallizing. Apologies to my friends in Seattle.

SERVES 2 / PREP TIME: 10 MINUTES / COOK TIME: 15 MINUTES

Balsamic Vinaigrette

½ **medium lemon or small blood orange, juiced (1½ tablespoons)**
4 **tablespoons balsamic vinegar**
Kosher salt
Freshly ground black pepper
3 **tablespoons extra-virgin olive oil**

- Whisk together the lemon juice, balsamic vinegar, a pinch of salt, and pepper to taste. Then drizzle in the olive oil, whisking. Taste for balance and adjust if necessary.

MAKES ½ CUP

Grilled Asparagus with Balsamic Vinaigrette

No fat, few calories, and off the charts on the aphrodisiac scale—no wonder asparagus is one of my favorite veggies. The Roman emperors had special "asparagus fleets" to gather the best of the crop for their meals (a.k.a. orgies). You, however, are on your own. Try to select straight spears with firm, crisp, unopened petals, the wider the better.

> 1 pound large asparagus
> 2 tablespoons extra-virgin olive oil
> Kosher salt
> Freshly ground black pepper
> ¼ cup Balsamic Vinaigrette

- Heat a grill pan on medium-high heat until it is very hot.
- Snap off the woody ends of the asparagus about 1 to 2 inches from the bottom.
- Toss the spears to coat in the olive oil and season with salt and pepper.
- Grill, turning occasionally until browned a bit, about 5 minutes. They should be tender but still crisp on the inside.
- Remove to a serving platter and drizzle with Balsamic Vinaigrette.

SERVES 2 / PREP TIME: 10 MINUTES / COOK TIME: 5 TO 10 MINUTES

1"

½"

¼"

⅛"

sometimes size does matter

You can probably forgive measurements in the bedroom, but in the kitchen, uniformity of size makes all the difference. In a *pico de gallo*, you don't want one onion bit to be the size of a pearl and another the size of a life raft. Here's what to do when a recipe calls for wielding a knife:

CHOP: Cut coarsely with a knife
JULIENNE: Cut very finely into matchstick-thick strips
MINCE: Chop into very fine pieces, about ⅛-inch square
DICE: Chop into ¼-to ½-inch-thick cubes
CUBE: Chop into cubes up to 1 inch thick.
GRATE: Finely shred using a grater or food processor
SHAVE: Paper-thin pieces often best achieved with a veggie peeler

CROSS-SPECIES MATING:
CARNIVORES AND HERBIVORES

I am a carnivore. If you want to get with me, baby, you should know I partake in veal saltimbocca, hot Italian sausage sandwiches, and bacon double cheeseburgers on a regular basis. (Let it be known that I also love vegetables. I'm not pitting meat versus veggies in some twisted culinary rendition of *Celebrity Deathmatch*, although I know for a fact that either could kick tofu's ass single-handedly.) However, nearly 30 million Americans have experimented with vegetarianism, so it's not unlikely that you'll date one of them at some point. So what do you do if, like me, you're a lifelong meat lover and you suddenly find yourself falling for a herbivore? Go for it.

Don't worry, you will not have to change your evil lamb-chop-eating ways or burn your leather sneakers in a show of solidarity. But it's hard enough to find a decent, loving partner without rejecting him on the basis of what he does or does not eat. In fact, if he's committed to a meat-free existence, at least you know he can commit.

The prevailing issue, as with any opposing schools of thought in a relationship, is one of mutual respect. If your date is not a lover of dirty-water Central Park hot dogs smothered in mustard, so what? Just as long as he or she doesn't mind that you are. Respecting your partner's beliefs, be they political, moral, or dietary, is the crux of a healthy relationship. You don't want to be berated by your partner as an animal-murdering sicko. Conversely, please don't tease the vegetarians. They don't like it. Sometimes they bite.

If you've never been involved with a vegetarian, let me assure you that it does not mean you'll be doomed to a life of poser tofu disguised as "chicken" à la king. The notion of vegetarian food has come a long way since the wheat-germ-eating, om-chanting '60s. You like pasta marinara? That's vegetarian. You crave gooey mushroom and pepper pizza? You get my point. You don't have to succumb to bean curd to share a romantic meal with your date. You may not want to take your partner to Joe's House of Charred Animal Flesh for dinner, but Indian, Thai, Japanese, Mediterranean, Italian, Middle Eastern, and most Mexican restaurants will have plenty of choices for both of you.

If you're cooking at home, open your mind to what constitutes a meat-free meal and you may find you have more options than you might have imagined. Here are three scenarios:

GOOD: It's Sunday night. You grill up some veggie burgers for you and your partner, scoring huge points for self-sacrifice. With every mealy mouthful you down, you hope that the eventual payoff will be worth the culinary torture.

BETTER: It's Sunday night. You grill up some hamburgers for yourself and some veggie burgers for your partner, scoring huge points for thoughtfulness. Bonus points accrue when you ensure that your burgers don't cross the invisible line down the center of the grill.

BOOTY: It's Sunday night. You make a gorgeous Blue Cheese Arugula Salad with Honeyed Walnuts (see page 40), and an outrageous Spinach Linguine with Yellow

> HOW TO KNOW IF YOU'RE READY TO MOVE ON TO THE NEXT CHAPTER: YOU'RE STILL HAVING FUN.

Squash, Zucchini, and Lemon (see page 255) for both of you, scoring huge points for thoughtfulness *and* your culinary expertise. Eyes meet. Hearts pound. Hormones abound.

You will have to train yourself to be more ingredient-conscious when you cook for a vegetarian. One time, I spent hours painstakingly stirring a perfect homemade risotto for an herbivore friend. I was thoroughly pleased with myself until, with a deflated voice three octaves higher than normal, she remarked, "Oh, you used chicken stock? That's okayyyy . . ." It wasn't okay. I felt terrible. And it would have been just as simple to prepare with vegetable or miso stock instead. Good thing she was forgiving. Good thing I wasn't trying to sleep with her.

If you find yourself in a cross-species relationship, just check the ingredients of your favorite recipes, and if nothing walks, flies, or swims, prepare the dish with love and prepare to get busy.

4)

picnic à go-go

Okay, so providing you remember to body-dip in Skin-So-Soft beforehand, picnicking is a joyous thing, the perfect experience for you two to share together now while you're still courting. After all, this is an exciting time. You're learning new things about each other every second. You're both still on your best behavior. You could easily cut the sexual tension with a butter knife. And you likely haven't heard the other person make embarrassing body sounds yet. Life is very, very good. So get creative with your dates and plan a day out with your partner and an abundance of tongue-tempting goodies. All you really need is a thermos and a dream.

In a few years, this will be the kind of thing you'll moan about not doing more frequently.

> I live for summer picnics: sprawling across a fleecy blanket, the sun kissing my bare feet, the smell of freshly cut grass in the air, a glass of Chardonnay in my hand, and the man I love at my side whispering ever so sweetly, "Relax already. You're not going to get Lyme disease.

PICNICKING LIKE A PRO

When packing your picnic, save the froufrou basket for the honeymoon. I'm sorry, but even the most manly man couldn't pull off swinging a cute little basket with a blue and white gingham cloth peeking out the sides. I prefer a good insulated backpack or picnic bag—the key word being *insulated*. Plus it will close tightly.

I always stow a bunch of ice packs to keep everything fresh, but you can use Baggies filled with ice if they're well-sealed. Make sure your thermos is closed tightly too. Soggy food does not a naughty picnic make.

I can't tell you how many times I've gotten excited to pop open a bottle of wine on a picnic only to find myself spending twenty minutes trying to jam the cork into the bottle with my house keys. So remember to pack a corkscrew if wine is a part of your master picnic plan. Plus plenty of napkins, utensils, plastic cups, baby wipes if you're sloppy, antihistamines if you have allergies, and more condoms than you think you'll need (if you are, in fact, at that point in your relationship). It may seem like a lot of stuff to remember, but smart packing will help make your picnic foolproof. Just make sure to leave room for the food. Oh, right . . . the food.

GOOD: Stop at the supermarket and grab some Wonder bread, PB&J, a bag of chips, and a couple of liters of soda. I suppose this does constitute picnic food, but it ranks relatively low on the booty meter. Unless you're sixteen.

BETTER: Head to your local gourmet store before your journey and fill your basket with wedges of exotic cheeses, ripe luscious fruit, an array of deli meats, some fried chicken, and a loaf of freshly baked bread. Tote along a bottle of wine. Absolutely nothing wrong with this option, but it's not quite . . .

BOOTY: Start cooking the night before. Prepare a fiery Five-Spice Jerk Chicken Breast, some wonderful salads, and your favorite homemade cookie or brownie recipe. Fill a thermos with homemade lemonade or iced tea. The next morning, move it all from fridge to picnic pack and get ready to tip the desirability scale heavily in your favor.

Of course there's a bit more to creating the perfect alfresco meal than cooking:

➤ **KEEP COLD FOODS COLD AND WARM FOODS WARM.** If it's hot out, cold refreshing items like fruit salad, pasta salad, or cold chicken will hit the spot. Keep it all in the fridge until the last minute, then pack with ice packs in an insulated bag. Pack warm foods in aluminum foil to preserve the heat, then place in plastic bags to dodge cross-culinary drippage.

➤ **KEEP YOUR COOLER IN THE CAR WITH YOU.** Don't stow it in a hot trunk. It's not a hostage. It's not going to try to jump out.

➤ **AVOID MAYONNAISE.** If you're going to leave early in the day and won't be eating for several hours, avoid foods than can go bad quickly. Don't keep food out in the sun for more than an hour or so either.

➤ **FREEZE WATER BOTTLES THE NIGHT BEFORE.** The ice will melt, and you'll have frosty cold water to drink all day long, especially if you plan on doing things that might get you sweaty. Like playing Frisbee. Or heavy petting.

➤ **LIGHTEN YOUR LOAD.** Snag those little salt and pepper packets from your deli or pack mini plastic shakers. Put wet condiments in small plastic containers; they're lighter than glass and allow you to bring only the amount you'll need. And remember, those collapsible tables and chairs are nice, but the more stuff you schlepp, the more stuff you have to schlepp back. No matter how much you eat, your load somehow always seems heavier on the way home.

➤ **DRESS ACCORDINGLY.** Wear clothes you can roll around in! As cute as your white cutoffs or ecru linen pants look in the morning, you'll look like a *fashion don't* by the end of the day.

➤ **KEEP THE CRITTERS AWAY.** Don't wear perfume or cologne that will attract bugs. Definitely bring a repellant of sorts, and calamine lotion if you have particularly sweet skin. Citronella candles also help to fend off the nasty beasts.

➤ **TURN OFF YOUR CELL PHONE.** Your picnic will be a whole lot more charming without the *Lone Ranger* song (or whatever freaky ring your phone has) chiming from your backpack every three minutes.

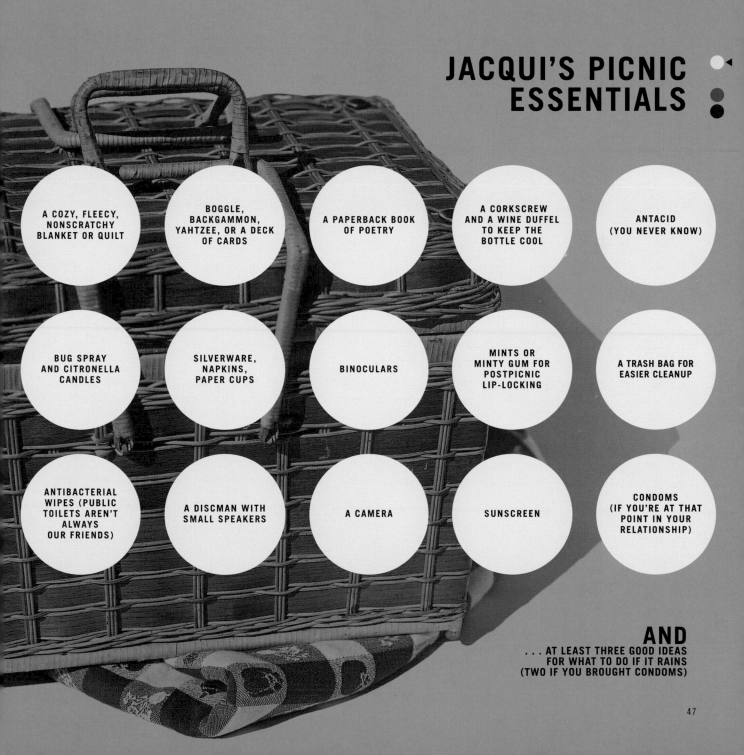

JACQUI'S PICNIC ESSENTIALS

A COZY, FLEECY, NONSCRATCHY BLANKET OR QUILT

BOGGLE, BACKGAMMON, YAHTZEE, OR A DECK OF CARDS

A PAPERBACK BOOK OF POETRY

A CORKSCREW AND A WINE DUFFEL TO KEEP THE BOTTLE COOL

ANTACID (YOU NEVER KNOW)

BUG SPRAY AND CITRONELLA CANDLES

SILVERWARE, NAPKINS, PAPER CUPS

BINOCULARS

MINTS OR MINTY GUM FOR POSTPICNIC LIP-LOCKING

A TRASH BAG FOR EASIER CLEANUP

ANTIBACTERIAL WIPES (PUBLIC TOILETS AREN'T ALWAYS OUR FRIENDS)

A DISCMAN WITH SMALL SPEAKERS

A CAMERA

SUNSCREEN

CONDOMS (IF YOU'RE AT THAT POINT IN YOUR RELATIONSHIP)

AND
. . . AT LEAST THREE GOOD IDEAS FOR WHAT TO DO IF IT RAINS (TWO IF YOU BROUGHT CONDOMS)

WARM-WEATHER PICNIC

In the warm-weather months, picnicking can be an activity unto itself, but it can also be part of a larger plan. Journey to a park and feed the ducks. Go for a bike ride. Get tickets to a minor-league baseball game and stuff yourself with grilled hot dogs and beer in the parking lot. Watch the monkeys do things to each other at the zoo. Catch an outdoor concert and sip wine illegally on the lawn. Hit golf balls. Steal away on a rented boat or hop a ferry and have a picnic at sea.

Don't feel obligated to make this whole picnic menu unless you're a crazy cooking fanatic like me. Mix and match recipes or scam a couple of mine and supplement with store-bought treats. Just don't forget the mandatory loaf of crusty bread, a wedge of cheese, a nice wine, and something sweet for dessert. Your lucky companion is not going to be able to keep his or her hands off you; you might want to consider picnicking somewhere deserted.

LUSCIOUS LEMONADES
I could drink lemonade in a blizzard, yet somehow it seems like the culinary equivalent of wearing linen after Labor Day. So I do my best to hold out for a nice day in April to make the first pitcher.

Use cool water, freshly squeezed lemon juice, and sugar to taste. Then get creative: Mix up lemons and limes; add fresh watermelon, strawberry, orange, or raspberry juice; garnish with fresh fruit or frozen berries. When I really want to impress, I freeze watermelon juice in ice trays and drop the sweet cubes in lemonade . . . gorgeous! Or use seltzer instead of water for a more adult taste, unless you think that defeats the purpose.

SHORTCUT: Although the jerk sauce is a cinch to make, companies like McCormick make really fabulous ones. Cheat on your recipes . . . not on your partner.

Five-Spice Jerk Chicken Breast

This gutsy jerk chicken recipe will give you a little taste of the islands, *mon*, every time. Marinate the chicken overnight so it really soaks up the sweet, peppery dressing. It's delicious with Red Stripe beer and ripe mangoes for dessert.

2 tablespoons extra-virgin olive oil
$\frac{1}{4}$ cup red onion, diced
2 cloves garlic, minced
$\frac{1}{8}$ cup diced habañero or Scotch bonnet peppers
$\frac{1}{2}$ teaspoon cayenne pepper
$\frac{1}{4}$ teaspoon green-curry powder
Dash cinnamon
Dash nutmeg
Dash allspice
Pinch kosher salt
Pinch freshly ground black pepper
$\frac{1}{8}$ cup mango juice
$\frac{1}{8}$ cup orange juice
2 tablespoons red-wine vinegar
1 whole chicken breast (about 1 pound), skin on, bone in, and cut in half

• Heat olive oil in a small frying pan, and add the onion and garlic. Sauté until the onion becomes translucent. Add the chilies and continue to cook until lightly brown.
• Mix together in a small bowl the cayenne pepper, green-curry powder, cinnamon, nutmeg, allspice, salt, and pepper. Then stir in the mango juice, orange juice, and vinegar. Add this mixture to the onion mixture and simmer on very low heat for about 20 minutes.
• Remove the jerk sauce from the heat and cool completely. Divide equally into two bowls. Cover one with plastic wrap and store in the refrigerator. Add the chicken to the other, cover with plastic wrap, and marinate overnight, turning once.
• The next morning, heat up the grill. Strain the excess sauce from the chicken, and grill, using the fresh sauce to baste the chicken as it cooks. Grill for 10 minutes on each side, or until the juices run clear when the meat is pricked to the bone. (Alternatively, place the chicken in an oven-proof dish, cover with the fresh sauce, and cook in a 350-degree oven for 20 minutes, or until the juices run clear when the meat is pricked to the bone.)

SERVES 2 / PREP TIME: 15 MINUTES / COOK TIME: ABOUT 40 MINUTES

Cold Grilled Mesquite Steak

Serve this simple tasty steak on top of the Roasted Corn and Arizona Bean Salad and you're golden. If you're a sandwich aficionado, layer the steak and salad between two slices of crusty Portuguese country bread. Or just pick up the steak, eat with your hands, and have your own Tom Jones experience.

2 small (8 ounces each) New York strip steaks
¼ cup olive oil
1 (1-ounce) package mesquite powder
Kosher salt
Freshly ground black pepper

• Rub the steaks with the olive oil and mesquite powder, coating evenly. Let marinate at least 30 minutes.

• Heat a grill pan over medium-high heat. Season the steaks with salt and pepper. For medium-rare, grill the steaks for 6 minutes on one side, then flip them and grill for 5 minutes more. Let the meat sit until cool, then slice into half-inch strips.

NOTE: If you are unable to find mesquite powder, substitute dried chipotle chili powder.

SERVES 2 / PREP TIME: 5 MINUTES / COOK TIME: 10 TO 12 MINUTES

Pasta Salad with Snappy Green Peas and Pancetta

This delightful salad will benefit if you buy the sweetest peas you can find. I like sugar snaps. If you're feeling a little frisky, add a few chili flakes and heat things up even more on your picnic.

3 ounces pancetta, cut into $\frac{1}{4}$-inch dice
1 clove garlic, minced
$\frac{1}{4}$ cup white wine
$\frac{1}{4}$ cup chicken stock
1 teaspoon red-wine vinegar
$\frac{1}{2}$ pound orechiette or penne
$\frac{1}{4}$ pound fresh shelled peas, blanched and shocked
Red-pepper flakes (optional)
Kosher salt
Black pepper
Shaved Parmigiano-Reggiano

• Cook the pancetta in a small frying pan over medium heat for 2 minutes. Add the garlic, and cook until the bacon is chewy, not crispy.
   • Lower the heat and add the white wine, chicken stock, and vinegar. Simmer for 5 minutes.
   • Boil the pasta according to package directions, or until al dente. Drain, and place in a bowl.
   • Add the pancetta mixture and the peas to the pasta, and season to taste. Garnish with the shaved Parmesan cheese.

SERVES 2 / PREP TIME: 10 MINUTES / COOK TIME: ABOUT 20 MINUTES

Roasted Corn and Arizona Bean Salad

This salad is a colorful, crunchy nibble to accompany the jerk chicken or the steak. If you don't have access to an outdoor grill, use a stovetop grill pan. And definitely chop the cilantro last so it won't become discolored. Your food should be as tempting to the eye as to the tongue, a lot like you.

2 large ears corn, shucked
1 tablespoon plus 1 teaspoon extra-virgin olive oil
1 (15-ounce) can black beans, drained
1 (15-ounce) can garbanzo beans, drained
2 large tomatoes, diced
½ yellow pepper, diced
½ red pepper, diced
¼ cup red onion, diced
⅛ cup chopped cilantro leaves
1 tablespoon balsamic vinegar
1 teaspoon diced jalapeños (optional)
1 teaspoon cumin powder, toasted (optional)
Juice of 1 lime
Kosher salt
Freshly ground black pepper

• Bring a pot of water to a boil. Add the corn, and cook for 5 minutes. Remove the corn from the pot, brush the ears with 1 teaspoon of the olive oil, and cook on a grill or a hot grill pan until slightly blackened.

• Slice the corn off the cobs. Combine with all the remaining ingredients, and add to your picnic cooler.

SERVES 2 / PREP TIME: 15 MINUTES / COOK TIME: ABOUT 7 MINUTES

COLD HANDS, WARM HEART

Picnics are great in the summer, but why stop when October rolls around? There are few things more romantic than an autumn picnic. Go somewhere where you can watch the leaves change or go apple picking. Take a hayride. Bird-watch. Visit a local winery, then find a nice patch of grass to sleep on until you're sober. Ride horses. Tailgate at a local football game. Sneak onto an empty beach in sweaters and scarves and snuggle while your bare feet burrow into the cool sand and hot cider warms your fingers. (Guys, this is a great opportunity to be a gentleman and see how cute your shivering date looks in your jacket.)

When the temperature forces you to pull your woolly mittens from the back of the closet, it doesn't mean picnic season is over. Bundle up, fill a thermos of (spiked?) homemade hot cocoa, and head for an outdoor skating rink. Propel yourselves down a golf-course slope on a sleigh with hot homemade chili waiting for you at the bottom. If the weather turns really nasty on the big day, just open a blanket in the living room and picnic right there on the floor. If things heat up, at least you won't have to worry about being arrested for indecent exposure.

When you're planning a cool-weather picnic, the food part is easy. Just make what you normally would when the weather's warm, then add a few thermoses full of hot soups and toasty beverages. If you don't feel like cooking, simply tote along your own homemade hot drinks, then stop at a deli counter and grab some barbecued chicken, coleslaw, and potato salad. At least you won't have to worry about the mayo going bad.

For those without exhibitionist tendencies, the following yummy drink recipes are a great way to keep hands warm on a cool day. Besides, I find something oddly comforting about wrapping my palms around a plastic cup and slurping like a six-year-old.

Feeling Thirteen Again: Foolproof S'mores

Roasting marshmallows over an outdoor fire and assembling hot, gooey s'mores will bring any couple back to adolescence faster than regression therapy. When you're done eating, make out in the glow of the flames. I swear it's every bit as thrilling as it was during your Clearasil years. The recipe is foolproof, but in no way fooling-around-proof.

Marshmallows
Sticks
Fire
Chocolate bars
Graham crackers

- Roast the marshmallows on sticks over the fire until gooey.
- Sandwich with a chunk of chocolate between two graham crackers.
- Lick your fingers. Lick each other's fingers. Make out with abandon.

Homemade Hot Cocoa (spiking optional)

Hot cocoa plays into that whole Heidi and the naughty yodeler fantasy for me. Please, please, please do not use skim milk. Hot cocoa with skim milk is definitely not booty-friendly. Whipped cream is optional; getting it on in a mocha-cocoa way, not optional.

2 tablespoons unsweetened good-quality cocoa powder (I like Fry's)
1 tablespoon granulated sugar
Dash cinnamon (optional)
2 cups whole milk
Splash Baileys Irish Cream, Kahlúa, peppermint schnapps, or crème de cacao (optional)
Minimarshmallows (optional)
Whipped cream (optional)

• Mix together in a small bowl the cocoa powder, sugar, cinnamon (if using), and 1 tablespoon of the milk to form a paste.
• Heat the rest of the milk in a small saucepan, being careful not to scald the liquid. Add the chocolate paste, stirring often. (If you like it dark and dirty, make more paste.)
• Pour into mugs or a thermos, adding liqueur, marshmallows, or whipped cream as you desire. Find a cold place and snuggle up.

SERVES 2 / PREP TIME: 5 MINUTES / COOK TIME: ABOUT 3 MINUTES

Spiced Hot Apple Cider (with kick or without)

Hot spiced cider can warm up even the coldest environment. When it's simmering on my stovetop, the fragrance alone makes me want to curl up under a blanket with my boy and not emerge until spring. Finish it off with a splash of Calvados or brandy. Blissful.

4 cups high-quality unpasteurized apple cider
1 teaspoon cinnamon
1 teaspoon brown sugar
Pinch orange zest
Dash ground cloves

• Mix all of the ingredients, and gently simmer for 3 to 5 minutes.

SERVES 2 / PREP TIME: 5 MINUTES / COOK TIME: ABOUT 5 MINUTES

Picnicking is more intimate than you might imagine. While it's hard to get into each other's space across a four-top at Casa del Antonio, you'll find that when you're spread out on a blanket, fingers touch and limbs become entwined far more readily. If you had any question at all about the chemistry between you and your date, it will certainly resolve itself by the time your little outing is through. Think of your picnic experience as a relationship gauge. If you each spend the entire meal on your own sides of the blanket, using Tupperware containers as a division line, you might want to shake hands and part as friends afterward. Of course, if your date sees you as an opportunity to earn his merit badge in premature public groping, that's no good either. There's a wonderful, thrilling place somewhere in the middle where a hand on the leg is welcome, kisses last far longer than they should outside the privacy of your own home, and you're starting to mentally clear your calendar every night for the next six months.

THAT'S WHEN YOU KNOW IT'S TIME FOR THAT FIRST MIND-BLOWING HOMEMADE MEAL.

5)

is this the one?

Time to bring out the big guns. You're going to provide an oral experience that will bring you a hair away from the first morning-after breakfast. You know what I'm talking about: that one incredible, homemade, grand-slam, home-run, crowd-goes-wild dinner for two.

This is no small undertaking. As I've mentioned, prepare a gourmet meal too quickly and he'll bolt with the napkin still tucked into his collar. So, before you polish Grandma's silver, you'd better spend some time contemplating whether this person is worthy of your culinary gifts. It doesn't mean he or she necessarily has to be the person you're going to spend the rest of your life with, have babies with, and fight with on major holidays, but there should at least be some semblance of that possibility.

There comes a point when you start losing count of dates and start keeping track of weeks. You're picturing this person naked on a regular basis and you're wondering if he or she looks cute spitting out toothpaste.

So how do you know if you two are ready to take it to the next level?

➤ **DO EITHER OF YOU FREAK AT THE WORD *RELATIONSHIP?*** Not a good sign. There should be some indication of potential commitment, like making plans that are a week or two away. The phrase "I've never been the marrying type" is not something you want to hear unless followed by "until I met you."

➤ **YOU CAN REALLY BE YOURSELF WHEN YOU'RE TOGETHER** You don't have to think about what you say or how you say it. You're not worried about what you eat; the whole spinach-in-your-teeth thing is becoming less of a concern. But you're still wearing your good underwear. In fact, he or she brings out the best in you *and* your underwear drawer.

➤ **YOU'RE NOT PLAYING ANY OF THOSE DUMB GAMES** like limiting your phone calls to two minutes and thirty-seven seconds or rejecting a Friday date offer after noon on Tuesday. In fact, your Friday dates should start to become assumed, i.e., your plans together aren't placeholders until courtside seats come along.

➤ **YOU NEVER LACK FOR THINGS TO TALK ABOUT.** In fact, there never seem to be enough hours in the day. He's genuinely interested in your life and you in his. And you're still discovering fun new things about one another—his high school prom disaster story, her battleship tattoo. If she can confide in you about personal stuff, that's a good sign. If he waits a month to tell you about his crazy aunt in the attic—not a good sign.

➤ **THE STUFF YOU HAVE IN COMMON STILL SEEMS TO OUTWEIGH THE DIFFERENCES,** most of which you can get over—like he's into dolphin figurines and you're not. As opposed to she's married and you're not.

➤ **YOU'RE NOT AFRAID TO BE AFFECTIONATE IN PUBLIC.** This means hand-holding or light touching, not getting to second base on the subway.

➤ **YOU REALLY LIKE ONE ANOTHER "THAT WAY."** I know, it's so seventh grade. But you shouldn't even have to bring up the subject. When you know it you just know it.

So you think this could be the one? Then stop your giggling and get your butt into the kitchen. It's time to go to work.

TAKE IT TO THE KITCHEN

The meal that put me over the brink (in a good way) came relatively quickly. It was date two and I was more than ready to succumb to my soon-to-be-boyfriend's cooking prowess. When I walked into his home, he had a glow on his brow, a towel slung over one shoulder, and that slightly rumpled I've-been-working-hard-in-the-kitchen-for-you-baby look. It doesn't get much sexier than that. He passed me a fabulous glass of Bordeaux and I joined him in the kitchen.

He was making homemade pasta for me. Homemade pasta! I mean, who does that for you? Either someone who really likes you, or someone who really, really wants to sleep with you. Fortunately it was both.

As he taught me how to hand-crank the noodles, we sounded vaguely like a porn soundtrack: "Go slowly . . . no, not too hard . . . now put your hands down here and pull gently . . . now switch hands . . . oh, yeah, that's it . . ." Very delicious, and very, very hot. When he fed his exquisite tomato-butter sauce to me off a wooden spoon, blowing on it so I wouldn't burn my lips, it was practically a kiss. Do the same with whatever you're making. It's a sensory experience to share and an easy way to get in each other's body space.

The meal was amazing. Afterward, still reeling from the experience, I was offered my first-ever glass of port, and I haven't been the same since. So don't skimp on the wine—it works!

This is a good time to use the dining room if you have one. The flickering fluorescent bulb in the kitchen doesn't say "sexy." It says, "I need three cc's of saline drip, stat!" Set the table nicely, light the candles, and use the good silver if you're inclined. This time it's okay. You both know why you're here.

After dinner, don't worry about washing up. A sink full of dirty dishes in the morning is a booty trophy. This could be The Night. Enjoy it!

CHECK YOUR EQUIPMENT: THE BEDROOM

If you're going to make the morning-after meal that follows, you want to make sure your bedroom and bathroom are as well stocked as your kitchen pantry is. You know what I'm talking about. Now, don't be nervous, getting intimate is your biological imperative. It's going to feel very natural and spontaneous. Just as long as you prepare for it:

➤ **CANDLES** In the bedroom *and* the bathroom. Better to light a candle than to curse the darkness—or your flaws in the unflattering light of a seventy-five-watt bulb when you skulk in there naked to pee at three A.M.

➤ **EXTRA TOOTHBRUSHES** It's considerate. Just make sure to keep them hidden so you don't look like a whore. Or a dentist.

➤ **GOOD SHEETS AND AT LEAST TWO PILLOWS** It's nice to share a bed, but sharing a pillow is a whole different thing. Have two. Three-hundred-plus-thread count sheets are always pleasant, even if they do end up in a heap on the floor. And if you've got stuffed animals on the bed, toss them in the closet.

➤ **TWO THIRSTY BATH TOWELS** No matter how intimate I am with a guy, I don't want him wiping toothpaste off his mouth on the same towel I use to dry off my bum. Nor would he, come to think of it. Make sure you have a spare one out, but don't make it look obvious. Prepared is good; overanxious is not.

➤ **CONTACT LENS SOLUTION** Even if you don't wear contact lenses, your new paramour might, and you don't want to give him or her a reason to leave early in the morning. Just pretend that your myopic brother left the bottle at your house on the last visit.

➤ **CONDOMS** Safe sex is the only sex as far as I'm concerned. Those flavored condoms are kind of fun. But whatever turns you on . . .

The items you don't have in the bedroom are also meaningful. Toss that autographed picture of a shirtless Scott Baio, or your special collector's edition Victoria's Secret catalog. Items like these tell a potential partner that your bedroom is used to pleasure yourself and not someone else. And personally, I don't want to get naked anywhere in the vicinity of lingerie models. So get the greased-babe calendars and the like out of the bedroom if I'm headed your way. Besides, it's bad Feng Shui.

THE MEAL YOU'LL TELL YOUR KIDS ABOUT

This meal makes memories, and could very well make a relationship. Start with the Homemade Fettuccine with Tomato-Butter Sauce, or substitute fresh or dried pasta if you don't have a pasta machine. It's still magnificent. Garnish at table with a fresh grating of Parmigiano-Reggiano. Then bring out the peppery Bistecca alla Fiorentina and serve with the simple string bean salad. If your date is raring for more—at the table—bring out the Chocolate Soufflé Cake and watch his or her jaw drop. There's something about a guy presenting a homemade chocolate cake to me that instantly makes him desirable.

Culinary overkill warning: If you've made the fettuccine from scratch, don't make the cake! It may lead your date to believe you're already picking out china patterns and a wedding singer.

Homemade Fettuccine

Trust me, this recipe practically guarantees booty, all for the small price of some flour and eggs. It's so easy, anyone with a pasta maker can do it. The sauce is my honey's Italian grandmother's recipe and is equal parts simple and sublime. It calls for canned plum tomatoes but if you want to use fresh ones, knock yourself out.

3 cups all-purpose flour
4 large eggs
½ teaspoon olive oil
Pinch salt

• Pour the flour into a mound on a smooth work surface. Stick two fingers gently into the center of the mound, turning them slowly to make a crater. You'll end up with something that looks like a volcano. Break the eggs, one at a time, into the crater. Add the olive oil and salt to the eggs. Using a fork, beat the eggs gently until well mixed, then gradually incorporate some of the flour from the volcano into the eggs. Be careful not to break the walls of the volcano, or the eggs will erupt and run off the counter!

• Using the fork, continue to stir the flour into the eggs until fully incorporated. Using both hands, swiftly bring the remaining flour over the egg mixture until it's completely covered. Begin working the dough with your hands until all the flour is mixed into the eggs. (Add a little flour if it's too sticky.) Knead the dough for only a few minutes. It should feel moist, but not tacky.

• Gather the dough into a ball and cut it into 6 pieces. Lightly flour the pasta machine and a cookie sheet (or a countertop). Flatten one ball and pass it through the machine on the widest setting (usually #1). Pass the dough through each setting twice, up to and including setting #6. Cut the ribbon of dough in half crosswise, then pass each half through the widest cutter setting (fettuccine) of the machine. Lay the pasta on the cookie sheet. Repeat with the remaining balls.

• Bring a large pot of salted water to a boil.

• Drop the pasta in the water and stir well. It should take only a minute or two until it floats to the surface. Taste a piece as soon as it rises. Don't overcook! Drain immediately. Smother with Tomato-Butter Sauce (recipe to follow) and lots of scrumptious, fresh Parmigiano-Reggiano.

THIS MEAL IS DESIGNED TO SERVE 2 / PREP TIME: 30 TO 40 MINUTES / COOK TIME: ABOUT 3 MINUTES

Tomato-Butter Sauce

2 cans (28 ounces each) whole peeled tomatoes, drained, reserving liquid, or 2½ pounds
fresh ripe plum tomatoes, peeled, seeded, and coarsely chopped
1 medium onion, peeled and halved
8 tablespoons butter (1 stick)
Kosher salt
Freshly ground black pepper
⅛ pound Parmigiano-Reggiano, freshly grated

• If using canned tomatoes, cut them in half and squeeze out seeds and excess water thoroughly. Then roughly chop them. Combine the tomatoes and the reserved liquid with the onion and the butter in a large skillet or saucepan. Simmer over low heat, occasionally mashing the tomatoes with a fork, until the tomatoes have reduced, about 35 to 40 minutes.

• Remove and discard the onion halves. Add salt and pepper to taste. Serve over pasta with a generous sprinkle of cheese (not from a can, please).

SERVES 2 IF YOU LIKE YOUR PASTA WET, LIKE I DO, BUT CAN SERVE UP TO 6 / PREP
TIME: 5 TO 10 MINUTES / COOK TIME: 35 TO 40 MINUTES

Bistecca alla Fiorentina

This is going to be the tasty tour de force of your first big-deal meal together, and yet it's easier than undoing a bra strap with one hand. Make sure to order the steak from your butcher in advance; most supermarkets don't have two-and-a-half-inch-thick T-bones lying around. And use really good olive oil. It makes a difference. Add it right after the steak is cooked; it will warm up and the scent will blossom for the future love of your life.

> 1 T-bone steak, 1½ to 2 inches thick (about 2 pounds)
> Freshly ground black pepper
> Kosher salt
> 1 clove garlic, peeled
> Extra-virgin olive oil for drizzling

• Cover both sides of the steak with pepper. Let the meat sit for 15 to 30 minutes at room temperature.

• Heat a cast-iron skillet or grill pan over high heat for 10 to 15 minutes, until it begins to smoke and a droplet of water sizzles and steams on contact. Make sure to turn on the exhaust fan or open the windows—the smoke is coming! Add the meat to the pan, and sear one side for 6 minutes, then flip it and cook until it's done to your liking, about 6 minutes for medium-rare. Don't move the steak around while it cooks or it won't sear as well.

• When the steak is almost done to your taste, sprinkle the kosher salt all over one side, then cook that side for just 30 seconds. This will form an amazingly crunchy, tasty crust.

• Remove the steak from the heat, and rub the garlic clove over the bone until the garlic melts onto it. Transfer the steak to a cutting board and drizzle with a little bit of olive oil. Let sit for 5 minutes. Carve off half-inch slices and serve immediately.

NOTE: If you like your steak rare and your partner likes it medium, carve the steak, then touch the rare slices to the hot pan to sear them a bit more. Don't overdo it unless you plan on serving Shoe Leather alla Fiorentina. And if you don't have a pepper mill, wrap whole peppercorns in a towel and pummel them with a hammer. Then tomorrow, go buy a pepper mill already! First thing. Or maybe second thing . . .

SERVES 2 / PREP TIME: 30 MINUTES / COOK TIME: 12 MINUTES

Lemon-Garlic String Bean Salad

This salad is just the right side dish to serve with the steak: not too fussy, not too difficult, but still impressively tasty. You don't want to go all out on your meals just yet. Whatever would you do for an encore? Make the string beans an hour or so before dinner; they'll get even better as they marinate in the garlicky dressing.

1 clove garlic, peeled
1½ tablespoons extra-virgin olive oil
¾ pound young string beans, washed and trimmed
Kosher salt
Freshly ground black pepper
Juice of 1 lemon

• Smack the garlic clove with the side of a knife to crush it slightly. Rub garlic over the inside of a large serving bowl to release its essence, then leave the clove in the bottom of the bowl and add the olive oil.

• Bring a large pot of salted water to a boil. Meanwhile, set a large bowl of ice water next to the sink. Blanch the string beans in the boiling water for 3 to 5 minutes, depending on the thickness. (Size does matter.) Drain, and plunge the beans immediately into the bowl of ice water. Let them cool for 1 minute, strain well, and set aside.

• Using a fork, remove the garlic from the bowl. Add the green beans, salt, and pepper to taste, and toss well. Add half the lemon juice to start, then adjust the salt and pepper. Add more lemon if necessary, but use less if you're having a wonderful bottle of wine with dinner.

SERVES 2 / PREP TIME: 10 MINUTES

SHORTCUT: Homemade is best, but mixes are hardly a compromise. If the idea of baking the whole shebang from scratch makes you anxious, feel free to share the credit with Betty Crocker (she won't mind). Then mix up the chocolate glaze and add the shavings, which takes about 3 minutes. Or simply buy a cake from a bakery. Those professionals do know what they're doing.

Chocolate Soufflé Cake with Chocolate Glaze and Shaved Chocolate

This sinful chocolate cake will make anyone's eyes roll back in his head. It's even better when (maybe a little later in your relationship) you save a piece and use it for body paint. I highly recommend serving this cake with a nice Fonseca port. The combo of rich, melting chocolate and sweet, fruity wine is orally orgasmic.

FOR CHOCOLATE SOUFFLÉ CAKE:
Butter and sugar for coating the pan
8 ounces semisweet or bittersweet chocolate, chopped
6 tablespoons unsalted butter (¾ stick), softened
2 tablespoons rum, Kahlúa, or other liqueur
6 large eggs, separated and at room temperature
¼ teaspoon cream of tartar (optional)
½ cup sugar

FOR CHOCOLATE GLAZE:
8 ounces semisweet or bittersweet chocolate
½ cup heavy cream
1 teaspoon light corn syrup
1 2-inch square chocolate, shaved, for garnish

• Preheat the oven to 375 degrees. Butter a 9-inch springform pan, coat with sugar, and set aside.
• Melt the chocolate with the butter in a bowl set over simmering water, stirring until smooth.
• Remove from the heat and let the chocolate mixture cool for 10 minutes. Whisk in the rum or liqueur and the egg yolks.
• Beat the egg whites until foamy, using an electric mixer with the whip attachment on medium speed. Add the cream of tartar, if using, and gradually beat in the sugar on high speed until the peaks are just stiff and glossy but not dry.
• Whisk one-third of the egg whites into the chocolate mixture to loosen it. Then, with a spatula, gently fold in the remaining whites, one-half at a time.
• Gently pour the mixture into the springform pan and smooth the top. Bake until the soufflé rises up and the edge looks set, about 25 to 30 minutes. Allow to cool completely on a wire rack.
• Meanwhile, place the chocolate for the glaze in a large mixing bowl.
• Put the heavy cream in a small saucepan, bring it to a simmer, then pour it over the chocolate. Let stand for 3 minutes, then whisk gently until smooth. Stir in the corn syrup.
• To glaze the cake, gently flatten the puffed edges of the soufflé and unmold the sides of the springform pan. Set the cake on a wire rack over a baking sheet and pour the glaze over the top. Shaking the wire rack encourages the glaze to run down the sides. (Come on, glaze.

I know you can do it!) Allow the glaze to set at room temperature, then garnish with chocolate shavings.

NOTE: For greater success with chocolate shavings, make sure the chocolate is the temperature of a warm room. Use a vegetable peeler or the largest openings on a box grater over waxed paper to grate the chocolate, and sprinkle the shavings from the paper onto the cake.

NOTE: As an alternative to glazing, prepare the soufflé mixture, and pour half of it into the springform pan. Sprinkle 1¼ cups (6 ounces) semisweet chocolate chips over the mixture, then pour in the remaining mixture. Bake as above, allow to cool for 15 minutes, remove from the pan, and sprinkle the top with powdered sugar.

• Serve warm with vanilla ice cream.

SERVES 8 TO 10, OR 2 PEOPLE FOR 4 NIGHTS OF ADULT FUN / PREP TIME: 30 MINUTES
COOK TIME: 25 TO 35 MINUTES

TOO FUNK TO DRUCK. Ah, yes, the elusive alcohol question. As with food, there's such a thing as overdoing it. There's nothing worse than waking up in the morning filled with horror and regret, and still having to face a sinkful of pots and pans. Plus too much booze affects performance. You want your first night of lust to be memorable and not because it ended before it began.

THE MORNING-AFTER BREAKFAST You open your eyes. Next to you, this delicious amalgam of limbs and hair and sweet flesh, who's still dreaming of last night's dinner and (you?) dessert. The sheets are rumpled. Clothes are everywhere. Your dogs need to be let out but you worry that your knees won't support you. Take a big breath. You're in deep now and there's only one thing to do: Go deeper. Steady yourself and race to the kitchen (with a quick pit stop in the bathroom for a little oral hygiene). You're going to prepare the mother of all morning meals—or maybe it's already afternoon. Either way, this is a job for luscious Lobster Eggs Benedict. Some of you may think that this is an insane undertaking, but I tell you, it's completely worthwhile. If homemade fettuccine says, "Let's fall in love," then Lobster Eggs Benedict says, "Let's have a really hot ongoing relationship." Bring your masterpiece back to bed on a tray with a side of spicy, homey home fries, a pot of coffee, and a glass of fresh orange juice or a mimosa. Your bedmate will never want to leave. Which is pretty much the point. If the recipe is a bit beyond your skills or inclination, make something simpler. Even a plate of home-made scrambled eggs provides the perfect excuse to stay in bed together till noon (at least). Besides, waking up in someone else's bed the first time can be extremely disquieting. The smell of toast or freshly brewed coffee alone can help put your new love muffin at ease. If you've finished all the champagne in the house the night before or the idea of cooking right now is too much for your heavy head to handle, there ain't nothing wrong with diner food. Run out and grab a few orders of eggs, greasy potatoes, bacon, and toast. Surviving a mild hangover together can indeed be a fabulous experience.

COFFEE
TUTORIAL

You might call me a highly caffeinated person (and you wouldn't be the first). I'm mad for Jamaican Blue Mountain, European dark roasts, Arabica, Kona . . . you name it. Coffee is one of the great passions in my life, and although I try to give it up at least twice a year, it keeps pulling me back. Currently I am back on the bean in a big way. If you two have stayed up all night teaching each other Tantric sex secrets, a strong cup of coffee (or four) is going to be mandatory in the morning. Although, as with booty, the quality of your coffee is more important than sheer quantity. When you're with a new lover, waking up to a perfect cup of coffee implies that this day, like your relationship, will be filled with promise and opportunity. Waking up to nasty coffee is always a bad omen, the equivalent of saying you will wake up unsatisfied and miserable every day for the rest of your life. So think carefully before you dump instant coffee in a mug and bring it to that sleepy new person in your bed. A bad cup o' joe in the morning may get the job done, but do you really want your partner to describe anything you do as "Well, I guess it got the job done"?

Prepare the brew properly and you will be rewarded with better flavor and aroma. A recent study of scents revealed that in America the smell of coffee is most associated with home. Follow these instructions and your lover's nose will tell him that he's found his home right there with you.

➤ Coffee that's been prepared with a French press or dripped through a gold filter is the ultimate. Percolators are viable alternatives, but instant-coffee crystals are not. If you're using paper filters, wash them in hot water to get rid of some of the papery taste.

➤ Buy freshly roasted beans and store them in a tightly sealed container for no more than a couple of weeks, max. If you grind them yourself just before you use them, they'll stay fresher longer. Just make sure you're using the right grind for your coffeemaker.

➤ Always use fresh, cool water (distilled or purified is a plus), and make sure the coffeepot is clean.

➤ For regular-strength brew, use about two tablespoons of ground beans for every three-quarters cup of water. For extra-strength, he-kept-me-up-all-night coffee, use four tablespoons to a cup of water.

➤ Don't burn your coffee or keep it warming for more than twenty minutes. Reheating the pot is practically a sin.

Once the coffee is made (and made well), remembering exactly how your partner likes it earns you big, big booty points. Everyone's got different preferences, and for those of us in Coffee Freaks Anonymous, it may be a bit more complex than one lump or two. Coffee drinkers define themselves by their morning beverage to some extent. So if a man gets how I take mine, I feel like he gets me—it's easy on the milk and hold the sugar (I love coffee ice cream but do not want to drink it for breakfast). I also need my Kona served to me piping hot in a big, heavy white mug. Styrofoam between my lips is about as pleasurable as wearing polyester underwear. And six ounces of strong, nearly black, kick-you-out-of-bed coffee served in anything pink or baby blue is all wrong, like a construction worker in drag. It's even more impressive that my honey knows how to make it just the way I like it considering he never touches the stuff himself.

One last thought about coffee: Don't forget it's considered an aphrodisiac. Now that things are starting to heat up in your relationship, brew a surprise pot any old time of day and put that extra energy to good use.

Post-Coital Lobster Eggs Benedict

If your lover impressed you the night before, then it's only fair to impress him right back in the morning with this. It's sheer luxury on an English muffin, and sounds more complicated than it actually is.

FOR LOBSTER:
 1 to 1½-pounds lobster
 4 tablespoons butter (½ stick)
 2 cups champagne or sparkling wine

FOR HOLLANDAISE SAUCE:
 ½ cup melted butter (1 stick)
 3 egg yolks
 1 tablespoon freshly squeezed lemon juice
 ½ teaspoon salt
 Pinch dry mustard or cayenne pepper

 1 English muffin, split and lightly toasted

FOR POACHED EGGS:
 4 eggs
 1 teaspoon vinegar, any type
 1 teaspoon salt

 Small bunch of arugula, washed
 Caviar for garnish (optional)
 Chives for garnish (optional)

• Bring 1 inch of water to a boil in a large covered pot. Plunge the lobster into the pot, cover, allow the water to return to a boil, and cook for 8 to 10 minutes.

• Remove the lobster, and let it sit until cool enough to handle. Remove the meat from the shells.

• Melt the butter in a medium saucepan over low heat, then add the champagne, and simmer for 1 minute.

• Turn off the heat, add the lobster, and let it sit while you prepare the rest of the meal.

• To prepare the hollandaise sauce, melt the butter in a small saucepan over low heat or in the microwave. Do not lct it brown.

• Combine the egg yolks, lemon juice, salt, and dry mustard or cayenne in a blender. Pulse, and drizzle in the butter. The mixture will begin to thicken. If the sauce is too thick, add a few drops of warm water. Taste, and adjust the seasoning. Transfer the sauce to a container nesting in a bowl of hot water to keep it warm while you continue.

• Toast the English muffins, and keep warm.

• To poach the eggs, heat 2 to 3 inches of water in a deep, small skillet until almost boiling. Add the vinegar and salt. Crack the eggs into two small cups and carefully slide one at a time into the simmering water. Reduce the heat if necessary, to keep the water just below a simmer. At this point, cover the pan or begin to spoon water over the tops of the eggs. Cook for 3 to 5 minutes, just until the white is set and the yolk has filmed over. (If an egg sinks to the bottom, wait until it is almost set before you try to dislodge it.) Remove the eggs with a slotted spoon and press against a paper towel to drain any excess water.

• To assemble, place each English muffin half on a plate. Then, top with arugula, lobster meat, and then a poached egg. Top each half with 4 tablespoons of the hollandaise, and serve immediately. If you're inclined, garnish with Ossetra or Sevruga caviar, wasabi-infused green caviar, or just simple chopped chives.

SERVES 2 / PREP TIME: 10 MINUTES / COOK TIME: 25 TO 30 MINUTES

timing is everything in the kitchen too

If you're attempting the complete breakfast, with the lobster eggs benedict, home fries, and mimosas, I bow at your altar. The order in which you do everything will make all the difference. It will keep your eggs from being runny, and you from ditching the whole thing and resorting to cereal and toast.

1. Make the mimosas first. Sip while you cook.
2. Start boiling the water for the poached eggs.
3. Make your home fries then pop them in the oven on low.
4. Toast your English muffins just slightly crispy for texture, then put them in the oven too.
5. Set the table or breakfast tray.
6. Make the champagne butter sauce.
7. Put the presteamed lobster in the champagne butter sauce.
8. Poach the eggs.
9. Prepare the hollandaise sauce.
10. Assemble. Serve. Eat. Go back to bed. Tell no tales.

Jalapeño Home Fries

Potatoes are our starchy friends. Once I discovered that they were also aphrodisiacs, I could justify eating even more of them. The jalapeño and cayenne in this recipe make coffee-shop home fries pale in comparison. And I've found that these potatoes are even better reheated the next day—or when you're hungry again after round two.

    1 tablespoon olive oil
    ¾ cup diced red onion (½-inch dice; about 1 large onion)
    2 cups diced Idaho or russet potatoes, skins on (½-inch dice; about 2 medium potatoes)
    1 cup diced sweet bell peppers (½-inch dice; about 1 large pepper)
    ½ teaspoon minced jalapeño pepper (about ½ pepper)
    1 small clove garlic, minced
    Dash cayenne pepper
    Kosher salt
    Freshly ground black pepper

• Warm the olive oil in a large iron skillet, and cook the onion over medium heat until it turns translucent. Add the potatoes, peppers, and garlic, stirring constantly. While stirring, add cayenne, salt, and pepper to taste. Cook until crispy and golden brown.

SERVES 2 / PREP TIME: 20 MINUTES / COOK TIME: ABOUT 30 MINUTES

Funky Mimosas

If you want to get funky, add a dash of Grand Marnier or Cointreau. If you want to get really funky, sugar the rims of the glasses and garnish with an orange slice.

    ½ bottle (325 ml) champagne
    12 ounces freshly squeezed orange juice
    3 ounces Triple Sec
    Sugar for garnish
    Orange slices for garnish

• Combine in a pitcher champagne, orange juice, and Triple Sec. Give it a gentle mix. I think mimosas are best served in champagne flutes. Before pouring the mimosas, wet the rims of the flutes with orange wedges and roll in sugar. Garnish with orange slices.

MAKES 1 PITCHER, SERVES 2 / PREP TIME: 5 MINUTES

KEEP IN MIND THAT SOMETIMES, THE FIRST TIME ISN'T THE BEST TIME. THE KISS, PERHAPS. THE FONDLING, OKAY. BUT THE OTHER STUFF? YOU'RE NOT EXACTLY COMFORT-ABLE WITH EACH OTHER'S BODIES YET, AND I CAN ASSURE YOU THAT THE REALLY INTI-MATE STUFF WILL GET BETTER ONLY IF YOU PROMISE TO PRACTICE DILI-GENTLY. CONGRATU-LATIONS. YOU HAVE A NEW HOBBY. ON TO PHASE II!

THE
MARA
OF

phase II

The Marathon of Lust creeps up on you slowly. One minute you're thinking, *Gee, I kinda like this person,* and the next thing you know, nothing matters *except* this person—and all the things you're doing with your clothes off. The bills are going unpaid, the phone unanswered, work unfinished, and dishes unwashed. You boink. You cuddle. You sleep. You boink again. You can't keep your hands off each other in public; that is, if you leave the house at all. Is it love? You're

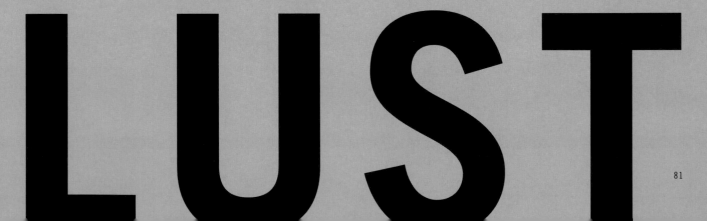

too sleep-deprived to say, but it's definitely a step in the right direc-tion—if you play your cards right.

When you're caught in the clutches of the Marathon of Lust, you can get away without calling friends. You can even skip work for a day or two. The one thing you can't avoid is eating. The following chap-ters should help you out even when eating is the very last thing on your delightfully smutty minds.

6)

when cooking is the last thing on your mind

When things get hot, the object of your desire consumes your every thought, and frankly, the only energy you may want to exert in the kitchen is on top of the counter. Naked. Even boiling water for pasta can seem like a chore after a late afternoon interlude, and washing the pot afterward? We both know it's not going to happen. So call me crazy for writing a cookbook with a chapter that tells you not to cook, but go ahead and don't cook. Just don't stop eating. This is the Marathon of Lust and not a sex-filled hunger strike. You're going to need your strength.

When I told friends about this book, some of them laughed, "Who cooks when they're in lust?" And I thought, they're right. Who am I to tell people to spend hours rolling homemade pasta dough when cooking is low on their list of priorities?

Thus, I present the miraculous world of take-out for those times when the best night out is a night in.

TAKE IT OFF TAKE-OUT

Even to a dedicated chef, take-out is never a cop-out. It's just another way of saying "five-course meal in bed with no clean up," a fine idea at any stage of a relationship. Ordering in is not only conducive to indoor sports, I find it's a precursor to them. When you phone in for dinner, the subtext is that you'll be able to act on whatever urges arise during that second glass of Chianti.

No doubt about it, I'm a home-delivery whore. I couldn't tell you the phone number of the local police precinct, but ask me who delivers the best chicken tikka masala in Manhattan and I can reel off three numbers by heart. I am a walking, talking encyclopedia of the take-out industry. I know which seemingly cheap New York Italian place charges double for daily pasta specials. I know which Los Angeles hole-in-the-wall will deliver unbelievable Thai food to your door in twenty minutes flat. I know that for an extra five bucks, there's a Mexican joint in North Dallas that will send burritos to the Holiday Inn Express after midnight. I even know how to fulfill my eat-in fantasies over-

It's easy enough to pull that little white slip out of the fortune cookie and insert one of your own creation. Try something like "You will get lucky on the back porch tonight," or "You will scream like a banshee before morning." How impressed your sweetheart will be when her fortune comes true!

seas, when an intercontinental hotel room tryst demands resourcefulness.

But if you can't get duck à l'orange delivered in your neck of the woods, don't sweat it. Sometimes, the raunchier the food the better. Cheap Chinese is a particular turn-on of mine, especially if I'm being fed sesame noodles out of a carton by candlelight. (Maybe it's the chopsticks—good manual dexterity in a man turns me on.) Even pizza delivery has been known to make me sweaty with anticipation. I'm infatuated with the idea of some young buck racing to feed me in thirty minutes or "give it to me free." And any lover who's ever witnessed me in a private moment with a to-go diner burger knows that I don't just eat it, I make sweet sloppy love to it.

Whatever your take-out food of choice, just remember to dim the lights, use the good cutlery, and make the meal into an event—and don't forget the cocktails.

BIG MACS AND CHARDONNAY

Foodies spend an excessive amount of time trying to conclude whether a Bordeaux or a Burgundy goes better with a filet mignon for a simple reason: to derive the most possible pleasure out of the meal. But are *two all-beef patties special sauce lettuce cheese pickles onions on a sesame seed bun* any less deserving of the ideal beverage? I think not.

In my household, take-out food doesn't officially become Booty Food until wine pairings come into play. Pizza is just pizza. But pizza along with a blanket on the living room floor, a few candles, and a bottle of Valpolicella is the prelude to an evening you wouldn't tell your mom about.

One day every delivery guy will have a sommelier riding shotgun. Until then, consider these suggestions for take-out/adult-beverage combinations an ample substitute:

➤ **CHINESE:** To me, those little white take-out boxes are the culinary version of a thong hanging from the lamp. Chinese food is like quickie nourishment, and there's nothing wrong with being hungry (or horny) again in an hour. Whether you're into shrimp dumplings, sweet and sour Szechuan spare ribs, or General Tsao's chicken, wash it all down with a light white wine. I like a gewürztraminer because it contains exotic Asian-style fruit and is sweet enough to hold up to those fiery spices. A Pinot Blanc is a less intense alternative, or seek out a six-pack of Chinese beer, like Tsing Dao. You can't go wrong with a beer that was literally made for Chinese food.

➤ **PIZZA:** When it comes to pizza, my wine of choice is red, red, and red. From a smoothly balanced Valpolicella to a classic Chianti, a velvety Amarone, or an earthy Montepulciano, virtually any Italian red wine will complement sausage, mushroom, and extra cheese perfectly.

➤ **MEXICAN:** A big, bold Spanish Rioja is the way to go with quesadillas or burritos, particularly if they're filled with beef. Even a tostada salad needs a heavier wine to do

MARATHON OF LUST SYMPTOMS

SEVERE SLEEP DEPRIVATION

SORE MUSCLES IN UNUSUAL PLACES

LOSS OF INTEREST IN ANYTHING REMOTELY WORK-RELATED

INABILITY TO KEEP UP WITH DAILY CHORES

YOU HAVE SEVENTY-TWO UNPLAYED MESSAGES

NO IDEA WHAT'S GOING ON IN THE SPORTING WORLD

DIDN'T WE JUST BUY THAT BOX OF CONDOMS YESTERDAY?

NOTICEABLE CHANGE IN SKIN FROM LACK OF UV EXPOSURE

OH, DAMN, MY PLANTS . . .

justice to the guacamole and the sour cream. If you're talking tacos or my favorite, carne asada, then you need a bottle (or two) of a full-bodied red, like a large red Zinfandel. It can handle anything your local Mexican joint can dish out (except maybe the heartburn).

➤ **ITALIAN:** This is a marathon, so why not do what marathoners do: load up on the carbs. I find there's nothing quite like making love all day, then ordering a fish pasta, like linguine with white clam sauce. Get an ensalata mista on the side and serve with a chilled bottle of Pinot Grigio or Orvieto Classico. They're both fabulous and reasonably priced. If you've saved room, finish with a little torta della nona—literally "Grandma's Tart"—something a kinky Italian Red Riding Hood might tote along for dessert.

➤ **DELI:** I don't believe you'll ever find the perfect wine for a six-decker corned beef sandwich, so don't bother. Instead, use your time to track down a couple of bottles of a good ale or lager. But beware of the food coma. A big deli meal may make you a little sleepy, so consider a long nap after lunch with your partner. Chances are you'll both need the rest anyway.

➤ **FAST FOOD:** Sharing your adolescent passions with your significant other can be extremely gratifying—I have had a love affair with McDonald's for as long as I can remember. Before there were boys there were Big Macs. But forget red wine with meat here; I take my Big Mac with a Chardonnay. There is something magical about the way the creamy special sauce plays off the buttery, oaky Chardonnay. And don't forget the fries—two orders at least.

➤ **ROTISSERIE CHICKEN OR BARBECUE:** Arguably the best part of ordering rotisserie chicken is the side dishes. Two are generally included free, but why stop there? Bring home little containers of chicken noodle soup, mac and cheese, roasted potatoes, Caesar salad, creamed spinach, cornbread stuffing, spicy string beans, and a basket of buttermilk biscuits. If you're really hungry, go for the chicken-and-rib combo—and a bottle of fruity Pinot Noir. This is the kind of food that's meant to be eaten savagely. Lick your fingers all you want (and your partner's).

➤ **SUSHI:** Sushi is so light and healthy, if it weren't for all that protein in the yellowfin tuna roll, I'd be hard-pressed to call it Booty Food. Order more rolls than you could possibly eat, heap on the fresh ginger, and turn the evening into an Asian aphrodisiac feast. To quell the wasabi fires, sip from a chilled bottle of good sake.

➤ **DINER BREAKFASTS:** Ordering in greasy morning-after diner food has always been the highlight of my lust life. If you have a phone by your bed, all the better. Dial up your local breakfast joint, then make a quick, no-clothes-necessary trip to the kitchen to mix up a batch of mimosas or Bloody Marys. Enjoy and remain in bed for the better part of the day.

WHAT DO YOU MEAN YOU DON'T DELIVER TO HORSESHOE CREEK?

Thankfully for my love life, I am able to get Malaysian, Jamaican, kosher deli, or patisserie delivered right to my doorstep. However, in most parts of the country, amorous foodies aren't as fortunate. Here are some solutions for those living in the land of "We don't deliver." Many cities have the equivalent of food taxis—companies that work with thirty or so different restaurants and will deliver from any of them for a small fee. You just have to throw on a robe, go to the door, pay the nice man, eat, and get back to bed. Phone your favorite restaurant and order something to go, then call the local cab company to pick it up for you. You pay the fare and you're back in booty. The prepared-foods section of the supermarket can be a surprisingly decent substitute for home delivery. In fact, the next time you find yourself in the checkout line late at night, glance over at the express lane. If there's a couple with devilish smiles on their faces and a rotisserie chicken in their hands, you'll know exactly where they're headed. If you don't have taxis in your town, make good use of the nearest drive-thru. Even Big Macs can be reheated at home before you're on to round two.

DINNER AND A MOVIE

(OR AT LEAST SOME OF A MOVIE)

As long as you've got all those boxes of stir-fried whatever lying around, why not stick with the reclusive theme of the evening and watch a video? (In my book of Booty Food etiquette, Marathon of Lust–ers should be banned from movie theaters altogether. Dark spaces are just too great a temptation to your sense of public decorum.) Renting movies makes you feel like you're actually doing something besides watching TV, even though all you're really doing is watching TV, and it proffers a fine opportunity to cuddle . . . and more. There's only one drawback: You start snuggling during the first act, hands start to wander during act two, and the next thing you know, the VCR is on auto-rewind and your pants are under the sofa. It doesn't matter if it's the greatest film of all time; couples in lust do not see the ends of movies. Period.

Then again, you should still be trying to get to know each other in a less biblical sense, comparing all your likes and dislikes in the world, and that includes films. Conflicting tastes in movies can be a relationship-killer for me. I can forgive a man who snores. I can overlook his passion for klezmer music. But if he in any way dismisses *Lady and the Tramp* or *Joe Versus the Volcano*, I'm going to write him off as a cynical, unromantic stuffed shirt, and I'm certainly not going to neglect my friends and family one more day for him. It's also important to me that my partner has the same fanatical love of the classics as I do. I've easily seen *The Godfather* six hundred times, yet when I flip on the tube and it's showing, I have to stop my life and go along for the ride once again. If I discover that he demonstrates the same affection for *Child's Play VII: Chucky's Nightmare at Girls' Camp*, I might reconsider the relationship—and my current phone number. Bonding over shared interests makes the Marathon of Lust even more intimate than the name infers. This doesn't, however, mean that couples have to have 100 percent identical tastes. I'm sure that a Steven Seagal man and a Meryl Streep gal can find a happy medium somewhere in the video store. Where, I don't know. But I have faith.

Incidentally, the most romantic movie experiences often don't involve romantic movies. The first summer I spent with my love, we decided we couldn't wait to celebrate Christmas together. So one hot July night, we stayed up till the wee hours watching my *Rudolph the Red-Nosed Reindeer* video and the like. We ate cinnamon donuts in bed, drank hot chocolate, and counted the days until December.

And don't forget to laugh! How well you get silly together is every bit as important as how well you get sexy together. Before you even think about moving forward in this relationship, hit the comedy section and make sure you have at least one movie-watching experience where you laugh so hard, the popcorn comes out of your nose.

no-cook aphrodisiac movie munchies

If turning on the oven seems an unlikely activity, hit the aphrodisiac chart for ready-made Booty Food suggestions. Black licorice whips, minty candies, or dark chocolate-walnut turtles are especially apt choices when there's an audience of two in the house. Or try one of these creative snack ideas that take little more work than raiding the pantry. You may never go back to Jujubes again.

— Frozen M&M's mixed with hot popcorn
— A bowl of sun-dried fruit: cherries, apricots, dates, pineapple, mangoes
— Hot popcorn sprinkled with chili powder
— Pumpkin seeds toasted with cayenne and cumin

7)

foods that promote round two

If you want the Marathon of Lust to live up to its name, you'll need the stamina and energy one can only get from protein. My favorite Booty Foods that keep you fueled for an encore performance are cheese, eggs, and seafood. They've got everything you need to recharge your still tingling body for the second round of bliss. And the third. And the eighty-third.

Your lips say "Yes" but your blood sugar level says "Balance Bar." You can't avoid it—you'll have to emerge from beneath the rumpled, sweaty sheets and eat sometime. However, man cannot live by chocolate strawberries alone. Especially when man is getting naked with woman several times a day.

CHEESE, NATURE'S VIAGRA

I once met an aging writer/psychologist who had really been around the block in a Hemingwayesque kind of way. He recounted a story about hiding away in a Paris hotel for a long weekend with his paramour, a few bottles of wine, and a dozen exotic French cheeses. It was the first time I had ever thought of cheese as sexy. Let's just say I was blushing by the end of his tale, and I don't blush easily.

Now that I regard those curds and whey with newfound awe and appreciation, they figure prominently into my own Booty Food experiences. Some of my most religious sexual experiences have been inspired by cheese, although any old variety simply will not do. When it comes to cheese, my motto is "the stinkier the better." I'm talking barely legal, someone needs to wash his socks, clothespin on the nose, who let the French guy in here, alligator ass, "who cut the cheese?" cheese. Young, ripe, blacklisted cheese is the Lolita of the food world, or like the naughty schoolgirl who called her history teacher to his undoing.

I mean, really, what could be sexier than illegal food? I make my way into one of the contraband fromageries near me, wink twice, give the secret handshake, and suddenly the most remarkable wheels of unlawfully imported cheese appear before me, tempting me to take them home if I dare. Blanche DuBois may have feared dying after eating an unwashed grape, but if I expire from feasting on an unpasteurized French triple crème, so be it. I'll go down with a sly little grin on my face.

CHEESE NAT

URE'S VIAGRA

I happen to love red wine with all cheese, although the majority of well-respected wine experts (most of whom, by the way, I have no desire to sleep with) would disagree with me. Red Zinfandel is my go-to red. It seems to hold up to even the most powerful of cheeses. If you're worried about staining the sheets, whites like sauternes and Pinot Blanc are classic and versatile. You can also try to pair cheese with wine from similar regions: Camembert with a Saint-Emilion, California Cheddar with a Napa Chardonnay, Asiago with a Bardolino. But don't sweat it too much. Wine and cheese are really sweet on each other and they always find a way to work out their differences.

WHAM, BAM, THANK YOU MA'AM CHEESE

None of these delicious, cheesy snacks take more than a moment to make, so you can refuel and get back to booty faster.

• Scoop ricotta over fruit salad instead of yogurt.
• Slice sharp Cheddar over Granny Smith apples.
• Microwave a flour tortilla stuffed with goat cheese, cilantro and diced red onions
• Crumble Stilton over mesclun lettuce, and top with balsamic vinegar and walnuts.
• Sprinkle paper-thin shavings of Asiago over steamed asparagus.
• Spread fresh chèvre in a baked potato with fresh-cut chives.
• Top crisp crackers with smoked Gouda and exotic chutneys.
• Grate Fontina over pasta as an alternative to Parmesan.

AROUND THE WORLD IN 8 BILLION CALORIES

If the most exotic cheese you've tried is Brie (not that there's anything wrong with that), prepare to have your eyes opened and your sexual appetite increased tenfold. You are about to be privy to cheeses so soft you could eat them with a spoon, so musky they get the pheromones flying, so lovingly handcrafted that the labels may bear handwritten notes recording the date and time they were wrapped. Try and top that, cheese-in-a-can.

The chart on page 96 is just a shortlist of the varieties that feed my insatiable addiction. To find some of them you'll have to seek out gourmet stores, specialty shops, or on-line purveyors that carry artisanal cheeses. It's entirely worth the effort. When you sample exotic cheeses from around the world you'll feel like you're making love in a Tuscan villa, a Spanish castle, and a Loire Valley château without ever flashing a passport.

THE CHEESE TRAY

One of the greatest things about cheese is that it's so splendid on its own, it needs hardly any preparation at all. At minimum you can throw on a robe (or not), tiptoe into the kitchen, and in moments emerge with a gorgeous cheese plate for two.

➤ **START WITH THE CHEESE:** Choose three to seven cheeses and mingle tastes, textures, colors, shapes, and regions. You can go as rich as you want if you're having a light entrée or if the cheese plate is a meal in itself, which it very well could be.

➤ **ACCOMPANIMENTS:** I prefer cheese the way the French eat it—right off the knife, or at most with a little fruit. I skip the bread because it competes with the flavor and fills me up too quickly, but you can eat cheese any way it turns you on. Smother it across crisp flatbreads, multigrain crackers, crusty peasant bread, fresh sourdough baguette rounds, or olive-dappled breads to your heart's content. Cheese is great with fruit, so surround yours with heaps of fresh apples or pears, plump strawberries, seedless grapes, or get crazy with traditional cheese accompaniments, like figs, dates, or quince paste. I know it sounds peculiar, but if you can find it, you'll impress the pants off any foodie paramour.

➤ **SERVING:** Lay your cheeses out whole on a big wooden block or a nice plate. Provide a separate serving knife for each cheese so the flavors don't intermingle; cheeses and their respective knives should always be monogamous. You'll need a cheese spreader for soft cheeses. Hard cheeses are best cut with a cheese shaver, sharp knife, or wire. Although in the end, if your beloved is lying naked in bed waiting for you to return with the goods, I'll be shocked if you're worrying about cutlery.

If you like...	You'll go nuts over...
SWISS (firm, full-flavored, nutty)	Gruyère (Switzerland) Tête de Moine (Switzerland) Raclette (Switzerland) Emmentaler (Switzerland) Istara (France) Leerdammer (Holland)
AGED CHEDDAR (sharp and powerful)	Cantal (France) English Farmhouse Cheddar (UK) Sao Jorge (Spain)
MOZZARELLA (soft, mild, shreddable)	Fontina (Italy) Halloumi (Cyprus)
BLUE CHEESE (rich, blue-veined, extremely pungent)	Cabrales (Spain) Gorgonzola Dolce (Italy) Roquefort (France) Shropshire Blue (UK) Stilton (UK) Fourme d'Ambert (France)
GOAT CHEESE (creamy, tangy, crumbly)	Chèvre d'Or (France) Chevrochon (France) Peilloute (France) Valençay (France)
BRIE (spoonable, buttery, decadent)	Camembert (France) Epoisses (France) Explorateur (France) Pierre Robert (France) Pont L'Evêque (France) Reblochon (France) St. André (France) Vacherin (France) Taleggio (Italy)
PARMESAN (hard and nutty with a nice bite)	Asiago (Italy) Manchego (Spain) Parmigiano-Reggiano (Italy) Pecorino Romano (Italy)
AMERICAN (smooth and mild)	Havarti (Denmark) Tilsit (Denmark)

Cheese Fondue

The only food hotter than cheese is hot cheese. If you want to keep me home from school for a week, just make me a grilled cheese sandwich, mozzarella sticks, or this yummy cheese fondue. Be sure your cheese is at room temperature before you melt it and always use low heat so the oils won't separate.

  1 tablespoon cornstarch
  1 tablespoon sweet vermouth
  1½ cups of your favorite dry white wine
  1 pound Gruyère, grated
  Crusty French sourdough bread, cut into bite-size cubes
  2 or 3 green apples, sliced
  6 to 8 slices crispy bacon, chopped fine

• Mix together the cornstarch and vermouth in a small cup and set aside.

• Bring wine to a simmer in a medium saucepan over medium heat. Add the cheese a bit at a time, stirring with a wooden spoon as the cheese melts.

• Add the cornstarch mixture to the cheese mixture, and stir until it thickens.

• Transfer to a groovy fondue pot and place over a Sterno.

• Use fondue forks to spear cubes of bread and slices of apple, dip into the pot, roll in bacon bits, and eat.

SERVES 2 / PREP TIME: 5 MINUTES / COOK TIME: 5 TO 10 MINUTES

According to ancient Swedish custom, anyone who drops their bread in the fondue pot must kiss everyone else at the table. Could get interesting . . .

SEAFOOD: FOR TWO OF YOUR FAVORITE ORGANS

You've heard that fish is brain food, but in my opinion it's bedroom food. Seafood is special-occasion food to me, and when I feel like Little Miss Fancy Pants I'm more likely to take them off.

Seafood is elegant, clean, and light enough to keep your sleek loving machine fully fueled but never weighed down. And physiologically, seafood is awe-inspiring. Fish oils have been proven to lead to better concentration, creativity, and dexterity, the very things you'll need when you're on your fourth round of lovemaking that day. Seafood is brimming with vitamin A (the better to see you with, my dear); vitamin D, for healthy bones and teeth (the better to nibble you with, my dear); and zinc, for memory (the better to remember your name in the morning, my dear). And let's not forget all that protein, which you'll certainly need to keep up your strength after six straight hours of taking the lord's name in vain.

With all this good stuff inside, seafood can very well power you through days when you're exerting more energy than usual. Start the morning with scrambled eggs and lox, munch on some sweet rock shrimp for lunch, and if you're not seafooded out, move into nighttime with a few dozen oysters. There should be decency laws against doing so, but, fortunately for you, there aren't.

Reality check: Cooking is still probably not the first thing on your mind. The odds that you're going to tumble out of bed and start whipping up some crazy sea bass dish are slim to none. The following recipes are two of my favorite oceanic nibbles for their combination of scrumptiousness and speedy prep time. They're the next easiest thing to ordering in sushi.

the booty food hierarchy of seafood

When you have a new lover, don't let a pesky little thing like exhaustion stand in your way. Here are varieties of seafood arranged by protein content so you can plan a menu according to how much energy you'll be exerting soon afterward; a romantic evening for two calls for oysters, while round-the-clock gymnas-tics is definitely a job for yellowfin tuna. If you're going for the record, scallops (with a whopping 29 grams of protein) could be as integral to your romantic ambitions as mood lighting and hearing-impaired neighbors. With seafood in your belly, you'll be getting so much *sumpin' sumpin',* you ain't never leaving the house.

Oysters (a dozen) . . . 12 grams of protein	Lobster . . . . 20 grams of protein	Bluefish . . . . 21 grams of protein
Monkfish . . . . 15 grams of protein	Flounder . . . . 20 grams of protein	Swordfish . . . . 21 grams of protein
Squid . . . . 15 grams of protein	Rockfish . . . . 20 grams of protein	Rainbow trout . . . . . . 22 grams of protein
Sea trout . . . . 18 grams of protein	Mussels . . . . 20 grams of protein	Clams (a dozen) . . . . 22 grams of protein
Shad . . . . 18 grams of protein	Sea bass . . . . 20 grams of protein	Atlantic salmon . . . . 22 grams of protein
Blue crab . . . . 19 grams of protein	Whitefish . . . . 20 grams of protein	Shrimp (6 large) . . . 22 grams of protein
Catfish . . . . 19 grams of protein	Mackerel . . . . 21 grams of protein	Fresh Yellowfin Tuna 25 grams of protein
Cod . . . . 19 grams of protein	Pollock . . . . 21 grams of protein	Scallops (6 large) . . . 29 grams of protein
Striped bass . . . . 19 grams of protein	Sole . . . . 21 grams of protein	Source: New York Seafood Council (nyseafood.org)

Bacon-Wrapped Sea Scallops

This dish is definitely worth getting out of bed for. Grab the biggest, plumpest sea scallops you can find, fry up some fatty bacon, put the two together, and you've got a luscious, pure-protein love potion. Follow with a bout of naked Twister, with or without the board.

12 strips bacon
6 large sea scallops, cleaned and removed from shell (you can wash and save shell for garnish, if available)
3 sprigs fresh rosemary
Juice of 1 lemon
Splash white wine
Freshly ground black pepper

• Preheat the oven to broil.
• Fry the bacon in a medium nonstick skillet over medium heat until slightly browned but still pliable, about 2 minutes. Remove the bacon from the pan, and save the rendered bacon fat.
• Wrap the outside of each scallop with 2 strips of bacon, and place on a nonstick cookie sheet. Pick the leaves off 1 rosemary sprig and sprinkle over each scallop.
• Broil for 3 minutes on each side, until the scallops just get firm and the bacon crisps.
• While the scallops are broiling, add the lemon juice and white wine to the bacon fat. Reduce over high heat for a minute or two. This will be used as a sauce for the scallops.
• Remove the scallops from the oven, cover with sauce, sprinkle with pepper, and garnish with remaining rosemary sprigs.

SERVES 2 / PREP TIME: 5 TO 10 MINUTES / COOK TIME: 10 MINUTES

Shrimp cocktail was literally the best thing that happened to me until I discovered the opposite sex. As an adolescent I saw it as a mysteriously refined dish that one encountered only at fancy hotels or country clubs, and eating it was like my ticket into the forbidden world of adults. I've had a love affair with shrimp cocktail ever since. This is erotic finger food at its finest.

Classic Shrimp Cocktail with Horseradish Sauce
1 (12-ounce) bottle lager beer
10 jumbo shrimp (under 15 count)

• Bring the lager to a boil, and add the shrimp. Boil for 3 minutes, or until shrimp are opaque.
• Chill shrimp in ice water, removing them after a minute or so. Serve with horseradish sauce.
NOTE: If desired, the shrimp can be cooked in a court bouillon instead of lager (see recipe below).

SERVES 2 / PREP TIME: 5 TO 10 MINUTES / COOK TIME: 3 MINUTES

Court Bouillon
$\frac{1}{2}$ bottle (325 ml) white wine
$2\frac{1}{2}$ quarts water
1 bay leaf
2 sprigs thyme
4 sprigs parsley
5 black peppercorns
$\frac{1}{2}$ cup roughly chopped carrots
$\frac{1}{2}$ cup roughly chopped celery
$\frac{1}{2}$ cup roughly chopped fennel
$\frac{1}{2}$ cup roughly chopped onion

• Bring the wine and water to a boil. Add the remaining ingredients, and simmer for 45 minutes.

MAKES 5 CUPS / PREP TIME: 10 MINUTES / COOK TIME: 45 MINUTES

Horseradish Sauce
$\frac{1}{2}$ cup ketchup
2 heaping tablespoons very finely grated fresh horseradish
Juice of $\frac{1}{2}$ small lemon (about 2 teaspoons)
Dash Tabasco sauce
Dash Worcestershire sauce

• Combine all ingredients, and mix together.

MAKES $\frac{1}{2}$ CUP / PREP TIME: 10 MINUTES

PSST . . . OYSTERS ARE APHRO-DISIACS. DON'T TELL ANYONE

If you buy into the idea of aphrodisiacs, then you buy into the idea of oysters as love chow. When Aphrodite, the goddess of love, was born, she sprang forth from the ocean in an oyster shell. So I guess you could say that the word *aphrodisiac* itself was born from an oyster. Ever since then, most cultures around the world have acknowledged the mollusk's less-than-angelic reputation. Those crazy ancient Romans sent slaves out to gather oysters from the sea, then served them with abandon in order to help the women (um) loosen up at parties. Casanova reportedly ate dozens of them every day, often in the bathtub with a courtesan or two. I've even read that eating oysters can raise a man's sperm count, but I can't vouch for it. All I know is that they work for me.

Case in point: When my sweetie and I were planning our first date, I was still emerging from a cloud of hell from a particularly bloody breakup. I told him I needed to take it slow. In his own excitement, my man showed up for our first date carrying beautiful flowers and exclaiming that we were heading to Blue Ribbon—a fabulous little restaurant in downtown Manhattan—for champagne and oysters. At that point I cut him off.

"Whoa there, Seabiscuit! Oysters and champagne are definitely Go foods. I said 'slow,' remember? And Blue Ribbon? That place doesn't just inspire foreplay, it *is* foreplay. New idea, please."

We skipped Blue Ribbon and instead headed for a friend's neighborhood fish joint. Despite my best efforts to resist, those bluepoints on the menu just called my name. We fell in love over twelve plump fresh oysters and four glasses of bubbly right there at the front table, and it took every ounce of resolve not to jump him on the spot. The moral of the story? I have few morals when oysters are present. I'm telling you—this stuff works.

Fresh Oysters with Red Wine Mignonette

Although oysters can be eaten raw with just a dollop of Worcestershire sauce and lemon, I love eating them in the classic French style, with a simple red wine vinegar and shallot mignonette. Serve with chilled champagne for a combination that is quintessentially Booty Food. If home cooks want to venture into the naughty land of oyster, purchase yours live and fresh. Rinse them under cold running water, scrubbing the shells to remove the schmutz. Always serve oysters as soon as possible. Always turn the ringer off your phone.

FOR RED WINE MIGNONETTE:
¼ cup red-wine vinegar
2 teaspoons minced shallots
Pinch finely chopped parsley
¼ teaspoon sugar
Kosher salt to taste
1 teaspoon freshly ground black pepper

• Combine all the ingredients and stir.

MAKES ⅓ CUP / PREP TIME: 5 MINUTES

FOR OYSTERS:
1 dozen oysters

• Shuck the oysters, leaving them on the half-shell, or reassemble preshucked oysters. Serve them on a plate of crushed ice and spoon on the mignonette.

SERVES 2 / PREP TIME: 20 MINUTES

I'M A LOVER, NOT A SHUCKER. Shucking, for those new to the mollusk world, can be downright dangerous. Ask your fishmonger to shuck the oysters for you, and to pack them, and their liquor, in a spill-proof container. Have him wash and bag your shells separately. Refrigerate well until use, which shouldn't be more than 4 to 5 hours before serving. Reassemble when it's time for booty and come off looking like a seafood sex god.

OYSTERS MAKE ME HOT. PASS IT ON . . .
One night my man and I cozied up at a corner table with two dozen fresh Wellfleet oysters and a killer bottle of Cristal. We sat inappropriately close, giggling, kissing and feeding each other. At one point I prepared an oyster with the perfect amount of mignonette, fed it to him, then followed it with a long, deep kiss. To my surprise and delight, he passed it right back to me with his mouth. The more kisses, the more oyster passing, the more desperate our cry of "Check, please!"

I suggest you only attempt the pass-along oyster game in the privacy of your own home. Unless you've mastered the delayed-gratification thing, it could definitely lead to coatroom sex.

EGGS: BREAKFAST OF CHAMPIONS

What could be a more appropriate nosh for a couple who's spending the entire day in bed than breakfast food? Breakfast can be foreplay. It can be afterplay. And if you're really in lust, it can be afterplay that becomes foreplay all over again. Eggs play no small part in this equation. They just seem to be made for couples with little on their minds besides each other. They're sexy, they're easy (it's hard to mess up a plate of scrambleds too badly), and they're definitely aphrodisiacs. Why does an egg put you in the mood for love? Like, duh, it's an egg. Its purpose is to make babies. So there is logic in the notion that eating one will make you want to make babies—or at least have a great time practicing. If I'm going to cook anything at all during the Marathon of Lust, it's going to be this.

I've determined that there are two categories of egg preparation: high eggs and low eggs. The high ones usually take place on Sunday mornings and involve fresh, fluffy omelets, a beautifully set table, several rounds of mimosas, and a pair of stiletto slippers from the Frederick's of Hollywood catalog. Low eggs mean my man is going to be my eggs-and-bacon bitch. It's quick, it's raunchy, I'm wearing sweats or nothing at all, and it's no less fulfilling than going the omelet route. Try both—you've got nothing to lose except inhibitions. Just be sure not to attempt any recipe with splatter potential while unclothed. Naked bacon-and-eggs cooking can lead to the burn unit, and I have the scars to prove it.

Huevos Rancheros are my favorite kind of eggs to make, the best of both worlds. They're somehow gourmet and down and dirty all at once. Add a pitcher of Bloody Marys and you've got the ultimate anytime breakfast meal.

If you want to get highfalutin with Bloody Marys, improve upon the classic celery-stalk garnish. Instead, top with a whole shrimp and a pickled string bean. It looks amazing and tastes even better. Or use pickled hot peppers, pickled okra, pickled cauliflower—pretty much anything from the pickle aisle. You could even moisten the rim of the glass and roll it in celery salt before filling with vodka-tomato goodness.

Spicy Bloody Marys

Shelf-stable Bloody Mary mixes are no match for homemade, and this one literally takes minutes to make. The secret to a perfect Bloody Mary is liberal use of fresh horseradish and a good squeeze of lemon. Add the vodka later if you have guests who prefer to stay sober before noon.

20 ounces tomato juice
4 ounces vodka
4 tablespoons Worcestershire sauce
1 tablespoon Tabasco sauce
2 teaspoons fresh horseradish, grated
Kosher salt
Freshly ground black pepper
Dash celery salt for drink, and lots to salt rims of glasses
Juice of $\frac{1}{2}$ lemon
1 lime, quartered, for garnish

• Combine all the ingredients except for the lime, and mix well. Serve over ice in salted glasses and garnish with lime.

MAKES 1 PITCHER, ENOUGH FOR 2 PEOPLE / PREP TIME: 10 MINUTES

Huevos Rancheros

Fried eggs get a kick from onions, peppers, and jalapeños in this Mexican rendition of stick-to-the-ribs breakfast food. Aphrodisiac content: eggs, black beans, cheese, and onions; this recipe will not only fuel you for round two, it will probably inspire it.

FOR SALSA ROJA:
6 large plum tomatoes, cut in half
1 red bell pepper, halved, stem and seeds removed
2 cloves garlic, minced
Olive oil
Kosher salt
Freshly ground black pepper
$\frac{1}{2}$ teaspoon chipotle paste
$\frac{1}{2}$ teaspoon cayenne pepper
Splash red-wine vinegar

• Preheat the oven to 375 degrees.
• Place the tomatoes and bell pepper in a roasting pan. Sprinkle with garlic, olive oil, salt, and pepper, and roast for 30 minutes, until the vegetables begin to soften and color.
• Place the roasted vegetables and their pan juices in a food processor, and add the chipotle, cayenne, and vinegar. Blend until smooth.

EASY

• Pour the mixture into a small saucepan and heat on low for 10 minutes. Adjust seasoning if necessary.

FOR BEANS:
2 tablespoons olive oil
$\frac{1}{4}$ white onion, diced
1 clove garlic, minced
$\frac{1}{2}$ small jalapeño pepper, minced, stem and seeds removed
1 (14$\frac{1}{2}$-ounce) can black beans, rinsed and drained
Chopped cilantro
Pinch cayenne pepper
Pinch cumin
Pinch chipotle powder or paste
Kosher salt
Freshly ground black pepper
Splash water

• Heat the olive oil in a medium saucepan, and sauté the onion, garlic, and jalapeño pepper without achieving color. Add the beans to the saucepan, then add the rest of the ingredients, and simmer on low heat for 10 minutes. Add more water if necessary.

FOR EGGS:
2 (8- to 10-inch) flour tortillas
$\frac{1}{8}$ cup olive oil
Kosher salt
4 tablespoons butter ($\frac{1}{2}$ stick)
4 large eggs
2 cups ($\frac{1}{2}$ pound) sharp Cheddar, grated
$\frac{1}{4}$ cup sour cream
Cilantro for garnish

TO ASSEMBLE:
• Preheat the oven to 400 degrees.
• Brush one side of the tortillas with oil and sprinkle with salt. Place in the oven, oiled side down, for 3 minutes. Remove from the oven.
• Melt the butter in a medium skillet, and fry the eggs to your liking. (I like mine sunny-side up, but even scrambled would do.) Remove the eggs from the pan.
• Place the tortillas on a cookie sheet, crisp side down; add the beans, then the eggs, the sauce, and, finally, the cheese. Bake in the oven until the cheese is melted, top with sour cream, garnish with cilantro, and serve.

SERVES 2 / PREP TIME: 20 MINUTES / COOK TIME: ABOUT 40 MINUTES

KEEPING YOUR BODY IN PRIME SHAPE FOR PLEASURE DOESN'T HAVE TO INVOLVE CREATINE SHAKES AND WHEATGRASS SHOTS. WOULDN'T YOU RATHER INDULGE IN A DOZEN FRESH OYSTERS OR A GORGEOUS CHEESE TRAY DINE FOR TWO? GET YOUR FILL OF PROTEIN IN ONE OF ITS MORE DELECTABLE FORMS AND THE LAST THING YOU'LL BE THINKING ABOUT IS NUTRITIONAL CONTENT; YOU'LL BE TOO BUSY FULFILLING YOUR EVERY MARATHON OF LUST FANTASY. FOR THE FIFTH TIME. THIS AFTERNOON.

dessert's on me

I didn't fully realize *my* Dessert's on Me fantasy until one particularly noteworthy evening when I literally wore my chocolate birthday cake to bed. From then on, it's been hard to peek inside my fridge without devising ways in which its contents could be nibbled off me or a compliant partner. Jellies, jams, sauces, chutneys, nut butters—you name it. If it's edible and spreadable, you can serve it up with a heaping side order of you.

Food and foreplay go together like a naughty boy and a good spanking. I've been intrigued with the concept of erotic culinary experiences ever since a blindfolded Kim Basinger had honey drizzled on her awesomely long tongue in *9½ Weeks*.

PLAY WITH YOUR FOOD

If you're new to the realm of adult-food fun, all you need is a sense of adventure, a good appetite, and, most important, a partner you're truly comfortable with. This is pretty intimate stuff after all. Those who still feel vulnerable naked with the lights on will definitely not enjoy being naked with the lights on and melon juice dripping from their hair. Needless to say, this is not an approved first-date activity.

The easiest way to bring food and foreplay together is simply to feed your partner. Pick any sort of food at all, although I am partial to desserts (I like getting hopped up on sugar, then having sex). Take a spoonful of whatever delicacy you're serving and bring it to your partner's lips. That's all there is to it; I guarantee hormones will take over from there. For intermediate gastro-erotic aficionados, lose the spoon and feed your lover with your hands. Not only is it a turn-on to have your fingers eagerly sucked clean, your partner will be every bit as stimulated. There's a sexy, submissive thing about being fed, and it will, decidedly, initiate activities not suitable for children under eighteen.

To get a bit more risqué with the contents of your pantry, let your imagination run amok; I'm sure you can concoct plenty of serving suggestions that would never appear on the side of the box. Drip gooey honey or real maple syrup on parts of your body that need a little nibbling. Spray whipped cream downward starting at your belly button. Put a dab of strawberry jam just behind your ear, or anywhere that's pining for a soft wet tongue. You can even bind a love slave's wrists with shoestring licorice whips, then bite them off when you're ready to release him on his own recognizance. ("Do you promise to be a bad boy? Okay, then . . .")

One way to up the ante is to inject the element of surprise. (The greatest thing about the chocolate-birthday-cake incident was that my honey completely blindsided me with it.) To keep things unexpected, add a blindfold to the equation. Feed your lover, alternating different flavors, textures, temperatures. Just when she's starting to enjoy the hot sesame noodles, surprise her with an icy strawberry popsicle. Dip each of your fingers in a different ingredient—cayenne, cinnamon sugar, Marshmallow Fluff—and make sure she systematically licks each one good and clean. Or alternate crunchy apple slices with the silky pulp of a fresh mango. (Have you eaten a mango lately? It's the epicurean substitute for a moist tongue. Try one and you'll definitely understand why ancient Indians used to apply it to their genitals to get in the mood.)

Then there's chocolate.

Some claim chocolate is better than sex, but I think it's better with sex. Blindfold your unsuspecting partner and drizzle chocolate syrup on his or her tongue. Kiss and share the sensation. Dip ripe, luscious strawberries into Nutella, then pass it to your beau with your lips. Or find that chocolate-shell stuff that hardens as it cools. It's intended for ice cream, but I'll bet it would taste far better on you. Chocolate soufflé, chocolate brownies, chocolate cupcakes, chocolate mousse—if it's got cocoa butter at the top of the ingredient list and you incorporate it into your sexual escapades, be warned that things could get no hotter. One of you just might spontaneously combust before the night is through.

THE TRUTH ABOUT CHOCOLATE. As with oysters, there's a reason chocolate is associated with love and lust. In a word: science. Chocolate contains more than three hundred chemicals with mood-altering effects. One is an amphetaminelike substance that supposedly stimulates the brain the same way falling in love does, increasing endorphins and generally making you feel good all over. Plus there's caffeine, which gets the heart pumping and is a neurotransmitter a whole lot like the THC found in marijuana. Of course you'd have to eat about twenty-five pounds of chocolate to get high, but I'm pretty sure I could do it.

twisted-tasting menus

An alternative to exploring random flavors you find in your kitchen: Devise a theme for your dessert perversion, creating a twisted-tasting menu of sorts. Here are a few suggestions, each of which serve two very, very well.

• **NAME THAT FRUIT:** Strawberries, peaches, plums, watermelon, fresh berries, and a snug blindfold

• **CHOCOLATE THREE-WAY:** Hot fudge, chocolate ice cream, chocolate pudding

• **PLEASURE AND PAIN:** Tabasco, honey, chili peppers, cantaloupe (in that order)

• **DO "IT" YOURSELF SUNDAES:** Your favorite flavors of ice cream, hot fudge, butterscotch sauce, whipped cream, maraschino cherries

• **EROTIC MASTERPIECE:** Chocolate syrup, strawberry sauce, blueberry coulis, maple syrup, honey; apply like finger paints to a human canvas

The only rule if you're into fetish-food play is that there are no rules. But there are a few common-sense tips I can offer, if only to help you have as much fun as you possibly can.

➤ **STICK WITH FOODS THAT TASTE GOOD.** It's fairly intuitive, but there's a reason Brussels sprouts are not Booty Food. Food that tastes good makes you feel good; food that tastes healthy makes you feel like jogging. It's just not the same thing.

➤ **CONSIDER THE CLEAN-UP FACTOR.** If you're going to get crazy messy, you might want to get busy in the bathtub or on the kitchen floor, or lay a plastic sheet over the bed to minimize the damage. Day-old congealed chocolate on the duvet isn't particularly a turn-on.

➤ **WASH HANDS AFTER HANDLING SPICY PEPPERS** if you plan on handling each other afterward. Imagine mistaking the tube of Icy Hot for the tube of K-Y jelly and you get the idea.

➤ **DON'T WORRY ABOUT HOW YOU LOOK.** So, you've got chocolate pudding in your ear and vanilla frosting between your toes. She does too.

➤ **FINISH THE EPISODE WITH A HOT BATH OR SHOWER.** You don't want to remain sticky the next morning. Besides, sweet or oily stuff left on the body is not a great idea for a woman. Enough said?

If you're so inclined, you can prepare your own kinky accoutrements from scratch. My favorite homemade edible spreadables are a cinch to make. Whipping them up seems less like cooking and more like foreplay—it's exciting to consider how the fruits of your labors might be reaped later on. Don't worry about the calories. I've never heard of one couple remarking, "Boy, that chocolate-pudding episode was fun, but we should really try it again next time with nonfat yogurt."

Double Chocolate Raspberry Pudding

Pudding brings out your inner child whether you're eating it right out of the mixing bowl or finding other novel uses for it. Utilize this recipe to temporarily tattoo your name onto your lover's body, then go claim your spoils.

$\frac{1}{2}$ cup sugar
$\frac{1}{2}$ teaspoon salt
4 tablespoons unsweetened cocoa
$1\frac{1}{2}$ tablespoons cornstarch
$\frac{1}{8}$ cup warm whole milk
1 cup heavy cream
1 ounce semisweet chocolate, grated
1 ounce white chocolate, grated
Splash Chambord (raspberry liqueur)
$\frac{1}{2}$ tablespoon vanilla

• Mix together the sugar, salt, cocoa, cornstarch, and milk in a small bowl until it makes a paste.

• Heat the cream in a small saucepan until just before scalding, then add the dark and white chocolate, stir, and add the cocoa paste. Mix well and bring to a boil, stirring constantly. Add the Chambord and the vanilla. When the pudding begins to thicken, remove it from the heat and let it rest for 2 minutes.

• Pour into temperature-resistant bowls or ramekins, and refrigerate until set (at least 30 minutes). Let cool completely before eating or using as body paint.

MAKES ABOUT 2 CUPS / PREP TIME: 5 MINUTES COOK TIME: 3 TO 5 MINUTES

Chocolate Cream Frosting

Good frosting is often the only reason to eat cake. If you don't eat the whole batch in one sitting, use what's left to frost cupcakes the next day. Then you'll have something new to play with that night.

> 1 (1-pound) box confectioners' sugar
> ¹/₈ teaspoon salt
> ¹/₂ cup milk
> 1 teaspoon vanilla, or 1 tablespoon rum
> 4 ounces unsweetened chocolate
> 4 tablespoons butter (¹/₂ stick)

- Place the sugar in a large bowl. Add the salt, milk, and vanilla or rum; whisk well.
- Melt the chocolate and butter together in a heat-proof bowl over hot water. Add the chocolate mixture to the sugar mixture, and mix well.
- Let stand, stirring occasionally, until thick enough to spread.

MAKES 2¹/₂ CUPS / PREP TIME: 10 MINUTES

Hot Butterscotch Sauce

Hot fudge gets most of the attention in the ice cream parlor, but that doesn't mean butterscotch needs your sympathy. With just the right combination of butter, brown sugar, and corn syrup, you've got a caramel love sauce that can hold its own against any dessert topping.

> 1 cup firmly packed brown sugar
> ¹/₃ cup heavy cream
> 3 tablespoons light corn syrup
> 4 tablespoons butter
> 2 teaspoons rum (optional)

- Combine the first 4 ingredients in a small saucepan, and bring to a boil. Stir until the mixture is thickened and smooth, about 3 or 4 minutes, then stir in the rum, if desired.
- Cool to room temperature, and serve over butter-pecan, chocolate, coffee, or vanilla ice cream, or . . .

MAKES 1¹/₄ CUPS / PREP TIME: 10 MINUTES / COOK TIME: 5 MINUTES

Whipped Cream from Scratch (with variations)

I love Reddi-wip (so named because it gets me ready for anything), but plenty of foodies would sooner skip dessert toppings altogether than buy the stuff in a can. Add a touch of real maple syrup or fruit coulis for a flavored body topping unmatched by anything you could find in one of those adult novelty stores.

>   **1 pint heavy cream or whipping cream, well chilled**
>   **2 tablespoons superfine or powdered sugar, or 2 tablespoons maple syrup**
>   **½ teaspoon vanilla extract**

• Begin whipping the cream, and when it starts to thicken, add the sugar or syrup and the vanilla extract. Continue whipping until soft peaks appear.
    • For flavored whipped cream fold in some berry coulis (see recipe below).

MAKES ABOUT 4 CUPS / PREP TIME: 7 MINUTES

Three-Berry Coulis

>   **1 pint strawberries**
>   **½ pint blueberries**
>   **½ pint raspberries**
>   **Juice of 2 lemons**
>   **4 tablespoons sugar**

• Combine all the ingredients in a blender or food processor and puree until smooth. Fold into whipped cream. If you have some coulis left over, save it to serve over vanilla ice cream or to make a berry smoothie.

MAKES ABOUT 4 CUPS / PREP TIME: 5 MINUTES

ONCE YOU'VE TRULY PUT FOOD AND BOOTY TOGETHER, EVERYTHING WILL START TO LOOK LIKE BOOTY FOOD TO YOU. IN FACT, IT MAY BE CHALLENGING TO REVERT TO HAVING ONE AT A TIME. ISN'T IT GREAT TO BE A CONSENTING ADULT?

9)

afternoon delights (nooky hooky)

Nooky Hooky is all about immediate gratification, both in the culinary and the carnal arenas. Forget the candles and caviar, the food is fast and so is the loving. And it's only made more hot by the fact that your illicit lunchtime romp will necessarily entail lies, deception, and complete disregard for responsibility.

You can't call in sick to work forever. Someone's got to bring home the proverbial bacon so that you can afford all those overdue fines at the video store. Don't worry about missing quality booty time during the day—that's why God invented lunch hour.

GET-OUT-OF-WORK-FREE CARD

If you're hoping to secure a two- or three-hour-long lunch break that you might spend in a horizontal position, leave your ethics at the door. You've got to come up with a big, fat, unabashed lie to account for your prolonged absence from work. Just be sure to follow a few common-sense rules and no one will be the wiser.

➤ **THE MOST CREDIBLE NOOKY HOOKY ALIBIS ARE SPECIFIC.** Details make all the difference. For example, don't say you have a dentist appointment; describe that you have a consultation with an oral surgeon regarding a wisdom-tooth extraction. Or, instead of telling your boss that you're bringing your cat to the vet, state that you're taking her to a feline osteoarthritis specialist across town. Who would question that?

➤ **CONCOCT AN EXCUSE WITH AN INFINITE TIME SPAN.** Client meetings won't last forever, but waiting on line at the DMV certainly might.

➤ **MAKE SURE YOUR ALIBI CHECKS OUT** (or, better yet, can't be checked out). It would be dreadful to say you're visiting your brother in prison, only to have him show up at your office to surprise you for lunch.

> **BE CONSISTENT.** Make sure to relate the same excuse to each of your coworkers. You don't need the office gossip describing your dermatologist appointment to the HR director, who thinks you're having your tires rotated.

> **KEEP UP THE CHARADE.** If your boss is expecting you to return to work with a mouth full of novocaine, you'd better darn well be slobbering when you run into her in the hallway.

If worse comes to worst, make note of the escape routes at your place of employment—a service elevator, fire escape, or back entrance may be the means to a perfectly justifiable end.

NOOKY HOOKY BASICS

Nooky Hooky can be spontaneous ("Honey, I can't wait another second to see you. I'll be at your place in ten minutes"), but I like planning it in advance. It's a complete turn-on to spend the entire morning fantasizing about the midday interlude to come. In the morning, leave a provocative Polaroid of yourself in your baby's briefcase or jacket pocket. Write a sexy note with it explaining all the things you're going to do to each other at noon. (Just make sure your lover is discreet and trustworthy; it would kind of suck to find your naked photo on the Internet somewhere down the road.) At the same time, get everything in place for your rendezvous. Set out the dishes, defrost the soup, check the batteries in the video camera (if that's your thing). You don't want to spend one iota of your lunchtime setting up.

If you arrive home before your partner, change into a robe or simply wait naked between the sheets. Nooky Hooky is all about cutting to the chase—no fumbling with belt buckles or bra closures, no prolonged foreplay, no mood lighting. Racing against the clock isn't a negative, it's part of the excitement, so don't try to fight it.

Out of necessity, your meal should be a quickie as well. Unless you're not expected back at work for a week, stay away from oysters and chilled champagne. My menu of choice is the grammar-school snow-day combo of hot, creamy soup with a toasty grilled-cheese sandwich. It's sexy and comforting all at once. You can prepare the soup in advance, then simmer to reheat while you're making the grilled cheese. But if you'd rather whip up a couple of roast beef sandwiches or finish off the leftover rotisserie chicken in the fridge, go right ahead. Just make sure you do it in a hurry.

You might prefer eating at the end of your indiscretion once you've worked up an appetite. Just make sure to save a few minutes! If need be, wrap up the sandwich, thermos the soup, and eat on the way back to work with a big smile.

HOTEL NOOKY HOOKY

If you live more than a quick drive from work, your home probably isn't the ideal Nooky Hooky location. This isn't to say that hotels are a compromise; on the contrary: What could be sexier than a midday romp between sheets that you don't have to wash afterward?

If you're going the swanky-hotel route, be sure to ask for an early check-in or you may not get much further than first base in the lobby. Arrange to have lunch sent up when you arrive (emphasis on *when you arrive*), ideally something simple that will keep for an hour, like salad, soup, cold sandwiches, or pasta. If you can get away with an extended lunch—or you're not planning on going back to work at all—then do dial up for room service.

Room service is the height of decadence if you think about it. A single push of a button is generally all it takes for a white-linen-clad table overflowing with Booty Food to come rolling into my room. The waiter sets my table, pours my wine, serves my food, then goes on his merry way until I call him to take it away. It's the Western equivalent of having your own personal geisha, and it definitely puts me in the mood. I don't care that they charge $14 for a Belgian waffle, I'm not getting busy in a hotel until I've at least ordered up *something*.

I'm not the only one who thinks of room service as essential foreplay. The W Hotel in New York's Times Square actually has a "Sex in the Sheets" option on its room-service menu. Ingredients: ice cream, hot fudge, caramel sauce, a Polaroid camera, and a plastic sheet for the bed. But you don't need a chichi New York hotel to have sexy food sent up to your room. Any number of Booty Food favorites are staples on most hotel menus, including shrimp cocktail, tomato soup, and chocolate cake. Check the kids' menu if you've got a hankering for a burger and fries or an ice cream sundae. Or order a cheesy omelet off the twenty-four-hour breakfast menu to fuel yourselves for a second interlude. Just be sure to hang the Do Not Disturb sign afterward.

Naturally you don't need to break the bank to get some during daylight hours. Throw caution to the wind and spend your afternoon in a sleazy $40 motel room. There's a lurid excitement in wolfing down fast food from the nearest drive-thru then getting it on as loudly as you want. Don't worry about the other guests—they practically *expect* it.

Just for fun, try checking in under a fake name to make your escapade seem all that much more illicit. Try using your "porn-star name"—the name of your first pet plus the street you grew up on. Mine is Cotton Sheffley and my man's is Tigger Lakeview. Feel free to borrow them. Just don't charge your room to us.

Only after you've thoroughly had your way with one another, mangled the sheets, and knocked the bad art off the wall should you return to polite society. You may find it hard to reacclimate after an afternoon in fantasyland, so take it slowly. Your best bet is to call it a wash and blow off work for the rest of the day, although I realize that may not be an option.

If you don't want to get caught when you return to the daily grind (nothing kills a post-coital buzz faster), simply try not to replay your lunch date in your head. It will be inexplicably hard to stop smiling, and your boss is going to wonder exactly what that "doctor" did to you. Hint: Let your mind wander to a painful bikini wax or Sister Mary Agnes. I'm sure you're much more attractive to your partner when you're gainfully employed.

NOTE: According to aphrodisiac lore, pumpkin seeds are a major aphrodisiac. Proceed with caution.

Five-Star Butternut Squash Soup

This delectable soup recipe was inspired by those you find on the room-service menu at upscale hotels. Indulge in a quick bowl or two after your noontime rendezvous and magically transform your abode into the honeymoon suite.

Using fresh pumpkin is best, but if you don't have a stray pumpkin lying around the house (the horror!), canned pumpkin-pie filling works just fine.

1 (3½-pound) butternut squash
1 small (2½-pound) pumpkin, halved, or 7 ounces canned pumpkin puree
1½ tablespoons olive oil
Kosher salt
Freshly ground black pepper
4 tablespoons butter (½ stick), plus 2 tablespoons
¼ cup crème fraîche
¼ teaspoon allspice
⅛ teaspoon cinnamon
¼ teaspoon nutmeg
3 cups vegetable stock (canned or homemade)
1 gram saffron
Cayenne-toasted pumpkin seeds for garnish
Splash cream (optional)

• Preheat the oven to 350 degrees.
• Slice the squash in half, then seed and gut it.
• Scoop out the pumpkin halves.
• Drizzle olive oil over the squash and the pumpkin, and sprinkle with salt and pepper. Add 1 teaspoon of butter to each half. Roast in a pan for 40 minutes, checking to make sure the vegetables don't burn.
• While the pumpkin and squash meat is still hot, spoon out the flesh, and place it in a food processor. Puree with 3 tablespoons of the butter, half the crème fraîche, the allspice, cinnamon, nutmeg, and salt and pepper.
• Combine the vegetable stock and saffron in a medium saucepan, and simmer on medium heat for 5 minutes to flower the saffron.
• Add the puree, and simmer briefly. Then add the remaining crème fraîche, and adjust the seasonings.
• For garnish, toast pumpkin seeds gently in 2 tablespoons of butter. Drain, and sprinkle with salt and a pinch of cayenne. Garnish the soup with the toasted seeds, and a splash of cream if you desire.

MAKES ABOUT 6 CUPS / PREP TIME: 20 MINUTES / COOK TIME: 45 MINUTES / PREP IN ADVANCE, THEN REHEAT IN SECONDS TO MAKE SURE YOU HAVE ENOUGH TIME FOR YOUR LUNCH-HOUR LOVE

Grilled Cheese with Sharp Cheddar and Bacon

Grilled Cheddar cheese sandwiches remind me of childhood, so I feel extra mischievous eating one for lunch naked in bed. If you're really short on time, skip the bacon. If you're a vegetarian, skip the bacon. If you don't want to wear clothes in the kitchen, skip the bacon.

> **6 strips bacon**
> **4 slices white rye bread (unseeded)**
> **4 tablespoons salted butter (½ stick), softened**
> **¼ pound sharp Cheddar, thinly sliced**
> **2 kosher dill pickles**

- Fry the bacon in a pan until just before crisp. Remove it, and drain on paper towels.
- Butter the outside of the bread, and assemble the sandwiches with slices of cheese and bacon.
- Melt 1 tablespoon of butter in a fresh frying pan, and cook the sandwiches over medium heat until golden brown, about 3 minutes on each side. You want to achieve a crisp outside and a gooey melted inside. (If the bread is browning too fast, either put a lid over the pan or put it in a 300-degree oven for 3 to 5 minutes, until the cheese melts.)
- Serve each sandwich with a kosher dill pickle.

SERVES 2 / PREP TIME: 5 MINUTES / COOK TIME: 6 MINUTES

Grilled Pecorino and Serrano Ham Sandwich

Add a European accent to your grilled cheese with this irresistible combination of cured Spanish serrano ham and Italian pecorino cheese. It's delicious with a big red wine if you've got the time.

> **4 tablespoons salted butter (½ stick), softened**
> **4 slices white rye bread (unseeded)**
> **¼ pound young pecorino cheese (like Pecorino Toscano), sliced**
> **¼ pound serrano ham**

- Butter the outside of the bread. Assemble sandwiches with slices of cheese and ham.
- Melt 1 tablespoon of butter in a frying pan. Cook the sandwiches over medium heat until golden brown, about 3 minutes on each side. You want to achieve a crisp outside and a gooey melted inside. (If the bread is browning too quickly, either place a lid over the pan or put it in a 300-degree oven for 3 to 5 minutes, until the cheese melts.)

SERVES 2 / PREP TIME: ABOUT 5 MINUTES / COOK TIME: ABOUT 6 MINUTES

Grilled Goat Cheese with Green Apple and Toasted Walnuts

This sweet, nutty grilled-cheese sandwich is doubly outstanding between two thick slices of a good multigrain bread. If you don't have the time to toast fresh walnuts, buy them roasted and put the extra minutes to better use.

4 tablespoons salted butter (½ stick), softened
4 slices multigrain bread
½ pound goat cheese, crumbled
1 Granny Smith apple (skin on), thinly sliced
10 halves toasted walnuts (see page 40)

- Butter the outside of the bread.
- Assemble sandwiches with crumbles of cheese, slices of apple, and walnuts.
- Melt 1 tablespoon of butter in a frying pan. Cook the sandwiches over medium heat until golden brown, about 3 minutes on each side. You want to achieve a crisp outside and a gooey melted inside. (If the bread browns too quickly, either cover the pan with a lid or put it in a 300-degree oven for 3 to 5 minutes, until the cheese melts.)

SERVES 2 / PREP TIME: 8 MINUTES / COOK TIME: 6 MINUTES

NOOKY HOOKY MENU CHECKLIST: ☑ IT'S FAST

say ahhhhh:
get-well food

SHARING GERMS . . . HOW ROMANTIC

It is impossible to spend days—or perhaps weeks—on end behaving like porn stars without getting at least a case of the sniffles. The relationship is still young and you likely haven't faced any major crises together yet. Getting sick is something of a test run for the bigger hurdles that are yet to come. (Incidentally, *sick* has fairly broad connotations—a nasty cold, a pulled muscle, a killer hangover, scurvy. Anything temporarily incapacitating will do for the purposes of this chapter, particularly if it lends itself to soup making.)

One minute you're performing moves that would put those pygmy-sized Olympic gymnasts to shame and the next, you can't find the energy to dispose of the sixteen tissues that have missed the trash can.

Hopefully you won't both become ill at the same time; it's no fun perspiring through your sheets without someone to cater to your every whim. Indeed, it's one of the best things about being part of a couple—you've got your own personal valet to run to the store and buy you gossipy magazines or the latest *SI*. To make you homemade chicken soup with a side of toast, just the way you like it. (A whisper-thin spread of marmalade? Lightly browned? Crusts off?) To surprise you with little gifts that momentarily make you forget that Bob Villa must have tiptoed into your bedroom in the middle of the night and worked over your throat with a square of sixty-grit sandpaper.

It's important to be a good patient. Admitting you need help isn't a sign of weakness but rather a sign of adulthood, the same as drinking martinis and pretending you watch PBS. Besides, any relationship-worthy person has a nurturing instinct. Don't let stubborn independence suffocate your sweetie's latent caretaker, yearning to breathe free.

Now, here's an important question to ask yourself when your hair is matted to your face and your pj's feel permanently affixed to your body: Do you mind that your partner is seeing you at your absolute worst? No, you say? You're both okay with it? Good sign.

Excellent sign. An even better sign is his insistence on returning to your bedside only when he is in possession of the very brand of cough syrup you've requested, plus a surprise bottle of vitamin C. On the other hand, if he suddenly has to work late when you call him asking for "sub bore oradge juice and sub bagazines," it's a good bet that he was only in it for the booty. In which case, kick his gluteus maximus to the curb with light speed. You'll thank me later.

YOUR INNER FLORENCE NIGHTINGALE

If your partner is the lucky winner of the virus du jour, the ball is in your court. Nurse him or her back to health, and it's fair to assume that you can take care of your sweetie emotionally as well.

One of my favorite bad-date stories is from a woman who severely slammed her finger in a door only moments before her date arrived to meet her. The poor guy didn't know what to do. She wanted him to declare, "Here's an ice pack. Here's a shot of tequila. Lie down on the couch. I'll call you later to make sure you're okay." Instead, he fumbled around without the slightest idea of how to take care of her and even (I can't believe this) attempted to tongue-kiss her when she handed him his jacket. He was a perfectly nice guy but perfectly clueless. The door may have, in fact, hit him in the keister on the way out. It just goes to prove that although the thought does count, sometimes competence counts more. Take control of the situation and your partner will start to feel better.

Don't overreact, though. An upset stomach doesn't necessitate programming 911 on your speed dial. Simply look at him with genuine sympathy—a big "awwww" goes a long way—and lay the back of your hand on his forehead (even if you don't know what you're feeling for). Make hot tea without asking first. Let him whine to his heart's content. And what better time to set a pot of homemade chicken soup simmering on the stovetop? If you've never attempted this before, your partner will be thoroughly impressed, even if he is not lucid enough to say so. Besides, you needn't worry about screwing it up; he can't taste anything anyway.

Of course, don't try to get intimate right now. Sick people aren't generally in the mood. Let your baby build up some strength, and in no time at all you'll be rewarded with some grateful, now-I'm-feeling-better booty.

THE PERFECT POT OF TEA

Sick or not, I love wrapping my palms around a mug of hot peppermint tea with a wedge of lemon and just a touch of honey. When my man brings a cup of chamomile to bed for me, it's a big warm hug.

Plopping a tea bag into a microwaved cup of water is to tea what Sanka crystals are to fresh java. Believe it or not, there's a science to brewing the perfect pot of tea. First, you

When I was sick once, and on the road, a boyfriend had chicken soup delivered to my hotel room from the best Jewish deli in town. How cool is that? I've never been too sick to appreciate a truly thoughtful gesture. Consider surprising your sniffling sweetheart with one of the following and showing him or her that you're in it for the long haul:

➤ Flowers and balloons—the goofier the better (laughter heals)
➤ Magazines
➤ Chocolate
➤ An assortment of jams and marmalades for toast
➤ Video rentals that require minimal attention
➤ Butterscotch candies
➤ Soft, fleecy socks
➤ A plush bathrobe
➤ Childhood toys like Silly Putty, a yo-yo, or a Slinky
➤ A coveted board game
➤ A guilty-pleasure novel
➤ Vitamin C tablets in erotic shapes (yes, they exist)

want to start with fresh cool water. Also, you should avoid reheating water that has already been boiled; the oxygen has escaped and the tea will taste flat.

GOOD: Bring a kettle of fresh cool water to a boil. Pour over a tea bag directly into a cup and steep to desired strength.

BETTER: Fill a kettle with fresh cold water. Add one tea bag per cup of water directly to a teapot, or a tea ball full of loose leaves. Bring to a boil, then serve.

BOOTY: Adhere to the proper British method of brewing a pot of tea. First, fill a kettle with fresh cold water and bring to a boil. When it nears boiling, pour a little water into a teapot, swirl it around to warm the pot, then pour it out. Scoop one heaping tablespoon of loose tea leaves per cup of water into the teapot (plus an extra for good measure), then pour the hot water from the kettle over the top. Stir quickly, then cover the pot with a tea cozy or a towel and let steep about five minutes. Pour through a tea strainer directly into a warmed cup or mug and serve with your choice of milk, lemon slices, honey, or sugar water.

NOTE: If your partner takes milk in tea, try pouring it into the cup before the tea. The hot water will cook the milk, giving the entire cup a richer, creamier flavor.

TWO GOOD REASONS TO GET SICK

If there's any benefit to getting sick, it's that you can eat whatever you feel like eating. If you want to suck down a whole tube of chocolate chip cookie dough, you're entitled. If you want to eat English muffins for dinner, that's okay. Didn't anyone ever tell you that calories don't count when you're not well?

My favorite sick foods in the world are real homemade chicken soup, and a basket full of hot-from-the-oven biscuits with sweet strawberry butter. Bring me a tray of these treats in bed along with a nice cup of tea and a glorious red rose and I'm moving into Phase III with you. Just as soon as I stop sneezing.

Real Homemade Chicken Soup

This chicken soup should be patented and regulated by the AMA. Its healing powers are unmistakable, and even when your taste buds are in remission it always hits the spot.

1 (4-pound) chicken, quartered
4 tablespoons ($\frac{1}{2}$ stick) butter, melted
Small bunch fresh thyme
Small bunch fresh oregano
Kosher salt
Freshly ground black pepper
2 strips bacon
$\frac{1}{2}$ white onion, diced
3 cloves garlic, minced
$1\frac{1}{2}$ tablespoons olive oil
4 celery stalks, diced
2 large carrots, peeled and diced
$\frac{1}{2}$ bulb fresh fennel, diced
1 parsnip, peeled and diced
16 cups cold water
8 ounces ($\frac{1}{2}$ pound) small dry pasta noodles of choice

• Preheat the oven to 400 degrees.
• Wash and dry the chicken. Place it, skin-side down, in a large, oiled roasting pan. Brush the chicken with melted butter, cover it with the thyme, oregano, kosher salt, and fresh pepper, and top with the bacon. Roast the chicken for 35 to 40 minutes, moving it to the lowest rack of the oven for the last 10 minutes of cooking.
• In an 8-quart stockpot, sauté the onion and garlic in olive oil until translucent. Add the celery, carrots, fennel, and parsnip. Add $\frac{1}{8}$ cup water, and simmer on high heat for 5 minutes. Add salt and pepper, then remove the veggies and set them aside.
• When the chicken is ready (the juices should run clear when the meat is pricked to the bone), set it aside until it cools, then remove the skin and bones, and cut the meat into small chunks. Save the skin and bones.
• Place the cooked herbs and bacon and the reserved skin and bones in the stockpot, and add 16 cups of cold water. Bring to a boil, then simmer for 35 minutes, skimming fat off occasionally. Remove the bones and strain. Add the reserved chicken and veggies, and bring to a boil. Add the pasta and cook until done, about 5 to 8 minutes. Add salt and pepper to taste.

MAKES 1 LARGE POT (SHOULD BE ENOUGH TO GET YOU THROUGH THE AVERAGE COMMON COLD) PREP TIME: 1 HOUR / COOK TIME: $1\frac{1}{2}$ HOURS

Biscuits with Strawberry Butter

Moms make you cinnamon toast when you're not feeling well, but lovers make you this. The hot, flaky biscuits are homey, while the sweet, decadent strawberry butter is just a little bit sexy. You'll surely be rewarded for your efforts the second the NyQuil goes back into the medicine cabinet.

FOR BISCUITS:
2 cups all-purpose flour
2$\frac{1}{2}$ teaspoons baking powder
$\frac{3}{4}$ teaspoon salt
1 tablespoon sugar
5 tablespoons unsalted butter, softened
$\frac{1}{2}$ cup milk
$\frac{1}{4}$ cup buttermilk

- Preheat the oven to 450 degrees.
- Mix the flour, baking powder, salt, and sugar together in a mixing bowl. Add the butter bit by bit, and mix slowly. Stir in the milk and the buttermilk.
- Drop the batter by heaping tablespoons onto a greased cookie sheet, and bake for 12 minutes, or until golden brown.

MAKES 10 BISCUITS / PREP TIME: 15 MINUTES / COOK TIME: 12 MINUTES

FOR STRAWBERRY BUTTER:
$\frac{1}{2}$ (13-ounce) jar high-quality strawberry jam
$\frac{1}{2}$ pound (2 sticks) salted butter, softened at room temperature for 15 minutes

- To make the berry butter, drain off any excess jam juice. Puree the jam in a food processor, then add the butter. Process until just combined, about 30 seconds. Don't overmix or it will start to separate. Add more butter or jam to taste. (I prefer a lot of berry.) Spread on warm biscuits or bodies.

SO, HAVE YOU SUR-
VIVED? HOW ABOUT
YOUR RELATION-
SHIP? IF IT HASN'T
FLAT-LINED BY NOW,
GIVE YOUR HONEY A
BIG GERM-FREE
SMOOCH. THE ONLY
THING YOU'RE GOING
TO CATCH NOW IS A
ONE-WAY FLIGHT TO
PHASE III.

phase III

You have spent a good deal of time getting to know your lover's thirty-seven distinctly different smiles and fifty-four different sounds of pleasure. You have made definitive New Year's Eve plans, even if it is only March. And no matter how many consecutive mornings you wake up together, there's no little voice in your head telling you to get out of Dodge. Surprise—you're not prisoner #8734200. You're simply half of a happy, healthy, well-fed couple, and that ain't half bad. What started as lust has become—dare I say it?—love. So now's the time to start acting like a team—in life and in the kitchen. Before you know it, you'll be regularly attending parties and dinners and weddings (oh, my!) together. You'll be trading keys and pet names. You may even meet the folks you could end up referring to as "my crazy in-laws." Your circle of friends will double, your recipe repertoire could triple, and let's not forget the best part of all: If things work out, you'll never have to make that long, cold post-coital drive home ever again.

11)

four hands are better than two

It's a lot like getting naked together—at first you fumble around a bit, not quite sure if what you're doing is right, wrong, or something she'll laugh about with her friends in the morning before phoning it in to the local radio call-in show. But eventually you get a feel for your partner's rhythms and adjust yours accordingly. Before you know it you're passing the coriander, peeling the potatoes, and stirring the risotto at precisely the right moments. Soon you'll want to do it every night. Or twice a night? Imagine two people in love racing home early from a party to . . . make lasagna. It could happen.

Remember the moment when you realized that sex would be a whole lot more interesting if you weren't the only one in the room? The same goes for cooking. Cooking well for someone is cool, but cooking well with someone . . . that's NC-17 hot.

Just as four burners can accomplish more than two burners, so can four hands, so make the most of them. You didn't come this far just to make spaghetti together, did you? Use more than three ingredients in a salad dressing! Be daring with your desserts! Try concocting something with squab or squid or quince or quail—the sky's the limit. Don't be afraid, you've got a teammate who can watch your back now—and the coconut-curry sauce while you make the nectarine pico de gallo. When the culinary victory is shared between you it will unquestionably be twice as sweet.

It may take some time to become the well-oiled machine in the kitchen that you two randy kids are in the bedroom, but in the end it will be well worth it. Cooking together can actually help build a healthy relationship on every level. Trust me—couples who cook together *cook* together.

TAKE MY SAUCEPAN . . . PLEASE

When cooking together in the kitchen or having someone else cook for you in your kitchen, control issues can really come up. Even though my man is an amazing cook, it took a lot of work on my part to give him more of a say at mealtimes, not to mention therapy sessions where I rehashed dreams about dying from eating undercooked chicken. But eventually I was able to hand over a saucepan without secretly watching

IS IT LOVE? You might prefer to do battle with a chainsaw-wielding serial killer than to say "I love you" first, but at least the latter rarely results in loss of limbs. If you do profess your love, at best your feelings will be returned and you two can run off and consummate the event immediately. At worst, you'll weed out *Not The One* from your life before things get too sticky. Either way, it's important to pay attention to the response you get when you utter those three little words. Hint: The phrase you are looking for is "I love you too."

through the keyhole in the door. Not only did our meals start to taste better when we worked together, our after-dinner activities became the stuff of legends. Give a guy a little power in the kitchen and suddenly he's Mr. Virility in the bedroom. Who knew?

I distinctly recall the night my honey blurted out that he would be my kitchen lackey no more. I was dismayed when the realization struck me: I had become the alpha chef in the relationship, delegating only the most menial tasks to the poor guy ("Farm boy, fetch me chicken stock . . ."). Then it dawned on me—I didn't want him to be my houseboy, I wanted him to be my co-chef. A life partner. In which case I would have to stop being an anal-retentive culinary psychopath, relinquish some control, and start treating him like an equal. Giving someone else the run of the kitchen can only be equated to handing over the keys to a new Ferrari. I freak out at the thought of him grinding steel wool into my pots and pans. I worry he'll rewrap the brown sugar too loosely. I even get a little twitchy at the possibility of him covering the cheese in aluminum foil. And to top it off, he's within arm's reach of several professionally sharpened chef's knives. But when you think about it, what's the worst thing that can happen if you pass the culinary baton? Even if something burns or a glass gets broken, these are just things, and no *thing* is more important than your relationship.

Treating a partner like an equal in the kitchen doesn't mean you have to be equals in the kitchen (a rare occurrence indeed). It just means you should respect that your sweetie has something to bring to the table too. Whether it's wine selecting, pancake flipping, or a magical ability to get last night's gunk off the grill pan, your better half is 50 percent of the team. That's why it's not called *your better sixteenth*.

Most likely, you two will have very different styles and habits to grapple with in the kitchen. What if the two of you have incompatible perspectives on butter versus margarine, 350 degrees versus 375 degrees, shaken versus stirred? I can only say employ your amazing compromising skills and it will bring you closer. Oven temperature is definitely not worth losing a relationship over. You're going to discover more and more of these differences now that polite courtship behavior is moving aside to make way for honesty. It's also possible that cooking disputes will ensue not because you two are different in the kitchen but too similar. I imagine an episode of *Cops* in which two officers are dispatched to an upper-middle-class domestic disturbance provoked by an overseasoned scallop dish. But having two great cooks in the kitchen doesn't have to spoil the broth. If you both believe your pesto recipe rocks, have a pesto cook-off. No matter whose is tops, you'll both win.

I am compelled to point out that not all issues exhibited in the kitchen are necessarily romance enders. A control freak and a daddy's girl might have a very fulfilling codependent relationship together.

Whatever your issues—because we all have them—if you can share the responsibilities, laugh about your missteps, and reap the rewards together in the kitchen, I have no doubt that you two will be doing the same in life.

KITCHENANALYSIS

If you two are struggling with the partnership while making dinner, I wouldn't be surprised if you're having problems other times too. The exact same skills are employed in both arenas—trust, communication, honesty, and compromise. So if you find yourself with a lover who barks, "That's not the way to make a salad dressing!" and snatches the vinegar away, I'd bet a million dollars that she's equally critical of you in other aspects of your life. Look at your own behavior in the kitchen and I'll bet you'll find parallels with your relationship.

ISSUE: He makes the most unbelievably perfect meal then sighs how undercooked or overseasoned it was. **TRANSLATION:** Perfectionist. He probably works ninety hours a week and truly believes he doesn't work hard enough; don't count on having a lot of vacation time together.

ISSUE: She's conveniently on the phone, in the shower, or otherwise engaged when you start to make dinner. This goes double when it's time to do the dishes. **TRANSLATION:** Daddy's girl. She's not looking for a partner but a surrogate parent—or a maid. I hope you're loaded.

ISSUE: If you cook for her, she tries to one-up you—make an apple pie one night, and she makes a *tarte tatin* the next. **TRANSLATION:** Hyper-competitive. Whatever diamond ring you buy her, better make sure it's bigger than the one her best friend just got.

ISSUE: In the beginning it was sweet that he never let you lift a finger in the kitchen, but you're starting to wonder how long this will last. **TRANSLATION:** Control freak. Soon he will give you an approved list of friends you may hang out with.

ISSUE: He throws out a perfectly tasty but slightly lopsided plum galette. **TRANSLATION:** Looks-obsessed. He'll encourage you to get a boob job, then leave you for a model anyway.

ISSUE: She can't plan a menu without getting your input first; she doesn't seem to trust her own judgment. **TRANSLATION:** Insecure. Be prepared for a lifetime of "Does this make my butt look big?"

ISSUE: He keeps opening the oven door to check on the soufflé, even after you've asked him not to. The soufflé falls. **TRANSLATION:** Impatient. He's going to want to put a bun in your oven before the ring is halfway on your finger.

FOUR-HANDED DINNER

This unbelievably tasty three-course meal hardly requires a culinary-school diploma, but for a single chef it would be something of a nightmare to pull off (I picture that Russian plate-spinning guy on *Ed Sullivan*). With two eager chefs at the helm, complex menus become exponentially easier, so divvy up the duties, roll up your sleeves, shake up a pitcher of martinis, and get busy. While one of you assumes grill duty, the other can simmer the sauce. While you chop the veggies, your partner can give you a neck massage. Isn't teamwork great? You'll be so energized by your joint accomplishments, you may never even get to dessert. Which is exactly why I'm recommending one that keeps in the freezer a good long time.

LOVE ME, LOVE MY DISHES. Being a team doesn't just mean doing the fun stuff together; sharing responsibilities comes with the territory. Offering to scrub the pots while she dries will only further secure you a place in her heart. Besides, it could be fun. Where there's hot, soapy water involved, can booty be far behind?

Grilled Sea Bass with Green Curry-Coconut
Sauce and Nectarine Pico de Gallo
(RECIPE ON PAGE 147)

Although gin has been referred to as "the panty remover," I can't even look at it without waves of nausea (despite the fact that the inciting incident took place back in the days of Kajagoogoo and trickle-down economics). There's nothing wrong with using a premium vodka instead.

Perfect Martinis

When it's time to give the Merlot a rest, I'm rather partial to icy martinis. It's very 007, and I am radically aroused by any man in a tuxedo who can engage in delightfully witty banter while saving the world. I like my martinis straight up, and dirty, of course—add a splash of olive juice and garnish with two to three olives.

Good-quality gin or vodka
Dry vermouth
Ice cubes
Olives or lemon rind for garnish

• Pour gin or vodka into an ice-filled martini shaker.
• Add 1 part vermouth to 5 parts gin or vodka, using a jigger (1¼ ounces) for proper measurements.
• Shake well, but not so vigorously that the ice breaks. Strain into well-chilled martini glasses.
• Garnish with olives or a twist of lemon. Or, to make your 'tinis tingle, garnish with giant olives stuffed with surprise goodies, like blue cheese, garlic, chili peppers, or almonds. Interestingly enough, they're all aphrodisiacs.

Crispy Calamari with Caper Aioli

This tangy, garlicky aioli is equally luxurious with oysters or clams, but I especially love it alongside tender calamari. I use rice flour to make the batter extra light and crunchy, but if your preference runs toward cornmeal or polenta, then be my guest.

1 egg yolk
Splash milk
$\frac{1}{4}$ cup corn polenta
$\frac{1}{4}$ cup rice flour
1 teaspoon cayenne pepper
Pinch kosher salt
1 quart vegetable oil
$\frac{1}{2}$ pound squid (Have your fishmonger thoroughly clean and prep the squid for calamari)

- Make an egg wash of yolk and milk in a medium bowl.
- In another medium bowl mix together the polenta, rice flour, cayenne pepper, and salt.
- Heat oil to 375 degrees in a large pot.
- Dip the squid in the egg wash, then roll it in the polenta mixture.
- Place the squid in the oil, and fry it until it's crisp on the outside and tender but cooked on the inside, about 4 to 5 minutes, or until golden. Place on paper towels to drain of excess grease.

SERVES 2 / PREP TIME: 15 MINUTES / COOK TIME: 5 MINUTES

Aioli

1 cup high-quality mayonnaise
3 tablespoons capers
1 clove garlic, minced
1 teaspoon red-wine vinegar
1 tablespoon lime juice
Kosher salt
Freshly ground black pepper

- Combine all the ingredients in a small bowl, mix well, and serve with the calamari.

MAKES ABOUT 1 CUP / PREP TIME: 5 MINUTES

NOTE: Spicy and creamy meets cool and fruity in this, one of my favorite grilling recipes. It tastes like Indonesia by way of New Mexico. Serve over tender, aromatic jasmine rice. The sauce also does wonders for chicken, by the way, so save some for the next night.

If you want to up the exotic quotient, serve this dish on a banana leaf, available in ethnic markets that feature Latin, Caribbean, or Far Eastern foods. It adds something to both the presentation and the flavor.

Grilled Sea Bass with Green Curry-Coconut Sauce and Nectarine Pico de Gallo

FOR GREEN CURRY-COCONUT SAUCE:
1 (15-ounce) can coconut cream, like Coco Lopez
2 teaspoons green-curry powder, or Thai green-curry paste
¼ teaspoon crushed red pepper
¼ cup whole milk
Kosher salt
Freshly ground black pepper

• Combine the coconut cream, green-curry powder, and red pepper in a medium saucepan. Bring to a boil for 5 minutes. Reduce the heat to medium. Add the milk, and simmer on low for 20 minutes. Add salt and pepper to taste.

FOR SEA BASS:
Oil for grill or grill pan
2 fillets of sea bass, 8 ounces each
⅛ cup green-curry sauce

• Wipe the grill or a grill pan with a little oil and preheat to medium heat.
• Lightly baste the fish on both sides with the curry sauce.
• Grill the fish for 3 to 5 minutes on each side, depending on the thickness.

SERVES 2 / PREP TIME: 5 MINUTES / COOK TIME: 25 MINUTES

FOR NECTARINE PICO DE GALLO:
8 large plum tomatoes, cubed
1 small red onion, diced
1 cup loosely packed chopped cilantro leaves (about 1 bunch)
Juice of 2 limes (about 5 tablespoons)
2 limes, peeled and cut into segments
1 peach, diced, skin on
1 nectarine, diced, skin on
1 teaspoon red-wine vinegar
Kosher salt
Freshly ground pepper

• Combine all the ingredients, fold together, and serve.

MAKES ABOUT 6 CUPS / PREP TIME: 10 MINUTES

HOW TO SUPREME CITRUS FRUIT This can be done on most citrus fruit: grapefruits, oranges, lemons, limes, you name it.

While holding fruit securely, cut off stem end and opposite end, making a flat surface on bottom so fruit stands upright. Cut rind away from fruit down to pulp area. Once all rind is removed, slice between the membrane and the pulp of each fruit segment and gently lift each segment out, leaving the membrane behind. You should have perfect segments of fruit that are pulp only. These are called supremes, and they live up to their name in an elegant and delectable way.

Indian Red Grapefruit Sorbet

This refreshing, tart sorbet is cool, clean, and effortless to make. It's just the thing to cleanse your palate after a spicy meal—and before a spicy evening. Sorbet is every bit as fun to play with as it is to eat. For a chilly thrill, skip the bowls and instead apply it to one of your lover's more lickable body parts.

> 1 cup sugar
> 1 cup water
> 1½ cups fresh ruby-red grapefruit juice
> 4 grapefruit supremes, broken into large bits
> ½ teaspoon grapefruit zest
> Fresh mint for garnish

• Make a simple syrup: Combine sugar and water in a medium saucepan, and bring to a boil. Once the combination is at a boil, reduce the heat, and stir until the sugar dissolves. Remove the syrup from the heat and let it cool.

• Put ½ cup of the grapefruit juice in a separate saucepan and reduce by half over high heat. Let cool, then add to the simple syrup. Add the rest of the grapefruit juice, the grapefruit pieces, and the zest. Stir until incorporated.

• Pour the mixture into an ice-cream maker, and follow instructions. If you don't have an ice-cream maker, pour the mixture into a shallow container appropriate for the freezer, and cover with plastic wrap. Place in the freezer for at least 2 hours.

• When ready to serve, break apart with a fork or an ice-cream scoop. Garnish the sorbet with mint.

SERVES 2 / PREP TIME: 10 MINUTES

FOUR-HANDED BRUNCH

Dinner isn't the only time you can put your hands together and put that drawer full of kitchen gadgets to good use. I love cooking alongside a man first thing in the morning, when we're refreshed, alert, and one whole glorious, stress-free day away from Monday. (Not to mention half-naked.) I'm convinced that brunch was invented as a way to inject alcohol into your mornings in a socially acceptable fashion. So grate some fresh horse-radish into those Bloodys, or put on the kettle for a pot of Blueberry "Tea." They'll help stave off the hunger while you tackle this yummy brunch menu built for two. The orange-infused French toast is delicious with chicken sausages and a batch of Jalapeño Home Fries from page 79. Or, if you're inclined, try the morning-after breakfast menu from chapter 5. It's doubly easier with double the manpower. Either way, feel free to bite off more than you think you can chew. Together you'll be able to accomplish more than you ever have before.

Grand Marnier French Toast

Elevate an otherwise blah breakfast into a randy morning meal with this boozy, bawdy take on the French-Canadian classic. Smoked chicken-apple sausage is the perfect side dish. Serve it on the same plate and allow it to soak up the sweet, citrusy maple syrup.

5 eggs
¼ cup milk
1½ ounces Grand Marnier
1 teaspoon orange zest
½ teaspoon cinnamon
Dash nutmeg
6 slices white rye bread (unseeded)
4 tablespoons (½ stick) butter
1 navel orange, cut into segments, for garnish
½ cup Maple-Citrus Syrup (see recipe below)

• Combine the eggs, milk, Grand Marnier, orange zest, cinnamon, and nutmeg in a bowl, and whisk well.
• Soak the bread in the egg mixture until just saturated.
• Melt the butter in a large skillet over medium heat. Add the bread, and cook until crisp on the outside, about 3 minutes per side.
• While the toast is cooking, peel and section the orange, then remove the membranes from the segments or supremes. (See technique on page 149.)
• Arrange the French toast on a plate, garnish with the orange segments, and serve with warm maple syrup.

SERVES 2 / PREP TIME: 20 TO 25 MINUTES / COOK TIME: 6 MINUTES

Maple-Citrus Syrup

½ cup orange juice
¼ cup lemon juice (about 2 lemons)
½ cup maple syrup
1 teaspoon orange zest

• Combine the citrus juices in a small saucepan, and cook on medium-high heat until the liquid is reduced by half. Add the maple syrup, and reduce by half again. Finish with the orange zest. Pour warm over the French toast.

MAKES ABOUT ½ CUP / PREP TIME: 10 MINUTES / COOK TIME: ABOUT 5 MINUTES

Fresh Fruit Salad with Yogurt and Honey

Fruit salad is easy and elegant any time of day, but it's especially refreshing alongside the rich French toast. Add a dash of rum and sugar for complexity, then top with plain yogurt and a sensual drizzle of honey.

$\frac{1}{2}$ **cup berries**
$\frac{1}{2}$ **cup cherries**
1 cup diced cantaloupe
1 cup diced honeydew
$\frac{1}{2}$ **cup orange segments**
$\frac{1}{2}$ **cup grapefruit segments**
$\frac{1}{2}$ **cup diced Granny Smith apple**
$\frac{1}{2}$ **cup grapes**
Dash sugar
Splash white rum
Yogurt
Granola
Honey

• Combine any combination of fruit in season, add a bit of sugar and rum, and serve over natural yogurt with granola and honey.

SERVES 4 TO 6 / PREP TIME: 20 MINUTES

Blueberry "Tea"

Teetotalers beware: This is not actually tea, it's alcohol masquerading as tea. In some kind of deliciously unexpected chemical reaction, adding a splash of Grand Marnier to strong black tea results in a blueberry aroma. It's an ideal hot, steamy drink for cold Sunday mornings.

2 bags black tea
2 ounces Grand Marnier
2 orange twists for garnish

• Brew a pot of strong black tea.
• Put spoons into snifters so as not to crack the glass, and pour an ounce of Grand Marnier into each snifter. Pour in strong black tea, and garnish with a twist of orange. Smells of blueberry . . .

SERVES 2 / PREP TIME: 5 MINUTES

CHECK YOUR EQUIPMENT:
THE GRADUATE COURSE

If you're committed to making food a significant part of your lives together, you need to be properly outfitted. And I don't mean that nurse costume. The "Check Your Equipment" lists in chapters 3 and 5 were great starting points, but the more challenging the recipes you undertake, the more you'll realize you're missing a few things. So instead of avoiding recipes that require rolling dough, go spend a few bucks on a rolling pin and open up your options. In fact, that's all stocking a kitchen is about—options. If a recipe calls for pressing vegetables through a food mill, you need a food mill. Simple as that.

It took me years to perfect my kitchen of love, so don't max out your credit cards on ice-cream makers and martini glasses all at once. Bit by bit, birthday gift by birthday gift (and anniversary gift and holiday gift), you will become master or mistress of your culinary domain. And lest you think I'm completely out of touch with reality, I'm well aware that a $300 mandolin and a full set of Riedel wineglasses are not life-or-death necessities. Most of the world will live perfectly contented lives without ever owning a professional wine-cooling system, but if you you've got the bucks and you love wine, why not start chilling it Booty Food-style?

➤ **BETTER BARWARE** Particularly for those who love entertaining, amassing stemware can quickly become an obsession. There are brandy snifters, champagne flutes, beer steins, martini glasses, margarita glasses, cordial glasses, highballs, tumblers, not to mention all the choices for wine alone. Let your drinking habits—and your cupboard space—be your guide; however, bear in mind that if you're going to be sipping Veuve Clicquot, there's no substitute for a proper champagne flute. Except maybe a belly button.

➤ **AN ITALIAN ESPRESSO POT** If you want to ensure that the tired "I'm tired" excuse never arises in your relationship, get your hands on a good-quality espresso pot. While you're at it, make sure you have a coffee grinder, a set of espresso cups, and a vegetable peeler to achieve those perfect little twists of lemon.

➤ **A CAVIAR DISH AND MOTHER-OF-PEARL SPOONS** When you've got the proper accoutrements, you'll be more likely to bring home the beluga. Besides, serving caviar in a cereal bowl is cute only if it's moving day and you're sitting on the floor eating over an upside-down packing box.

➤ **SOMETHING BETTER THAN A CORKSCREW** With the Screwpull, you can open a bottle of wine in about three seconds. It's a must if you're a big party thrower or an impatient wine drinker.

➤ **A FONDUE POT** You can't make fondue without one, critically limiting things you can do with cheese on a cold night.

➤ **AN OMELET PAN** If you serve omelets more frequently than once every presidential-election year, invest in a designated omelet pan and never use it for anything but. If you take very good care of it, it will take very good care of you.

➤ **A BREAKFAST TRAY** Breakfasts in bed are considerably sexier when you're not balancing plates on your knees, getting crumbs in the bed, and spilling hot coffee on the sheets.

➤ **FANCY KNIVES** Fill out your collection with cheese knives, fish knives, a meat cleaver, and chef's knives of varying lengths. You won't be sorry; I have more regrets about my high school prom than I do about my knife rack.

➤ **A WOK** Not everyone has hours to devote to cooking each night; a wok ensures that a hot homemade meal is never more than a few minutes away. I prefer a traditional wok over those newfangled electric types—if it was good enough for the Chinese for the last millennium or so, it's good enough for me.

➤ **FRIVOLOUS, FUN APPLIANCES** An ice-cream maker, a waffle iron, and a juicer are little luxuries that make life more fun. They're also likely to get more use now that you're in a couple; homemade ice-cream for one just isn't the same.

➤ **PLASTIC SQUIRT BOTTLES** The 99-cent secret to finishing your dishes like a professional chef. Fill bottles with infused oils, chocolate sauce, raspberry coulis, and the like. Apply like a pro in the kitchen and beyond.

➤ **COOKIE SHEETS, PIE TINS, CAKE PANS, WIRE COOLING RACK** If you're going to bake, bake. Microwaved brownies are not Booty Food.

appliances of love

It's an old joke that an appliance does not a romantic gift make, but I had an experience that led me to the opposite conclusion. Way back when, after spending three straight weeks with a particular guy, I discovered his love for fresh orange juice in the morning. I was so excited, I ran out and bought him a juicer and a box of ripe oranges. His previously loving, lusty vibe instantly turned frosty. Apparently any gift with an on/off switch that didn't come from a sex shop represented too much of a commitment to him. So, he was not The One for me. At least it only cost me $19.95 to find out.

➤ **FISH POACHER** I love All-Clad's version and couldn't have sexy seafood nights without one.

➤ **A GOOD MANDOLIN** A mandolin is a souped-up way to cut veggies like the pros do and make fancy fries to impress everyone you know. The Sonic Slice-O-Matic you see on the channel 57 infomercials is not a good mandolin, no matter which has-been celebrities tout its merits.

➤ **MORTAR AND PESTLE** Essential for grinding chili pastes, homemade guacamole, and fresh mint for pitchers of Mojitos. Sometimes there's just no substitute for 5th-century technology.

➤ **MISCELLANEOUS GADGETS** An egg poacher, a citrus press, a food mill, a lemon zester, a meat thermometer, and a truffle grater are all nice to have around for the few times you need them. (Come to think of it, the truffle grater isn't nice in my household, it's essential.) Also invest in fun serving utensils, like a pizza cutter, an ice-cream scoop, and a cake server—each one is an indication of a spirited household. I bet more rock stars own pizza cutters than state senators do.

BIG-TICKET ITEM$

If you can't afford these things now, write them down and save the list for your wedding registry or your Bob-and-Steve-commit-to-each-other-for-life party.

➤ **A TWO-BUTT KITCHEN** If you've got a one-butt kitchen, it's going to be difficult to do two-butt cooking without bumps and bruises and burns. Keep this in mind if your lease is up anytime soon.

➤ **WINE REFRIGERATOR** The sign of a true wine enthusiast, a wine-coolant system stores wine at the perfect temperature and humidity levels. And, most important, it makes more room in your fridge for cheese.

➤ **A HIGH-END GAS GRILL** Let's just say there's a reason some gas grills cost more than a Kia. See page 171 for a more detailed take on the charcoal-versus-gas debate.

➤ **DISHWASHER AND GARBAGE DISPOSAL** They'll set you back a few bucks, but will repay you tenfold with more free time after dinner

THE (GASP!) KEY EXCHANGE

You've quietly left your toothbrush in your lover's bathroom but you're not quite ready to send out "We're moving!" postcards in the mail. The logical intermediary step is an event I dub the Key Exchange, which, in any modern relationship, is as significant as the first fight over which of your eight parents to spend the holidays with. If you're offering that shiny token to convey, "I completely trust you, oh darling, oh love of my life, oh apple of my eye. My space is your space and one day it will be our space," hooray for you both. Celebrate with a sexy homemade dinner, then go have we-just-traded-keys sex. However, if you've only handed over the key to the inner sanctum to avoid walking down four flights of brownstone stairs every time your lover buzzes, that's not the Key Exchange. That's sloth.

Opening up your home and hearth to your sweetie displays a huge amount of confidence, and not just because you keep valuables lying around. Dropping $1.79 on a key at the hardware store is the same as pledging, "There will never be a mango in the fridge that you can't eat, a door you can't open, or a message on the answering machine that you can't hear." That's not to say you want your calls screened. In fact, there will be a lot of things you'll pray your partner will not do when he or she is home alone at your place. I've heard stories about guys rearranging their girlfriend's CD collections, girls throwing out the swimsuit issue in the bathroom, and, the worst offense of all—lovers who put the milk carton back empty. As someone who's given far too many keys away (and later changed far too many locks), I urge you to discuss any particular boundary issues now or skip directly to the chapter on breakup foods. And be specific—you may be okay with your girlfriend putting her feet up on your couch; you may not be okay with her reupholstering your couch.

➤ **PERSONAL SPACE BOUNDARIES:** Does proffering a key indicate, "Mi casa es tu casa," or "Mi casa es tu casa as long as I'm there too?"

➤ **PHONE BOUNDARIES:** Is it okay for her to answer when you're not home? Is it okay for her to answer when you are home? If she does answer, is it okay for her to hang up on telemarketers?

➤ **REFRIGERATOR BOUNDARIES:** Determine how much valuable fridge room you will allot to your honey's pulp-free orange juice, natural peanut butter, or protein powder. When you offer a key and a drawer, a little kitchen space comes included.

➤ **STUFF BOUNDARIES:** If you feel like you're being squeezed out of your own closet, it's reasonable to draw the line. However, if you're a guy who finds that a second bottle of shampoo in the bathroom propels you into a rant about man's biological inability to remain monogamous, head directly to the self-help section of the bookstore. Do not pass go. Do not collect women's phone numbers along the way.

Personally, I don't have a laundry list of relationship-ending boundary violations. If he wants to answer the phone, stock my medicine cabinet full of aftershave, or store his gym clothes in the closet, it doesn't freak me out at all. I only ask that I never come home to find him drinking my bottle of Chateau Latour with his ex-girlfriend.

I don't mean to convey that the Key Exchange is exclusively about rules and compromise and arguments about the ring of razor stubble left in the bathroom sink. Without trading keys, your sweetie would never come home to find you setting a vase of snapdragons on his dining room table. Or cooking her favorite dish for dinner after a heinous day at work. Or lying in his bed wearing nothing but a pair of fishnets, a few dollops of Cool Whip, and a smile.

12)

get out of the house, for god's sake

TWO FOR THE ROAD

Enter an exciting new phase in your relationship: the first trip. Although the main goal of your little jaunt might be getting busy in a strange and exotic location, there is an ulterior motive here. It's a chance to see how symbiotic you two are on the road, as traveling together is a critical factor in any healthy relationship. As I can attest, sometimes all it takes is a long weekend in Florida.

By now you've undoubtedly broken in (or just broken) the living room sofa, the kitchen floor, the dining room table, and maybe even a crawl space or two. But there should be more to your relationship than ravishing one another in every corner of the house. Like ravishing one another in a hotel.

After a month and a half together, my not-quite-yet significant other and I decided to spend the upcoming weekend in warmer climes. One day and a mad packing frenzy later, we were tooling around the beaches of St. Petersburg in a convertible. Despite the fact that our routines were off, we got along famously. We bonded over eighteen holes of mini golf, a fiercely competitive air-hockey match, and about $40 worth of old-skool video games in a boardwalk arcade. I have many romantic memories of that weekend—sipping Piña Coladas at the most amazing burger shack on the beach, slow-dancing to "My One and Only You" after dinner, and certainly the hours spent in our hotel room with the lights low and the cell phones off. But there's one moment that surpassed them all—locking the keys in the trunk of our car.

Now, don't get me wrong. It's not that I enjoy being stranded in a rest-stop parking lot, but the way he handled the situation was remarkable. Having been in similar predicaments with previous boyfriends, I was prepared for a gamut of reactions, from raging lunacy to absolute ineptitude. I'm happy to report that this time was different. He averted a would-be crisis with easy confidence and a refreshing sense of humor. I was awed. I was smitten. And for the first time, I was fully prepared to toss the little black book out the window—all because we locked the car keys in the trunk.

There are some things you just can't tell about a person until you get out of the house.

Even when you can map out every freckle on your partner's body by memory and predict his dinner order with the greatest of ease, I assure you there will be some completely unforeseen compatibility issues that arise once you hit the road together.

▶ **THE CONTROL FACTOR** Do you share the responsibilities of planning the trip, or does one of you insist on picking the locale, booking the hotel, driving, navigating, and declaring "We'll stop at a restroom when I'm good and ready, so deal with it"?

▶ **THE SPONTANEITY FACTOR** Is his or her overnight bag stuffed with brochures, travel guides, and a typewritten, double-spaced itinerary itemized in ten-minute increments? If you're driving a long distance, do you both like to get right to the destination, or do you prefer to meander through unexplored territory and scope out tag sales, county fairs, and the local girlie bars?

▶ **THE MARIO ANDRETTI FACTOR** Does one of you help state troopers fulfill their speeding-ticket quotas each month, while the other never strays far from the right lane? It seems that grannies-at-the-wheel fall in love with those with the need for speed. It may take some work to get used to your partner's driving style, but it will be near impossible to try to change it.

▶ **THE SNOB FACTOR** Does he get the willies from any hotel without white-gloved doormen at his beck and call? On the other hand, are you uncomfortable that the desk staff drops to its knees and salutes whenever you walk past? If your partner is Michelin three-star all the way while you prefer the communal living and mild danger of youth hostels, there's going to be some serious compromising in your futures.

▶ **THE MINIBAR FACTOR** There are two kinds of people in this world: those who love mini-bars, and those who would sooner die of dehydration than imbibe from that $12 bottle of Evian. Which category does each of you fall into?

▶ **THE SEATING PREFERENCE FACTOR** If you're flying, training, or bussing à deux, your preferred seat location can be surprisingly important. Is he an aisle or a window person? Are you both window people? Do you believe that a window man and a window woman can have a mutually fulfilling travel relationship?

Just because you're not the exact same kind of traveler doesn't mean you can't have an enjoyable trip together. You will just have to make your partner see the error of his or her ways. And yes, I do believe a window man and a window woman can find eternal bliss together—one-third of the trip you get the window, one-third of the trip your partner gets the window, and the rest of it you spend together in the restroom earning your Mile-High Club membership.

VARIATIONS
• For a Dirty Colada, add 1 shot of
Kahlúa.
• For a Dirty Chunky Monkey (the
only drink with a goofy name that I
am proud to order), add 1 shot of
Kahlúa, 1 banana, and 1 shot of
shredded coconut.

Piña Coladas

In a fine French restaurant, you do not want to order any drink that has ever, since its incep-
tion, arrived garnished with a little umbrella. However, in the comfort of your own warm-
weather vacation home, Piña Coladas should be the house drink. Make sure to clear your
schedule for some Club Med–inspired indoor activities afterward.

> 1 (15-ounce) can Coco Lopez coconut cream
> 1½ cups pineapple juice
> 4 ounces dark rum
> Ice
> Pineapple wedges (optional)
> Toasted coconut shavings (optional)

• Blend the first 4 ingredients to a thick consistency, and garnish with a pineapple wedge
and toasted coconut shavings, if desired.

SERVES 2 / PREP TIME: 10 MINUTES

THE APHRODISIAC NORTH AMERICAN TOUR

Food is a great excuse to travel. There are food festivals across the continent celebrating all things edible from strawberries to Spam. Of course, if you've got booty on the brain, some are more suitable than others.

JANUARY
- Florida Citrus Festival, Winter Haven, FL

APRIL
- Poteet Strawberry Festival, Poteet, TX
- Elmira Maple Syrup Festival, Elmira, Ontario,
- Spamarama, Austin, TX

MAY
- California Strawberry Festival, Oxnard, CA
- Castroville Artichoke Festival, Castroville, CA
- Greek Food Festival, Little Rock, AK
- Messick Mushroom Festival, Messick, MI

JUNE
- Virginia Pork Festival, Emporia, VA

JULY
- Gilroy Garlic Festival, Gilroy, CA
- Hopkins Raspberry Festival, Hopkins, MN
- Santa Barbara French Festival, Santa Barbara, CA
- National Cherry Festival, Traverse City, MI

AUGUST
- Olathe Sweet Corn Festival, Olathe, CO
- Los Angeles Tofu Festival, Los Angeles, CA
- Barnesville Potato Days Festival, Barnesville, MN
- National Lentil Festival, Pullman, WA
- Beef Empire Days, Garden City, KS

SEPTEMBER
- California Prune Festival, Yuba City, CA
- Grundy County Corn Festival, Morris, IL

OCTOBER
- The Whole Enchilada Fest, Las Cruces, NM
- OysterFest, Shelton, WA
- La Fiesta Del Los Chilies, Tucson, AZ
- Watonga Cheese Festival, Watonga, OK
- Suffolk Peanut Fest, Suffolk, VA
- Allardt Pumpkin Festival, Allardt, TN
- California Avocado Festival, Carpinteria, CA

NOVEMBER
- Verboort Sausage Fest, Verboort, OR
- Kona Coffee Cultural Festival, Kailua-Kona, HI
- Pickle Festival, Rosendale, NY

DECEMBER
- International Tamale Festival, Indio, CA

PALM TREES, WHITE SAND, AND AN OVERPRICED PLUMBER

Holing up in a hotel for two weeks with the phone off the hook and three meals' worth of room-service trays on the bedroom floor is a fine way to spend an extended holiday if you're independently wealthy. Instead, why not rent a property with a kitchen? Whether it's a European villa, a summer shack at the nearest beach, or a time-share condo on a ski slope, you'll not only have the man or woman of your dreams all to yourself, you'll get to play house like real live grown-ups. You'll shop for groceries, call repairmen, pay phone bills, change light bulbs, share a kitchen, and generally see how well you maneuver around the domestic hazards of pseudo-cohabitation. It's a fail-safe compatibility test that every couple should pass before taking the one-and-a-half-carat plunge.

Not that it's all work. You also get to try exotic new foods together, sip frosty blender drinks, wear out your sexiest CDs, and spend more time naked than Harvey Keitel.

Think of it as leasing a life partner with the option to buy.

Years ago, I rented a condo in the Dominican Republic with one of the grand passions of my life. We found a small, gated oasis in an undeveloped beach town and signed a three-week lease. When we weren't dozing on the beach or abusing the king-size bed with the mosquito-net canopy, a remarkably significant amount of our time revolved around food—when to eat, what to eat, where to find it. We shopped together at the rustic supermercado up the road, where we sniffed and sampled deliciously unpronounceable fruits and vegetables. We bought whole roasted chickens out of store windows, and sometimes right from people's homes. We procured dozens of plump oysters from men on the beach who had caught them only moments before, slurped them down on the spot, then bought a couple dozen more for happy hour back at our place. As my *papi* helped me slice up fresh mangoes for breakfast one morning, I became aware that with all this shopping and cooking and indoor bodysurfing, it was more than a vacation; it was a twenty-one-day glimpse into our future, and I liked what I was seeing. (If he had chosen to dedicate his life to something other than digging ditches in developing countries, I have no doubt we'd still be together today.) I am now convinced that every couple should have a similar experience if they're even starting to contemplate making the relationship legal.

When you arrive at your temporary pleasure palace there will be plenty of hurdles for you two to overcome as a team. Just try to think of new issues that arise as mere growing pains, good even though they feel bad.

▶ **WHAT ARE THE HOUSE RULES?** Establishing boundaries together is the first way to make this place "our" place. Consider: Can the screen door be left open? How high can you crank the AC? Can you wear shoes in the house? Can her friends visit the second week? Can his mother visit the second week?

INCONSIDERATE JERK, AISLE FIVE

If you two have been cooking and canoodling for a while, I'm sure you've been on numerous trips to the grocery store as a couple. Never mind that. Picking up veggies for one night's salad has absolutely nothing to do with stocking a vacation home together. It's like comparing apples to ostriches. This time you're choosing the food that will sustain you for an entire week or longer, and you're going to be less apt to be a good sport and compromise on your favorite brand of bacon or the flavor of your jelly.

Grocery stores are among my favorite places, but there's something about them that brings out people's shadowy alter egos. I'm convinced that bad grocery-shopping behavior parallels bad relationship behavior; the rogue grape and nut thief, who thinks he's entitled to pilfer a fistful of loose cashews from the bin without paying for them, is the same type of guy who will jam the parking meter with a soda-can pop top. Consider yourself forewarned if the hot lover you're sharing an Amagansett beach-house bedroom with enters the local IGA and mysteriously morphs into one the following types:

➤ **THE DELI LINEBACKER:** Would tackle his or her own grandmother in order to get number 27 instead of 28. **How you will spend your future together:** Illegally parking in handicapped zones.

➤ **THE FUZZY MATHEMATICIAN:** Will try to sneak through the express lane with logic like, "If a dozen eggs count as one item, so should a dozen cans of garbanzo beans." **How you will spend your future together:** Being audited for creative accounting on your joint income-tax returns.

➤ **THE SPENDTHRIFT GOURMET:** Will buy black truffles, imported red pepper tapenade, and the fancy potato chips, even if unemployed. **How you will spend your future together:** Begging the credit-card company with the 39 percent interest rate to give you a second chance.

➤ **THE TIGHTWAD:** Will try to convince you that the cheap, generic peanut butter is the same as the brand you've been loving since you were a kid. **How you will spend your future together:** Driving an extra five miles to the other supermarket to redeem a coupon for 15 cents off capers.

➤ **MR. OR MS. NO FRIEND OF THE ENVIRONMENT:** Will keep the freezer door open while deciding on a brand of frozen waffles. **How you will spend your future together:** Sneaking recyclables into the garbage.

➤ **THE CART HOG:** Will have one hand on the shopping cart at all times, even if it's empty, even if you're pushing it. **How you will spend your future together:** Fighting over who gets to be on top.

If perchance you do find yourself with one of the bad boys or girls of supermarket etiquette, don't throw in the towel just yet. Seeing as how you're far enough into a relationship that you're shopping together, I'm sure you'll find some delicate way to exorcise your lover of the shopping demon trapped within so you can get on with the most important aspect of your vacation: devouring all the food you've bought together. In bed.

➤ **HOW DO YOU DIVVY UP THE CHORES?** When there's cooking, mopping, gardening, and laundry to be done, do you work together, take turns, or commit your life savings to a live-in housekeeper? Above all, be sure to determine whose job it is to bring in the hammock cushion when it rains. This task alone can influence the outcome of your entire relationship.

➤ **WHO DOES THE HIRING AND FIRING?** You may be obligated to gardeners, housekeepers, pool cleaners, or garbage collectors. How do you deal with it when they show up an hour late, a day late, or a week late? And trust me, they will.

➤ **WHAT DO YOU DO WITH YOUR TIME?** Do you prefer the ocean side or the bay side? The bunny slope or the double black diamond trail? Eating out or eating in? Getting busy in the kitchen or getting busy in the hot tub? And, most important, do you need to be together every single minute of every day? You've got your whole lives to spend together—don't burn out on each other now.

➤ **WHO DEALS WITH THE CRAZY LANDLORD WHO WON'T RETURN YOUR SECURITY DEPOSIT BECAUSE YOU BROKE HER $2 WINEGLASS?** Okay, it was $2.50. But I swear it already had a crack in it.

Certainly the benefits of a vacation together far outweigh the obstacles. Sure, you may have to navigate the piranha-packed waters of summer real-estate agents to get there, but when thoughts of bills and bosses and political parties start to fade from memory, there are no remote controls to fight over, and you can imagine no more urgent task than toasting good-bye to the sun at precisely 8:23 P.M., it should be hard to argue about much at all. The key seems to be an ability to maneuver around challenges during the day, then still find your way back into each other's arms at night. If you two can do that, you're way ahead of the game.

Then again, have you gone shopping yet?

I'M SO JEALOUS THAT YOU'RE GOING ON VACATION! DROP ME A POSTCARD IF YOU GET A CHANCE AND ASSURE ME THAT EVEN THOUGH THE AC DIED, THE BEDROOM CEILING LEAKED, AND YOU LOST THE FIGHT ABOUT THE CHEAP PAPER TOWELS, YOU TWO ARE STILL COMPLETELY GAGA FOR EACH OTHER. IF SO, THINGS ARE LOOKING PRETTY PROMISING FOR THE TWO OF YOU. I WOULDN'T BE SURPRISED IF YOUR NEXT TRIP TOGETHER IS THE ONE YOU RETURN FROM WITH TAN LINES ON YOUR NEWLY ADORNED RING FINGERS.

13)

meet the friends already

A woman could present letters of recommendation from six ex-boyfriends and Hugh Hefner himself, but it wouldn't mean half as much as his buddy Chuck from college thinking she's cool. The same goes for a woman's gal pals. Without their express consent, add your relationship to the endangered species list.

There is one sticking point, however: None of your friends are talking to you right now.

Do you blame them? They've been temporarily traded in for love, lust, and skimpy lingerie. I'll bet you see the Chinese food delivery guy more often. But all is not lost. I'm sure your friends have been in love too and will allow you to beg for their forgiveness. So why not throw a fabulous little barbecue in their honor? It will not only give you all time to catch up over fantastic food, it will give them a chance to meet the person who's been replacing them on Saturday nights so they can come to their own conclusions about how terrific he is or isn't.

> You've heard that the way to a man's heart is through his stomach, but I believe a more direct route is through his friends' stomachs.

THEY LIKE ME! THEY REALLY LIKE ME!

I'm sure you can't wait to hook up all your single friends with your partner's still unattached pals, but I suggest that when entertaining, you keep your groups of friends separate at first. If you're too busy catching up with your own long-lost buddies, you're not going to have any time to make a good impression on your partner's—let alone serve the grub, refill the wineglasses, change the music, and keep the dog from eating your guests' coats. So I strongly urge you to plan two small gatherings, one for your closest group of friends and one for your sweetie's. You might want to limit invitees to your inner circle, as in the people in your life who would never say to your new lover, "I've heard so much about you. Especially that thing you do with your tongue." If your bestest, closest, you'd-die-without-'em confidants number in the triple digits, figure out a way to pare down the list. This is not an engagement party. This is not a bar mitzvah. It is simply a great opportunity to demonstrate what a passionate, caring person you are—and isn't that why your hunka' hunka' burning love fell hard for you in the first place?

Most of these suggestions are common sense, and if you have an ounce of etiquette in you, good behavior will come naturally. Besides, if your sweetie's friends are truly friends, they're not going to be looking for an excuse to reject you. They'll be hoping for an excuse to throw you an engagement party.

Of course having a party for your partner's friends isn't just about getting in good with the buddies. You can tell a lot about a romantic partner by who he or she chooses to spend time with. If all her friends are kind, decent people who say please and thank you and donate 50 percent of their incomes to charity, it's pretty unlikely that she's the selfish black sheep of the lot. There's some truth to that guilt (or innocence) by association thing. It's also important to examine how your lover behaves with his cohorts. If that flower-picking, Emily Dickinson–quoting nice guy you're in love with suddenly becomes a beer-guzzling, fistfight-picking cretin when his friends come to call, you're either going to have to learn to live with his alter ego or bow out gently, knowing you've been duped by a pro.

MEET-THE-FRIENDS SURVIVAL TACTICS

A party for your friends should be relatively easy to pull off—you at least know they like you. A party for your partner's friends, on the other hand, will rank up there with skydiving without a parachute; it's terrifying meeting the people who have influence over the outcome of a relationship that's important to you. But don't panic. Adhere to these suggestions and you'll make it through the event with a whole new fan club.

➤ **GET THE INSIDE SCOOP.** Friends like the idea that you were discussing them in between bouts of lip-locking; however, if you're going to rely on the old "I've heard so much about you!" you'd better have one or two examples to back it up. Also, get the physical descriptions down before the night begins. You don't want to congratulate the woman who just got fired, accidentally mistaking her for the woman who just got engaged.

➤ **DEMONSTRATE AFFECTION APPROPRIATELY.** Showing your girlfriend a little attention in front of her friends is a nice touch. Tongue-kissing her in front of her friends tells them she needs a relationship intervention.

➤ **KEEP CONFIDENCES.** Don't bring up people's deepest, darkest secrets in an effort to bond. Your partner may have confided in you about Peter's tax-evasion conviction or Susan's sexually experimental phase in college, but neither are appropriate conversation starters.

➤ **BE YOURSELF.** If you've been referred to as "the chick who stole David away from poker night," or "the guy who Lisa won't shut up about," it's only because they don't know you yet—they only know the effect you've had on their relationships. Be your own sweet self and I'm sure even the most relationship-cynical among them will see all the yummy qualities your partner sees in you. Besides, it's really hard to dislike the woman who's made you a killer margarita or the guy who made the shrimp dip you can't stop eating.

PICK A DATE, ANY DATE . . . People's calendars tend to be so jam-packed around the holidays, I prefer to celebrate occasions that are more likely to generate a *yes* than a *maybe* from my invitees. When is the last time you said, "I'm sorry, I already have Bastille Day plans?" Consider fun but underrated holidays, like Chinese New Year's, summer equinox, or the festival of San Gennaro. Plan a get-together around the big game or the season finale of the sitcom your friends never miss. Or channel your creativity and celebrate the birthday of your favorite musician, artist, or author. A Hemingway bash replete with cigars, conch fritters, and key lime pie could be fun. Save the Anaïs Nin party until you know your sweetie's friends a bit better.

VALIUM-FREE PARTY PLANNING

Putting out a bag of cheese curls is not throwing a party, no matter what the ads might tell you. On the other hand, serving a six-course sit-down dinner for thirty is not going to leave you a lot of time to get to know your lover's cronies, which pretty much defeats the entire purpose of the party. A casual, simple barbecue is an ideal way to feed your hungry revelers in that it allows you to hobnob with company while still flexing your culinary biceps. Fire up the grill and you may actually have as good a time as your guests.

There are many things I don't do well in life (I will definitely never be able to hold any job where a good working knowledge of trigonometry is required), but entertaining does not make that list. I absolutely live for the regalia of it all—Oscar parties, bridal showers, lawn parties, New Year's galas—give me an excuse and I'm cooking up a guest list. Sometimes I even consider moving just so I can send out housewarming invitations.

There are few things more fulfilling than bringing together your nearest and dearest, plying them with good food, wine, and music, then realizing that they're having the time of their lives. I put no less passion and effort into feeding my friends than if I were feeding a hot new lover. Rather like good sex (and I know you're an expert at that by now), hosting a successful barbecue—or any kind of party, for that matter—is as simple as making sure all of your guests leave with their eyes rolled back in ecstasy. Don't think that's a chore—it's actually the fun part. I get a thrill flitting from guest to guest, making sure the vegetarian has found enough to eat and the pregnant woman is taking advantage of the virgin punch. I adore manning the grill and cooking each burger to order. I get off on passing around the guacamole so that I can interact with each guest, even just for a moment, even if just to clarify that, no, the *Journey's Greatest Hits* CD that's playing is not a joke. If you can tailor the event to the maxi-

out, damn spot

Just call me the spill queen—I could knock over a glass of Bordeaux if it were nailed to the table. Of course from necessity comes invention; I can get all but the nastiest stains out of any sofa, carpet, or ball gown. If you're a guy who can make a glass of sangria magically disappear from your girlfriend's best friend's new white blouse, you become a stain-removing superhero. Just remember to have her take it off—in private—before you start dabbing.

- ➤ **RED WINE:** Blot the stain, then douse with club soda and continue to blot. If it's really tough, douse with more club soda, apply kosher salt, and scrub.
- ➤ **TOMATO SAUCE OR SALSA:** Sponge on cool water, then add a dab of liquid laundry detergent before laundering.
- ➤ **BUTTER OR OIL:** Pour a bit of liquid laundry detergent on it, then rinse with warm water.
- ➤ **COFFEE:** Rinse in cold water and a drop of clear dishwashing soap. Or soak in white vinegar and water.
- ➤ **MUSTARD:** Scrape off the extra without spreading the stain. Soak in all-fabric bleach before tossing in a hot wash.
- ➤ **LIPSTICK:** Coat in rubbing alcohol or spray with hairspray before washing.

mum enjoyment of each guest, even bigger gatherings will feel intimate. Just try to strike a happy medium. Invite too many guests and you can't spend much time with any one person; invite too few and you give yourself no opportunity to sneak into the bathroom with your honey to make out.

After hosting approximately 18 zillion barbecues, I have become a firm devotee of keeping the menu simple. I prefer nibbles and appetizers that can be made in advance, served cold or at room temperature, and don't require frantic last-minute assembly. All things being equal, wouldn't you rather put the energy into your guests than into your fingerling-potato-peeling technique? Keep the main fare easy as well. You can make just as grand an impression with an armada of burgers as with individual Roquefort soufflés, and the former will allow you to socialize while you cook. If you're not going to enjoy your own party, don't bother throwing one. They're expensive. Buy a big-screen TV instead.

Of course you don't have to max out your Visa (and your Discover card and your AmEx and your other Visa) to host a get-together that's the talk of your social circle. If you're on a budget, spend your money where it will be best noticed. For example, splurge on better bottles of wine, but make your own crudités and dips instead of buying them prepared. Or play a Tony Bennett CD instead of hiring Tony Bennett. After a few beverages, no one will know the difference anyway. If you can throw some dough toward a bartender, caterer, or clean-up crew (particularly if you're entertaining more than about twenty people), it's well worth the investment. Anything you can afford to have done for you professionally will give you more time to mingle, chat, and smile politely at long, boring stories.

THE GRILL OF VICTORY, THE AGONY OF BURNT MEAT

If you ask ten people what kind of grill they prefer, you'll get eleven different answers, none of them wrong. Here's where I stand:

GOOD: Electric. It's the easiest to use, but adds nothing to the flavor of the food. You might as well use your oven.

BETTER: Charcoal. This is a lot of work, since you have to understand things like banking coals and indirect grilling and how to time the preheating process so that you don't start eating at midnight. However, when done well, meat and vegetables will achieve that yummy, smoky barbecue flavor that's unmatched by other kinds of grills.

BOOTY: Gas. I like grilling with gas because it's fast, you can control the flame better, and it's easier to clean. Some people will want to kick my butt from here to Sheboygan for not recommending charcoal grilling above all else, but a man reeking of briquette smoke and lighter fluid doesn't exactly make me want to strip off my clothes and beg him to make me his bitch. Where flavor is concerned, yes, charcoal grills rock. Where booty is concerned, I'll take a gas grill any day.

BUDGET TIP Approach your favorite waiter at a local restaurant and ask if he wants to make a few bucks working your party. Or, if there's a culinary school nearby, employ a student chef to prepare a menu that you create together. You could end up having hired the next Mario Batali, dirt cheap!

Men and women seem to behave very differently toward grilling. Men enjoy poking and prodding the flame, showing women how big their flame is, and comparing it to the size of other guys' flames. Women, on the other hand, don't see the flame as much more than a means to an end. So, ladies: If your man is giving you a hard time about manning the grill, forgive him. For some reason he's convinced it's an extension of his manhood. Then again, many men have told me that chicks who play with fire are a definite turn-on. I, for one, can't get enough of it. Once I've got those tongs in hand, I'm not likely to give them up. Even my friends have come to expect that when they offer to help out around the grill, they'll assume basting duty at best. The tongs stay with me.

Then again, you might consider that it's even easier (and more fun!) to host a barbecue when you and your partner work together like the all-star team that you are. Amaze your friends with your collaborative skills in the party-throwing arena, and they will surely see that you two are destined to make beautiful barbecue sauce together forever more.

GRILL TO THRILL

For a hot time, call Williams-Sonoma. Ask for their grilling department and order off this list. Seeing my man agilely handling a full set of barbecue tools is about as hot as it gets for me.
– A grill brush for cleaning the grates
– A brush for basting
– A spatula with a wooden handle
– Heavy pot holders or mitts that come up to your elbows
– Skewers, ideally wooden and waterlogged, although metal will do
– Tongs, my favorite kind of gadget (not to be confused with thongs, my favorite kind of underwear)

DON'T GRILL TO KILL

Singed eyebrows and third-degree burns will sure take the festivity out of any gathering. Here are a few tips to ensure you remain a happy, healthy griller.
– Keep your barbecue clean. You will be terribly disappointed if your plans are foiled by a grill that needs to be soaked overnight or replaced completely.
– When you're not sure whether a piece of meat or chicken is done, cut into it before eating it. Better safe than dead.
– Don't spray cooking spray onto a lit grill.
– Don't take a walk when the food is on the fire.
– No more than one adult beverage before grilling.
– Don't wear moisturizer or suntan lotion if you're manning the grill. During one taping of *Hot Off the Grill*, I set my entire SPF 30-coated arm on fire! I was okay, but from then on, I scrubbed like a surgeon before going anywhere near that puppy.

The following are a few of my favorite grilling recipes. Perfectly seared, juicy, just-off-the-grill burgers are the ultimate barbecue fare, and for my nonbeef-eating friends, an irresistible quesadilla dripping with melted Brie and sweet slices of mango never makes them feel like they've been served second best. If you don't have a grill or you live somewhere very snowy, don't feel left out. All of these recipes are completely doable in a regular old kitchen.

Mango Brie Quesadillas with Pico de Gallo

This is a great summer recipe for when mangoes are in season and it's too hot to eat something heavy anyway. The quick preparation time betrays the amazing complexity of flavor—you'll find the creamy Brie, the sweet mango, and the piquant salsa mix it up like nobody's business.

16 (8- to 10-inch) flour tortillas
$\frac{1}{4}$ cup olive oil
Kosher salt
Freshly ground black pepper
4 large ripe mangoes
1 pound Brie
Pico de Gallo (see page 147) for garnish
1 bunch cilantro for garnish
Cilantro Crema (see recipe next page) for garnish
Chili oil for garnish

• Brush one side of each tortilla with olive oil and sprinkle with salt and pepper.
• Peel and cut the mangoes into long thin strips, about $\frac{1}{2}$ inch by 2 inches. Remove the rind from the Brie, and cut into similarly sized strips.
• Preheat a grill to medium-low heat. (These can also be cooked in a grill pan, a frying pan, or the oven: You want to achieve a crisp outside and a melted inside.)
• To assemble the quesadillas, sandwich the Brie and mango between 2 tortillas, oiled sides facing out. Grill for 2 minutes on each side, or until the outside is crisp and the filling is melted.
• Cut into quarters, and garnish with Pico de Gallo, cilantro leaves, Cilantro Crema, and a drizzle of chili oil.

SERVES ABOUT 15 / PREP TIME: 35 MINUTES / COOK TIME: ABOUT 10 MINUTES

Cilantro Crema

¾ cup sour cream
Juice of 1 lime
¾ cup loosely packed chopped chives (or scallion tops)
1 cup loosely packed cilantro leaves (about 1 bunch)
Pinch of kosher salt

• Combine the ingredients and puree in a blender until smooth. Put the mixture in a squeeze bottle, and use to garnish the quesadillas.

MAKES ABOUT ¾ CUP / PREP TIME: 10 MINUTES

The Burger to Cure All Ills

I am the last person in the world to dis a good Big Mac, but anyplace that serves thousands a day just can't put the same love and passion into their burgers that you can. Season the meat gently, grill for the exact amount of time, and garnish affectionately with fat slices of Vidalia onion and the ripest beefsteak tomato you can find. Dig in and any entertaining woes will magically dissipate. A great trick to perfect burgers: Don't handle the meat more than you need to. Find something else to do with your hands.

2 tablespoons (¼ stick) butter
½ white onion, diced
3 cloves garlic, minced
Dash oregano
Freshly ground black pepper
5 pounds lean ground sirloin
Kosher salt

• Preheat the grill to medium heat.
• Melt the butter in a small frying pan and sauté the onion and garlic until they are just about to achieve color. Remove from the heat and drain of butter.
• Add the onion, garlic, oregano, and pepper to the meat; form into 6-ounce patties.
• Grill until medium-rare for best results. Remove burgers from the heat and salt lightly.
NOTE: Number-one booty burger garnish—crisp bacon and melted blue cheese. (To melt the cheese quickly, be sure to close the grill.)

MAKES 10 TO 12 SERVINGS / PREP TIME: 15 MINUTES / COOK TIME: 10 MINUTES

Guacamole with Roasted Corn and Sour Cream

There is an ancient adage that he who makes the best guacamole has his choice of the women in the tribe. Okay, I made that up, but I'm always disproportionately impressed by amazing homemade guac. I like it made creamy with cool sour cream, crunchy with fresh kernels of roasted corn, and tangy with lots of fresh lime and a whole lot of garlic.

1 ear corn
1 teaspoon oil
5 large plum tomatoes, seeded and cut into ½-inch dice
3 tablespoons lime juice
6 large ripe avocados, peeled and cubed, 1 pit reserved
2 cloves garlic, minced
¼ teaspoon cayenne pepper
Kosher salt
Freshly ground black pepper
3 tablespoons sour cream

• Steam the corn on the cob for 2 minutes.
• Brush with oil, and slightly blacken the corn on a grill or in a grill pan.
• Cut the corn off the cob with a sharp knife.
• Put the tomatoes, lime juice, avocado cubes, garlic, and the seasonings in a medium bowl, and mash with a potato masher. Fold in the corn and the sour cream. Add the reserved avocado pit and cover with plastic wrap to help retain color. Serve with tortilla chips within one hour of preparation.

MAKES 6 CUPS / PREP TIME: 15 MINUTES / COOK TIME: 5 MINUTES

The Perfect Fries

Even though these thick hand-cut fries are easy to make, for weeks after your barbecue your guests will continue to discuss the fact that you actually made homemade fries. I like mine with a side of mayo that's been spiked with Tabasco, onion, and lime.

10 large Idaho potatoes
2 quarts vegetable oil
Kosher salt

• Hand-cut the potatoes into your favorite fry size, leaving the skins on, and put them in a bowl of ice water.
• Heat the oil to 330 degrees in a large, deep saucepan.
• Drain and dry the potatoes thoroughly.
• Using a basket, a metal spider, or a slotted spoon, lower the potatoes a bit at a time into

the hot oil. (Work in batches.) Have a plate with paper towels ready to absorb excess grease. Fry the potatoes until they just begin to color, about 10 minutes. Turn off the oil, remove the potatoes, and drain on paper towels. Set aside until cool.

• When you're ready to give the potatoes their second cooking, preheat the oven to 200 degrees, and reheat the oil to 375 degrees.

• Carefully put the potatoes back in the oil and cook for a few minutes, until brown and crispy. Drain on paper towels. Salt immediately, tossing the fries to coat them thoroughly. Place in the oven to keep warm until ready to serve.

MAKES ABOUT 10 SERVINGS / PREP TIME: 15 MINUTES / COOK TIME: 40 MINUTES

Boston Bibb Salad with Almonds, Oranges, and Parisian Mustard Vinaigrette

This salad is far more interesting than romaine and a bunch of tomatoes—no lettuce is as sensual as silky Boston Bibb, and the crunchy toasted almonds play against it perfectly. If you're short on time, you can substitute a can of drained mandarin oranges for the fresh ones and spend the extra time primping. Just be sure not to dress a tender lettuce like Boston Bibb in advance or it will get soggy. Serve the vinaigrette on the side and let your friends help themselves.

> 1 large head Boston Bibb lettuce
> 1 tablespoon butter
> $\frac{1}{2}$ cup slivered almonds
> 2 large navel oranges
> 2 tablespoons good-quality Dijon mustard
> 2 tablespoons red-wine vinegar
> Kosher salt
> Freshly ground black pepper
> 2 tablespoons extra-virgin olive oil

• Wash the lettuce thoroughly and dry gently.

• Melt the butter in a small frying pan over low heat, and gently toast the almonds for about 3 minutes, being careful not to brown either the nuts or the butter. Drain the almonds.

• Peel and section the oranges, and remove the membranes from the segments.

• Mix the mustard, vinegar, and a pinch each of salt and pepper in a blender, slowly drizzling in the oil until the dressing has a creamy consistency.

• Arrange the lettuce on plates, sprinkling with almonds and dotting with orange slices. Dress with the vinaigrette and serve immediately.

SERVES 2 / PREP TIME: 20 MINUTES

SOCIAL LUBRI-
CANTS. Certainly
not everyone is a big
fat lush. When
you're having a party,
it's important to
respect the imbibing
habits of your on-
the-wagon, pregnant,
or designated-driver
guests. If you're
serving Bloody
Marys, Piña Coladas,
or Pomegranate Mar-
garitas, offer to whip
up a virgin batch for
those who would
prefer theirs zero-
proof. Also, have
plenty of sodas and
fruit juices on hand,
and present them as
lovingly as if they
were mai tais. Your
alcohol-free friends
won't feel like pari-
ahs with a cranberry-
orange juice—club
soda concoction in
hand or a tall glass
of Red Zinger iced
tea garnished with a
twist of orange and
a bendy straw.
Remember, throwing
a brilliant party
entails considering
everyone's needs,
not just the ones who
make it easy for you.

Tinto de Verano con Limón (Summer Wine with Lemon)

I'm pretty sure *Tinto de Verano* is the Spanish expression for "let's get busy." I first tasted this easy, breezy sangria alternative during a steamy summer in Barrio Santa Cruz. It's lightly fizzy, slightly sweet, and a delightful complement to the strong Mediterranean flavors on the table.

1 (1.5-liter) magnum cheap but not skanky red wine
1 (12-ounce) can lemon-lime soda (preferably Fanta lemon or something that has the look of carbonated lemonade)
2 cups orange juice
$\frac{1}{8}$ cup lemon juice (about 1 small lemon)
$\frac{1}{8}$ cup brandy
$\frac{1}{8}$ cup Triple Sec
2 to 3 lemons, sliced into rounds
2 to 3 limes, sliced into rounds

• Combine all the liquid ingredients, and add the fruit. Serve over ice.

NOTE: If you prefer, the summer wine can be made the day before. Simply leave the sparkling soda out of the mixture, and add it just before serving. Other citrus fruits can be added for variations of taste and color.

MAKES ABOUT 15 SERVINGS (A LARGE PUNCH BOWL) / PREP TIME: 10 MINUTES

YOU CERTAINLY DON'T HAVE TO ADORE EVERY ONE OF YOUR PARTNER'S BUDDIES AND ADOPT THEM AS YOUR OWN, BUT YOU SHOULD AT LEAST KNOW THAT YOU'RE ABLE TO HANDLE THEM FOR A FEW HOURS AT A TIME. AND, OF COURSE, THEY YOU. BUT THE BEST REASON OF ALL TO ENTERTAIN FRIENDS: IT'S ESSENTIAL TO HAVE A LIFE OUTSIDE YOUR RELATIONSHIP. NOT EVERY ROMANTIC LIAISON LASTS FOREVER, BUT MANY FRIENDSHIPS DO. MAKE SURE YOU'RE GETTING A LITTLE PLATONIC ACTION ON THE SIDE AT ALL TIMES. SENDING OUT INVITATIONS IS A GOOD PLACE TO START.

14)

meet the parents: things to bring

Whether it's Sunday dinner at the parents' house or a three-day visit over a holiday weekend, ease your way into their lives with a great covered-dish recipe. Food not only can smooth the way to some great new relationships, it can put you both at ease in this, the most nerve-jangling of situations, the way little else can. It's the reason why I'd rather introduce my beau to my parents over dinner and not, say, big-game hunting.

Those stereotypes about the father who grills you like a CIA agent, the overprotective brother who wants to maim you, the evil mother who practices voodoo on a doll with your likeness—all true. Even so, meeting the folks is more than a torture test intended to weed out unworthy suitors; think of it as a joyous milestone, confirmation that you two are indeed an inextricable part of each other's lives.

WHO'S YOUR DADDY?

Committing to a relationship without meeting your significant other's parents is like standing on a golf course in a lightning storm with tin foil on your head—it's just dumb. A closer look at the gene pool gives you a world of insight into who you're getting in bed with, literally and figuratively. Sometimes the apple, as they say, does not fall far from the narcissistic, overbearing, chain-smoking tree.

I've encountered any number of in-law archetypes throughout my many years of dating. I've met Ozzie and Harriet version 2.0, who sat on the porch, plying me with lemonade and sugar cookies. I've dealt with the parents who loved my boyfriend's ex so much, they still invited her over on the holidays. I've dined with Stepford parents so devoid of personality that I could only imagine that their sexy son was adopted. There's been a single father who flirted with me, a single mother who flirted with me, and a crunchy couple who wanted to show me a photo of their son's childbirth (yes, the actual moment of birth) during dinner. I've even been so fortunate as to encounter several pairs of I-wouldn't-mind-if-they-were-my-parents parents.

Clearly all parents do not fit under the general heading "Parents" and so you should get a good sense of what subcategory they belong to previous to meeting them. I'm sure

Anything you decide to cook for them should be something you've made before successfully, so try out any new recipes on your honey first. The last thing you want to hear from your beau's mom is "Needs salt." Well, that and "You're almost as pretty as his last girlfriend!"

by now you and your partner have traded stories (horror and otherwise) about your respective folks, but how specific have you been? If your honey mentioned his Mom and Pop were a little old-fashioned, does that mean that they don't believe in premarital cohabitation, or that they don't believe in electricity? This is not the time for pulling punches or watering down the facts. If her dad's a raging boozer, better to find out now, before you offer to make margaritas.

No matter what kind of parents you're dealing with, food can be the great equalizer. Even your twice-divorced girlfriend and your church-deacon dad could find common ground over a bowl of fresh snap peas or a homemade artichoke dip. Small talk about food beats the heck out of almost any other topic in existence. Besides, it's hard to put your foot in your mouth when it's already full.

FOOD TO SOOTHE THE SAVAGE PARENTS

I don't recommend cooking an entire meal for the clan the first time you're slated to meet. Spending time in the kitchen fussing over a pot roast while your guests are there provides an all-too-convenient alternative to making conversation. Besides, it gives them the opportunity to look in your medicine cabinet. Avoid that trap altogether. If for some reason your partner's family is coming to your place, get to know each other over a few appetizers, then take everyone out to a restaurant. It's just safer that way. Believe me.

When you procure your first invitation to the folks' house (or you're taking your honey to meet your own folks), don't even think about showing up empty-handed. You might as well arrive with a safety pin through your nose and your parole officer on your arm. It doesn't matter if it's the first time you're meeting them or the fifty-first, your responsibility is to demonstrate what a fabulous, caring catch-of-all-catches your honey has deemed worthy of his or her affection. Bringing a great gourmet host/hostess gift is just one way of showing the 'rents what a sweetheart you are. Whether you're cracking open the cookbooks or raiding your favorite French patisserie, here are some tips to help you pick the right gourmet gift for the people who just might be paying for your wedding one day.

➤ **PICK WINE OVER HARD ALCOHOL.** A bottle of bourbon is something you bring to a bachelor party, not a dinner with the future in-laws. Whether or not they're big drinkers, a decent mid-priced bottle of wine shows you have class.

➤ **PLAY TO YOUR AUDIENCE.** If his or her parents come from the land of white bread and American cheese singles, stay away from anything with rare foreign ingredients in the recipe name. Pignoli tuiles might be your favorite holiday-time cookie, but save them for when the parents know you're not actually pretentious. On the other hand, if they're foodies themselves, better whip your own cream to top off that chocolate mousse. Reddi-wip will only make them pray for your relationship's speedy demise.

DINNER CONVERSATION STOPPERS

"I'M PRO–DEATH PENALTY, PASS THE STRING BEANS" IS NOT APPROPRIATE DINNER BANTER. THE FIRST TIME YOU MEET THE PARENTS, AVOID THE TRADITIONAL TABOO TOPICS—POLITICS, RELIGION, SEX, AND MONEY. ANY OTHER SUBJECTS THAT WILL INSPIRE DEBATE, ANIMOSITY, OR RAISED EYEBROWS MIGHT ALSO BE BETTER LEFT UNTIL LATER (I'M THINKING YOUR FIRST CHILD'S TENTH BIRTHDAY), INCLUDING THE FOLLOWING:

YOUR BAD CREDIT HISTORY

YOUR CRAZY PARENTS

YOUR COLLEGE DRUG EXPERIMENTATION

YOUR VISIT TO YOUR HONEY'S OTHER SET OF PARENTS

WHY THEY WON'T LET YOU SHARE A ROOM

HOW BAD THEIR DOG SMELLS

HOW THEY WON'T BE LIVING WITH YOU IN THEIR OLD AGE

SO THEY WON'T LET YOU SHARE A ROOM His parents know you went to Mexico together, and they can't truly expect that their full-grown son is a novice in the ways of the world, but in their home, you two are virgins. If you're spending the weekend and the parents put you in separate bedrooms, do not sneak into your baby's room in the middle of the night. It's rude, it's disrespectful, and, wait a minute . . . what about the laundry room in the basement?

➤ **BE AWARE OF ANY DIETARY CONCERNS.** Her lactose-intolerant stepmother will not appreciate a cheesecake, nor will his vegetarian sister be enamored of a meat-of-the-month selection.

➤ **DON'T TREAD IN ANYONE ELSE'S CULINARY TERRITORY.** The woman who brings a jar of homemade marinara the first time she meets her boyfriend's Sicilian mama is asking for trouble. Pick another region . . . any region . . . but stay away from Italy.

➤ **DON'T BRING SEX FOOD.** Oysters and caviar . . . bad idea. Anything that gives them the impression that you two know your way around the bedroom together is definitely not parent food.

There are plenty of benefits to putting your culinary skills to work for your partner's parents, the least of which are the conclusions they will be able to draw from your effort:

• You can read (a recipe, at least)
• You have money for food
• You will not starve their child
• You will not starve their grandchildren

So, if you're hoping to get four thumbs-up from Mom and Dad (or Mom and husband number 7, or Mom and life partner Carol), make the extra effort and scope out a great recipe for homemade preserves, pesto with basil from your garden, or a perfect dessert. Essentially, anything that fits into a Tupperware container or casserole dish will do. You just may peanut-butter-chocolate-chip brownie your way right into their hearts.

If your sweetie's family is from a different region than yours, give them a taste of your culinary heritage. If you hail from Georgia, bake your mom's famous peach pie. If you grew up in Vermont, concoct a dish made using real maple syrup. If you're from New-foundland, make something with seal. You could also learn about any particular interests the family has and use that to jog your creativity (and kiss some parental posterior in the process). If his dad's a master griller, a homemade barbecue sauce is not only incredibly thoughtful, it will certainly be put to good use. Suburban parents who grow their own veggies would adore your own herb-infused olive oil to dress freshly picked lettuces from their garden. Or, if her father spends every weekend of the winter ice fishing on a nearby lake, make a homemade marinade that would best complement the catch of the day.

You'll notice one consistent motif in each of these suggestions—none is designed to outshine someone else's cooking. Bringing a side dish, sauce, or dessert tells the chef of the house that you defer to his or her cooking prowess, and when that chef could become your mother-in-law one day, I can only say emphatically: Defer! Defer!

Here are a few special dishes from my recipe box that have become firm-and-fast parental favorites. They're also fabulous when you bring your lover to meet your own parents. I've found that nothing erases the passive-aggressive, I-give-your-relationship-a-month smile from your mom's face faster than a pot of homemade chili or a few dozen still-warm chocolate chip cookies. Especially when she finds out you two made them together.

Twice-Torched Sweet Potatoes

These sweet potatoes have thoroughly endeared me to my in-laws. They're creamy and comforting, made sweet with brown sugar, cinnamon, dark rum, and just a hint of nutmeg. When you're browning the marshmallow-top crust in the oven, be careful not to set them on fire (like I do almost every single Thanksgiving). Parents generally don't want their child dating someone who's burned their home to the ground.

5 pounds sweet potatoes (8 large)
8 tablespoons (1 stick) salted butter
$\frac{1}{4}$ cup heavy cream
2 ounces dark rum
$\frac{1}{4}$ cup firmly packed brown sugar
1 tablespoon cinnamon
Pinch nutmeg
Pinch kosher salt
Large bag marshmallows (buy an extra bag—or two—if you're a pyro like me)

• Bring salted water to a boil in a large pot. Meanwhile, peel and cut the potatoes into uniform $1\frac{1}{2}$ -inch pieces. When the water boils, add the sweet potatoes, and cook until a fork will easily go through them, about 30 minutes. Drain thoroughly.
• Preheat the oven to 400 degrees.
• Mash the potatoes until creamy and smooth. Add the butter, cream, rum, brown sugar, cinnamon, nutmeg, and salt. Mix with a hand mixer until incorporated.
• Place the potato mixture in a baking dish and top with marshmallows. Bake until the marshmallows just start to brown. Be careful: They catch on fire very easily. Let cool slightly, and serve.

SERVES ABOUT 8 TO 10 / PREP TIME: 15 MINUTES / COOK TIME: ABOUT 40 MINUTES

Creamy Mustard-Ale Bread Dip

This is not only a sensational dip to bring along to someone else's house, it's a great party recipe. Serve it in a hollowed-out loaf of crusty round bread and garnish with hard pretzels, crisp vegetables, or wedges of fresh bread. I guarantee someone will ask you for the recipe, then bring it back to your house a year later, passing it off as his own.

16 ounces cream cheese, softened
$\frac{1}{4}$ pound (1 stick) salted butter, softened
1 cup finely diced white onion
1 tablespoon dry mustard powder
About $\frac{1}{3}$ bottle dark ale
1 large round loaf dark rye, unsliced

• Combine the cream cheese and the butter in a large mixing bowl. (This is easier using an electric mixer.) Add the onion and the mustard powder, and stir until incorporated. Add the beer a bit at a time, taking care that the mixture doesn't become too wet.

• Slice the top off the bread and save it. Scoop out the inside of the bread, fill the bread with the dip, and return the lid to the top for presentation. Serve with any combination of rye bread, crackers, or veggies.

NOTE: For best results, make the dip the day before and refrigerate overnight to allow the flavor to grow. Assemble just before serving.

MAKES 6 CUPS / PREP TIME: 15 MINUTES

culinary gifts from the culinary-challenged

If whipping up a homemade lemon poppy seed loaf isn't your thing, you can still imply kitchen savvy with a smart gift. When I first met my honey's dad and his dad's wife, I brought them a pot of rosemary. Not only did they love it, every time I return for dinner I get to reap the rewards. Here are some ideas:

• A five-spice set
• A chip-and-dip platter
• Flavored mustards, exotic chutneys, or gourmet olive oil or vinegar
• A windowsill herb garden
• Cool cocktail napkins or great coasters

• A basket of unique hot sauces (for spice lovers only!)
• A proper teapot
• A potted plant or flower
• Hand-dipped candles

South of the Border Chili

Any schmuck can bring a salad to someone's house. Instead, opt for a pot of robust, spicy chili. Double the recipe if you've got a big family to feed. Double the cayenne if you've got an adventurous family to feed. And make sure that everyone at the table is a meat eater or skip the beef.

1 teaspoon olive oil
1 yellow onion, peeled and coarsely chopped
1 small red bell pepper, chopped
1 garlic clove, chopped
1 pound medium ground round beef
$\frac{1}{2}$ pound ground steak or lean ground sirloin
1 large (13-ounce) can stewed tomatoes, drained
1 (15-ounce) can red kidney beans, drained
$\frac{1}{4}$ teaspoon cayenne pepper
4 teaspoons New Mexico chili powder
2 teaspoons cumin
$\frac{1}{4}$ teaspoon dried oregano
1 bay leaf
1 ounce bittersweet or unsweetened chocolate, chopped
Kosher salt
Freshly ground black pepper

• Heat olive oil in a large, deep skillet. Sauté the onions, the red bell pepper, and the garlic without achieving color. Add the beef and gently brown. Drain off the renderings, and put them aside.

• Add the tomatoes, the beans, and all the dried seasonings.

• Simmer on low heat for 50 minutes, adding in the renderings to achieve desired consistency. Add the chocolate, cook 10 minutes more, and season with salt and pepper.

MAKES ABOUT 6 CUPS / PREP TIME: 20 MINUTES / COOK TIME: 1 HOUR

Classic Chocolate Chip Cookies

Even the most overprotective parents can't be suspicious of a suitor bearing fresh-baked chocolate chip cookies. Couples who bake cookies are happy couples, and this recipe is aces.

$1\frac{1}{2}$ cups unsifted flour
$\frac{1}{2}$ teaspoon baking soda
$\frac{1}{4}$ teaspoon salt
8 tablespoons butter (1 stick), softened
$\frac{1}{3}$ cup sugar
$\frac{1}{2}$ cup firmly packed brown sugar
1 teaspoon vanilla
1 large egg
8 ounces high-quality semisweet chocolate chips
$\frac{1}{2}$ cup chopped walnuts (optional)
$\frac{1}{4}$ cup raisins (optional)

• Preheat the oven to 375 degrees. Combine the flour, baking soda, and salt in a small bowl.

• Beat the butter, sugar, and brown sugar in a large bowl or mixer until creamy. Add the vanilla and egg, and beat a bit more, until blended. Slowly add in the flour mixture, and mix until incorporated. Stir in the chocolate chips and goodies of choice.

• Form the dough into teaspoon-size balls, and bake on a nonstick cookie sheet for 10 to 12 minutes, or until golden brown.

NOTE: Variations include white-chocolate chips or chunks and chopped macadamia nuts, or toffee chips and pecans. Or, for groovy dark-chocolate cookies, add 2 tablespoons of cocoa to the flour mixture, then lots of dark-chocolate chunks and sun-dried cherries.

MAKES $2\frac{1}{2}$ DOZEN (UNLESS YOU EAT TOO MUCH COOKIE DOUGH FROM THE BOWL) / PREP TIME: 15 MINUTES / COOK TIME: 10 TO 12 MINUTES

WHETHER YOU'RE PREPARING A LAVISH MEAL TO IMPRESS YOUR SWEETIE'S PARENTS OR SIMPLY MAKING A FAVORITE DESSERT, PREPARE IT WITH ALL THE LOVE IN THE WORLD. AFTER ALL, THEY DESERVE IT. NO MATTER HOW CRITICAL, UPTIGHT, EMBARRASSING, OR UTTERLY OUT OF THEIR GOURDS THEY MAY BE, THEY ARE STILL THE PEOPLE WHO GAVE BIRTH TO THE MOST INCREDIBLY PERFECT PERSON IN THE WORLD.

15)

he loves me,
he loves me not

From the cute kid next door who stomped on your sand castle and your heart at age six (Joey Gallelo, I'll never get over you!) to the hot Spanish teacher in seventh grade who for some unknown reason didn't return your affections, you have certainly suffered through the agony of romantic defeat in some fashion. And most likely it sent you scurrying for Hostess cupcakes. Food, of course, is no substitute for love, but when love leaves town, cream-filled crap definitely helps.

So, if you've been listening to Ray Charles's "Crying Time" over and over, thinking he had it better than you did, pay close attention to the advice—and the recipes—on the following pages. They can save you roughly $20,465 in psychotherapy.

No one is immune to heartbreak, although I hope someone develops a vaccine soon so I can buy stock in it.

LIFE SUCKS AND SO DOES SHE

Most people do not marry their junior-prom dates, move to the burbs, pump out a few puppies, and die together holding hands. If there's one Mr./Ms. Right for you, then inevitably there will be plenty of Mr./Ms. Wrongs. And whether you knew it all along or were surprised by the notion when your partner blurted out "It's not you, it's me" (or some other lame excuse) in the middle of a perfectly nice dinner (or so you thought), breaking up hurts like hell. It doesn't matter if you've been dating for a year or a minute; being dumped just plain sucks.

COULD BE WORSE: COULD BE IN THE PAPER

Poor Tom and Nicole, Julia and Benjamin, Elizabeth and Nicky/Michael/Mike/Eddie/ Richard/Richard/John/Larry. At least you can lick your wounds without worrying about 60-point tabloid headlines screaming [Your name here] TRADED IN FOR SEXY YOUNG THING! 40 LB. WEIGHT GAIN FOLLOWS.

Let's continue examining that half-full glass and consider all the benefits of being single again. Ladies: That cheap imitation Native American pottery that he brought you from the Phoenix airport gift shop and you kept on display for his benefit? *Hello, Goodwill?* Then there's the lacy thong that made foot-binding seem like a more reasonable fashion trend—back of the drawer for you, my wedgie-inducing friend. Gentlemen: Say hello to that Friday night pick-up game she always gave you a hard time about and adieu to 6 P.M. shaves. There will be no more girlie garbage to clutter up your otherwise manly bathroom. And can you say *lap dance?*

You may be losing a "we," but you're gaining an "I." The world's most celebrated couple of the year is going to be you and your big fat id. You don't have to explain why you didn't call/why you didn't return an e-mail/why you came home at 2 A.M. from a business dinner smelling like Jack and Coke. You don't have to justify Pop-Tarts for dinner. You don't have to conceal your forbidden devotion to *Facts of Life* reruns or pretend you don't read the wedding section of the paper first. You can be yourself at your absolute worst, and there's no one to tell you otherwise.

You've got your whole bed back, that top dresser drawer, and no one to finish the last ice cream bar in the freezer. At least until the real person you're supposed to spend your life with comes along. That's right . . . just keep repeating it until you believe it too.

GETTING OVER IT

As many times as you've gone through a breakup, you never get used to having your heart trampled like a German tourist in Pamplona during the running of the bulls. Fortunately there are techniques—and proven comfort foods—that will stave off a nagging desire to join the clergy.

I, for one, enjoy throwing myself headfirst into the estrogen ravine—scented candles, hot baths, the writing journal, the chocolate-covered Oreos. Immersing myself in a carnival of girliness somehow helps me to restore balance. (I'm not exactly sure what the male equivalent is—round-the-clock *SportsCenter* and a scratch-yourself marathon?) Music is also helpful. I've got an entire CD shelf full of what I call lamenting-chick music—you know, if a woman's private parts could sing, that's what it would sound like. I select a CD from that shelf—generally something of the Sarah McLachlan or k.d. lang ilk—curl up on the couch, and write bad poetry:

> *Little duck sauce packet*
> *Alone at the bottom of my refrigerator*
> *Poor, poor, lonely little duck sauce*
> *There is no egg roll for you.*
> *I am that duck sauce.*

I know, it's pathetic. But at least I'm not calling his house and hanging up thirty times a night.

It's healthy to cry, mope around, and feel sorry for yourself for a few days. Just don't stay in your flannel pajamas refusing to bathe for months on end. There's nothing like doing what feels good to help you . . . well, feel good. A few more tips to help you get back to your sexy self again:

➤ **TOSS HIS OR HER STUFF.** When you've quit smoking, you don't keep a pack around just in case. Likewise, toss your ex's stuff (in a bonfire?) or send it back. It's a very important step toward moving on, and, oh, so cathartic.

➤ **MAKE A LIST OF ALL THE THINGS THAT BOTHERED YOU ABOUT YOUR EX.** For example, you used to find it quirky and endearing that he used spray-hair-in-a-can, but now you realize it's just creepy. In fact, tell all your friends about it. That will make you feel really good!

➤ **PLAN ACTIVITIES.** A ski trip with friends, a day at a spa, or an overdue visit to Grandma will give you something to look forward to. Plus, now you have time to take a class. Study French cooking, Swahili, or, better yet, kickboxing, which I am convinced

BAD IDEA ALERT:
BOOTY CALLS Late one night, after six cosmos and an unfortunate run-in with "our song" on the radio, you might be inclined to call your ex-ex to help you get over the pain. Just remember that rebound sex (also known as the backslide) is a lot like eating a shopping cart full of Twinkies—fun at the time, nauseating in the morning. But in the end, whatever makes you happy is okay by me just as long as you're not hurting yourself or any small animals. Who knows—maybe a good, long, no-strings-attached make-out session is just what the cardiologist ordered.

was invented for the recently scorned. Be sure to find a gym where dating prospects outnumber you ten-to-one.

➤ **THROW YOURSELF INTO WORK.** It may be the last thing you want to do, but work gives you something to focus on besides your conviction that no one will ever call you "schmoopie" again.

➤ **VOLUNTEER.** Signing up for a shift at the local soup kitchen or a shelter for former child celebrities will make you realize that you really don't have it so bad after all.

➤ **SURROUND YOURSELF WITH GOOD FRIENDS.** Ask them to come to your house and cook for you. Go to the movies together. Shoot hoops together. Shoot tequila together. Just stay away from couples entering the Marathon of Lust phase—in your fragile state, third-wheel syndrome may lead to head-in-the-oven syndrome.

➤ **GO THERAPY SHOPPING.** Procure an Xbox or a digital camera. Buy new sheets, or, even better, a new mattress, and reclaim your bed. Yield to some completely insensible shoes and pay full price. The road to healing often starts with a good line of credit.

➤ **FLIRT LIKE THERE'S NO TOMORROW.** Allow your friends to drag you somewhere where there are plenty of available cuties, then make sure you get as much attention as possible. A returned flirtatious glance could be just the spark that reignites the fire in your new single self.

➤ **COOK FOR YOURSELF.** Muster up the energy, drag yourself into the kitchen, and make a raging first-date meal just for yourself. Who deserves your love, attention, and homemade fettuccine noodles more than you do? Not that ex of yours, that's for sure.

➤ **INDULGE IN GUILTY PLEASURES.** Listen to Styx and sing along so loudly that the neighbors call the cops. Play computer games until you develop eye strain. Get a massage every day for a week. Read the kinds of magazines you'd generally hide between the covers of *Newsweek*.

➤ **AND EAT!** Starving yourself will not help your psyche, but chocolate definitely will. It's a scientific fact.

BLUES FOR THE BLUES. I love the blues when I'm feeling melancholy. It reminds me that I'm not the first one to go through a bad case of heartache; some old guy from the Delta did it long before. Blues themes generally fall into one of the following categories (in case you're wondering why it's the official music of lonely-hearts clubs everywhere):

YOU SUCK

YOU CHEATED ON ME

YOU BROKE MY HEART

YOU LET ME DO THINGS FOR YOU BUT YOU WON'T SLEEP WITH ME

YOU'RE GOING TO LEAVE ME

YOU LEFT ME

YOU LEFT ME BUT YOU MIGHT COME BACK

YOU THINK I WON'T GET OVER YOU BUT I WILL

I'M GOING TO KILL MYSELF

I'M GOING TO KILL YOU

SOOTHE-THE-HEART COMFORT FOOD

Food and breakups go hand in hand. Let me rephrase that: Food *issues* and breakups go hand in hand. I know plenty of guys who walk around sporting a breakup spare tire a good six months after the split; however, I'm less worried about them than their counterparts, those otherwise healthy, Big Mac-loving Americans who suddenly can't eat a thing because they're sad. In my opinion, depriving your body of both regular sex and nutrition may be too much for you to bear at once. A better idea is to eat whatever you like. Calories? What are they? Chocolate will be considered a very important food group now. And carbs will become your best friend for a while, so get used to the idea.

My rule of thumb for breakup meals is the less you need to chew, the better. Pasta and potatoes are a given. Or pasta and potatoes and Stove Top stuffing. Or pasta and potatoes and Stove Top stuffing and Wonder bread. The closer it is to baby food, the more likely I'll be lying in bed with a plate of it on my unshaven legs. When I'm feeling down and out of it, all I want to do is dive into a box of mac and cheese that's intended to serve a family of seven, then wash it down with a big chocolate milkshake. If you're seriously at a low, just spoon the ice cream into your mouth, squirt in some chocolate syrup, take a swig of milk out of the carton, and swish. You'd be surprised at how good it makes you feel.

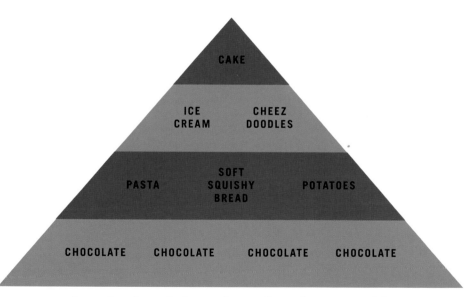

booty food breakup food pyramid

Stick to the breakup food pyramid and you'll be emotionally healthy in no time flat

English Shepherd's Pie

Whether you're pining over an ex or just having a rough day, shepherd's pie exhibits remarkable powers of emotional restoration. Although there are dozens of variations of this dish, I adore this combination of meat, onions, garlic, and potatoes mashed with butter and cream. It's heavy, warm, and fills the hole in my chest where my heart used to be. Besides, potato mashing can be very therapeutic.

6 large potatoes
8 tablespoons (1 stick) salted butter
½ large white onion, diced
1 clove garlic, passed through a garlic press
1 pound ground sirloin
½ cup water
Kosher salt
Freshly ground black pepper
⅓ cup half-and-half

- Preheat the oven to 375 degrees.
- Put salted water up to boil, peel the potatoes, and cut them into quarters. Boil until a fork pierces the potatoes easily: Be careful not to overcook.
- Melt 2 tablespoons of the butter. Add the onion and garlic, and cook on medium heat until brown. Add the meat, being sure to break it up completely. As you are browning the meat, add the water. Add salt and pepper, cover the pan to keep in the juices, and reduce to low heat.
- Drain the potatoes well; add 4 tablespoons of butter, the half-and-half, salt, and pepper, then whip until totally smooth and creamy, eliminating all lumps.
- Place the meat and its juices in a casserole dish. Top with mashed potatoes. Melt the remaining butter, brush on top of the potatoes, and bake for 20 minutes. Put the oven on broil, and broil for 2 minutes, until the top is slightly brown. Watch carefully so it doesn't burn!

SERVES 6 / PREP TIME: 30 MINUTES / COOK TIME: 40 MINUTES

White-Truffle Mac and Cheese

If you have the energy to make macaroni and cheese from scratch, this is a fairly simple recipe with most rewarding results. Sprinkle on the Parmesan and bread crumbs evenly and you'll have a nice, crackly crust on which to take out your aggressions. Douse the top with white truffle oil to remind yourself that life is good.

16 ounces (1 pound) elbow macaroni
3 tablespoons butter, plus 1 tablespoon to butter casserole
4 tablespoons all-purpose flour
4 cups milk
Kosher salt
Freshly ground black pepper
4½ cups (about 1 pound) grated sharp Cheddar
¼ cup grated Parmesan
¾ ounce white-truffle oil

- Preheat the oven to 350 degrees.
- Bring a large pot of salted water to a boil. Let the pasta cook until just al dente. Drain the pasta and set aside.
- Melt the butter in a large pot, and mix in the flour, stirring for 1 minute. Add milk a little at a time, stirring all the while, until the mixture just comes to a boil, about 10 minutes. Season with salt and pepper. Turn off the heat.
- Slowly stir in the 4 cups of Cheddar cheese, and half the Parmesan.
- Add the drained macaroni, mix well, then pour the mixture into a large buttered casserole dish.
- Bake the casserole for 25 minutes, then sprinkle the remaining Cheddar and Parmesan over the top and bake for 5 more minutes.
- Remove from the oven, and let cool a bit. Drizzle with the white-truffle oil and eat.

SERVES 8 / PREP TIME: ABOUT 15 MINUTES / COOK TIME: 30 MINUTES

NOTE: Different types of rice absorb liquid at different rates. If you prefer a creamier consistency, after the rice has been refrigerated you can thin it with the addition of warm milk or cream.

Rice Pudding

When I'm feeling down, there's no way I could eat crème brûlée or some fancy flan. Rice pudding is Grandma food, and Grandma food is comfort food. Top with a generous sprinkling of ground cinnamon and tons of raisins, then bring it to bed with a good trashy novel and a ton of Kleenex.

1 cup white rice
1¾ cups water
½ teaspoon salt
5 cups whole milk
½ cup sugar
¼ cup brown sugar
2 teaspoons tangerine zest
⅓ cup raisins
2 drops vanilla
1 teaspoon cinnamon

• Combine rice, water, and salt in a medium heavy-bottomed saucepan. Bring to a boil, turn down the heat, cover, and cook over low heat until the rice has absorbed all the water, about 10 minutes. Add the milk, sugar, brown sugar, and tangerine zest. Cook over medium heat for 30 minutes, stirring often. At this point the mixture should just about have a puddinglike consistency. Stir in the raisins, vanilla, and cinnamon. Place in a casserole dish and allow to cool. When cooled, cover with plastic wrap and refrigerate. Eat cold or—if you have an extraserious case of the blues—drizzle it with Hot Butterscotch Sauce (see page 118), if you can handle looking at the Marathon of Lust at this stage of the game.

MAKES ENOUGH FOR ONE WEEK OF MOURNING AN EX OR NURSING A HEARTBREAK OF ANY KIND. PREP TIME: 10 MINUTES / COOK TIME: 50 MINUTES

The Ultimate Chocolate Milk Shake

To this day, ice cream brings back memories of lying in a hospital bed newly tonsil-less and being told I could eat all the ice cream I wanted. If you've got a similar memory, let a rich, thick chocolate milk shake take you back to your happy place. Don't forget a bendy straw—bendy straws never fail to make people smile.

¾ cup whole milk
½ cup high-quality chocolate sauce
2 scoops chocolate ice cream
2 scoops vanilla ice cream

• Combine all the ingredients in a blender. Blend, being sure to keep a thick consistency. For best results, halve all the ingredients and blend, one shake at a time, in a milk-shake machine.

SERVES 2 / PREP TIME: 10 MINUTES

IN THE IMMORTAL WORDS OF A GREAT DISCO DIVA, NO MATTER HOW BADLY IT HURTS, YOU WILL SURVIVE. PICK YOURSELF UP, DUST YOURSELF OFF, AND HIT A COOKING CLASS FOR GOURMET SINGLES. WHEN YOU DO FIND THE ONE, IT WILL ONLY SERVE TO REMIND YOU THAT YOU HADN'T BEFORE.

MAKING UP IS HARD TO DO

If you linger in one of those "on and off" relationships, it's safe to suggest that it's not going to culminate in wallet-size photos of your eight children. But if you believe your breakup was only temporary ("So you mean I went through all that heartache and sixteen boxes of Stove Top stuffing for nothing?"), I applaud your efforts to repair the relationship.

If your ex shows up at your place at 2 A.M. begging for forgiveness, don't jump right into bed together. First you've got to make sure you're not the unwitting recipient of a booty call. Talk for a while. Figure out what went wrong and how you're both going to work to fix it. Some people are crazy about ex sex and are somehow convinced that they get one free pass with their former paramour. Uh . . . no. Holding off until the intentions are clear is the only infallible way to protect yourself from more pain. There's a fine line between forgiveness and masochism. So how do you know if you should give it another go?

➤ **YOU CAN HANDLE IT.** Absence does make the heart grow fonder. Of course, it makes some hearts brittle and black. Look into yours and decide whether you really can take this person back without compromising your self-esteem or your mental health.

➤ **YOU'RE THINKING WITH YOUR HEADS AND NOT OTHER ORGANS.** If you two have had some time apart and realize you're better off together, that's great. Just make sure that one of you isn't simply having a hard time finding another partner willing to spray whipped cream on his or her naughty bits.

➤ **YOUR ISSUES CAN BE RESOLVED.** Use this chart to help you determine whether your relationship hurdles are worth overcoming together, or if they're better off as chapters in your upcoming memoir:

FORGIVABLE SINS	UNFORGIVABLE SINS
He's scared of commitment	Monogamy is against his religion
She's emotional	She's emotionally void
He got you a vacuum for your birthday	He had a threesome on your birthday
She's a workaholic	She's a compulsive liar
He checks out other women	He checks out other guys
She's materialistic	She's a shoplifter
He's cheap	He's being arraigned for tax evasion
She's a big flirt	She's a big whore
He can't cook	He can't say "I love you"

KISS, MAKE UP, AND EAT

If I'm making up, breaking up, or considering the possibility of either, I stay far away from public eating establishments. I'm way too apt to make a scene, and it won't be a pretty one. If you and your partner are anything like I am, don't try to repair your relationship at a restaurant. Invite your still-sulking sweetie to your home for a drink or a light bite and keep the drama between the two of you. (The waiters at your local Szechuan restaurant will be grateful as well.)

If you're the chef for the night, don't knock yourself out. A six-course meal replete with after-dinner cordials is wrong on so many levels. First of all, it's too presumptuous—it will seem like you've prepared a "Woo-hoo! We're back together!" meal before you've actually agreed to reconcile. Second, it's impractical. When you two are having a heart-wrenching discussion about your (shaky?) future together, I'd be shocked if you could do much more than move your salad around on your plate. If my lover and I were supposed to spend the night talking out our problems and he served me cantaloupe soup, hand-pressed portobello-mushroom ravioli, and a pistachio-ginger flan, I would not be impressed. I would conclude that he spent the day preparing an insanely complex meal because even that was easier than spending the day reflecting about our problems. Making amends over dinner is fine; making amends with dinner is not. I'm not so easily fooled; if you want me back, I want to see some soul-searching. I want to feel some empathy. I want a lot of things from you, and cooking skills just don't make the list. Besides, you're better off keeping it bland. After a two-hour discussion about why your heart feels torn out, stomped on, then replaced upside down in your chest cavity, indigestion is a near-sure thing. Why encourage it with spicy bean burritos for two?

If you've got make-up-meal duty, stick with angel hair pasta in tomato-basil sauce, a lemon fettuccine, or just open up a couple of cans of alphabet soup. Perhaps the simplest comfort foods are more suitable—for both of you—than anything else.

Once you've kissed, made up, and sworn never to be more than twenty minutes apart ever again, then you can pull out the roasted duck with oyster sauce recipe, or make that

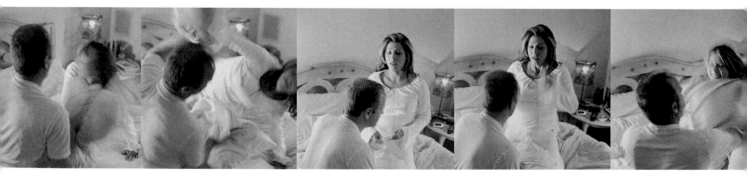

mako shark sashimi. A four-handed meal is a great way to ease back into happier times. Co-chefs have plenty of opportunities to say "I really care about you" without actually saying a word. It could be as simple as passing him a pot holder before he reaches for the hot saucepan, loosening the pickle jar that she always struggles with, or, with little fanfare, opening the bottle of wine you two were saving for a special occasion and sipping from it while you work. One of my favorite all-time postfight moments is when my honey and I are cooking together; he'll leave his cutting board for a moment, come up behind me, and wrap his arms around me while I stir the sauce. I know at that instant that no one will be sleeping on a sofa that night. The process of preparing food as a couple can indeed be as healing as the food itself.

If you really need to get yourself out of the doghouse, don't even think about asking for another set of hands in the kitchen. You've got to go it alone, and this meal better be a doozy. We're talking a dinner as romantic, thoughtful, and creative as your most romantic, thoughtful, creative meal to date. If you usually light a candle at dinner, light ten. The deeper the hole you've dug for yourself, the more all out you'll have to go in setting a mood and wowing your lover with dinner. Which, by the way, absolutely must include at least one of his or her favorite dishes. It doesn't matter if it's homemade paella or frozen fish sticks, there's no finer way to communicate that you're attuned to your partner's needs now, in the future, and in the very near future. I'm not kidding; if my honey goes all out on dinner for me, I can't help but think I'm in for a special treat later on when the lights are out.

You can also serve dishes that have special significance to the two of you. Make the pasta salad you ate on your first picnic together and picnic right on the bed. Re-create the meal you made the first night you said, "I love you." Re-create the meal you made the first night you said, "If we do it one more time, I think it's going to fall off." There's nothing like employing the smells, tastes, and sensory memories of food to hurl you back to happier and hornier days.

Baby Greens and Frisée with Bacon Vinaigrette and Warm Brie Croutons

This is a very special salad for very special occasions. The Brie croutons, still toasty from the oven, set off the sweet baby lettuces perfectly. Make sure the bacon is well browned and crisp, and serve while the dressing is still just a bit warm.

4 ounces baby oak-leaf lettuce or cut baby-lettuce mix
4 ounces frisée or curly endive (1 medium bunch)
½ pound pancetta (bacon); have butcher cut into ¼-inch slices
¼ pound Brie
1 small French baguette, sliced into ½-inch rounds
3 tablespoons red-wine vinegar
½ tablespoon smooth Dijon mustard
Kosher salt
Freshly ground black pepper
2 tablespoons extra-virgin olive oil

- Preheat the oven to 375 degrees.
- Wash and dry the lettuce thoroughly.
- Cut the pancetta into cubes. Cook the pancetta in a medium frying pan over high heat until it is almost crisp. Remove the bacon from the pan and drain on paper towels. Save the bacon-fat rendering in the frying pan.
- Cut the Brie into strips ¼-inch thick, and place the cheese on the baguette rounds. Bake for 5 minutes, or until the Brie is melted.
- Whisk together the red-wine vinegar, mustard, and a pinch of salt and pepper in a small bowl, then whisk in the olive oil and 1 tablespoon of the hot bacon fat.
- Add the pancetta and the vinaigrette to the frying pan, and heat for 1 minute.
- Place the lettuce in a large bowl, dress with the warm vinaigrette, and top with the Brie croutons. Serve and eat immediately.

SERVES 2 / PREP TIME: 20 MINUTES / COOK TIME: 15 MINUTES

Pork Tenderloin with Port-Infused Fig Sauce Served over Polenta

This dish is like an aphrodisiac orgy, best reserved for your one and only. The rich, savory port sauce coupled with fresh figs is unimaginably gratifying, making it the ultimate olive branch of the quarreling gastronome couple. Prepare it anytime you think your relationship (or your meal) needs a little pick-me-up.

20-ounce pork tenderloin
2 tablespoons chopped fresh sage, plus some whole leaves for garnish
⅛ cup olive oil
Kosher salt
Freshly ground black pepper
2 cups corn-grit polenta
5 cups water
1 cup chicken stock
3 tablespoons salted butter
1 cup shredded Parmesan
2 cups good-quality ruby port
8 ounces ripe black figs

• Place the pork, sage, olive oil, salt, and pepper in a dish. Cover, and refrigerate for at least 2 hours.

• Combine polenta, water, chicken stock, and a pinch of salt in a double boiler. Stir to incorporate. Cover, and cook for 2 hours on medium heat, checking the water frequently. After 2 hours, or when the liquid is absorbed and the polenta is soft, add butter and Parmesan cheese. Keep warm in the double boiler on low heat.

• Reduce the port by half in a medium saucepan over high heat.

• Peel and mash the figs, saving 2 for garnish. Add the mashed figs to the port syrup, and simmer on low heat for 10 minutes.

• Pan-roast the tenderloin in a large skillet over medium to high heat. Cook for about 15 minutes, or until the center of the pork is barely pink (145 degrees). Let the meat rest, then slice it into medallions.

• To assemble, spoon about a cup of polenta onto each plate, and top with pork medallions and sauce. Garnish with fig halves and sage leaves.

SERVES 2 / PREP TIME: 15 MINUTES / COOK TIME: ABOUT 2½ HOURS

Sautéed Spinach with Garlic

A simple sautéed spinach gets a kick with tangy garlic and a bit of lemon, making it a nice balance to the sweet port sauce in the entrée. Make sure to wash the spinach several times before preparing so that it's not inadvertently crunchy.

1 pound spinach
⅛ cup olive oil
3 cloves garlic, minced
Juice of ½ lemon
Kosher salt
Freshly ground black pepper
Splash water

- Wash the spinach thoroughly.
- Heat the oil in a large skillet over medium heat. Add the garlic, and cook until just before it achieves color. Add the spinach to the pan. Stir, and allow to wilt. Add the lemon juice, salt, pepper, and water, if necessary. Cover, and reduce heat. Cook until tender, about 3 minutes.

SERVES 2 / PREP TIME: 5 MINUTES / COOK TIME: 3 TO 5 MINUTES

Simply the Best Apple Pie

Who bakes a homey, all-American apple pie for his or her beloved in the 21st century? Only someone who's really in love. If you're not the apple-pie-baking type, it's an even cooler demonstration of your affection. Don't bother making the crust from scratch. Better to put your energy into devising your own original sins to keep you busy after dinner.

2 frozen piecrusts (like Orinoco)
6 large Granny Smith apples, peeled and cored
1¼ cups sugar
5 tablespoons flour
1 tablespoon cinnamon
¼ teaspoon nutmeg
Pinch kosher salt
3 tablespoons butter

- Preheat the oven to 425 degrees.
- Remove the piecrusts from the freezer so that they will be pliant when you're ready to use them. Take the top crust out of its tin, and set it aside. (If the crust breaks, roll it into a ball with your hands, then roll it out with a rolling pin.)
- Slice the apples about ½-inch thick, and place them in a medium bowl.
- Combine the sugar, flour, cinnamon, nutmeg, and salt in a larger bowl. Slowly start to incorporate the apples into the mixture with your hands. It will seem like you have too much filling—this is a good thing.
- Pour the apples into the bottom piecrust in the aluminum tin. It will be overflowing, so heap the apples toward the center. Sprinkle the remaining sugar mixture from the bowl evenly over the top of the apples. Dot with the butter, then add the top crust, gently stretching it to cover the pie. Using the back end of a fork, press the edges together to seal them. Make a few slits in the top crust to serve as air vents.
- Bake the pie at 425 degrees for 15 minutes, then lower the temperature to 400 degrees, and continue to bake for another 30 minutes, or until the crust is golden brown and the juices are bubbling. Serve warm with good vanilla ice cream.

MAKES 1 PIE / PREP TIME: 20 MINUTES / COOK TIME: 45 MINUTES

it's hard to say i'm sorry

Without a heartfelt apology on either (or both) of your parts, the relationship is going nowhere. Then again, working out your issues is going to be really hard if he or she won't even return your calls. Here are some wonderful door openers that say "my bad." Flowers are a given— particularly expensive ones—and, coupled with one of the following overly romantic gift ideas, you'll at least be assured a return phone call.

– A handwritten poem
– A heartfelt love letter with a photo of the two of you in happier days
– A limited-edition copy of his or her favorite classic novel
– A gourmet basket of the foods you first connected over
– A disposable camera with a note taped to it reading, "Let's Start Over"
– A $60,000 engagement ring from Harry Winston

THE BEST PART OF MAKING UP . . .

If the apologies seem heartfelt and the relationship now seems to be heading in a better direction, warn the neighbors—you are going to have mind-blowing, sheets on the floor, scream like a banshee, hot, sweaty make-up sex. You won't need candles or mood lighting in the bedroom. You might not even make it into the bedroom. It's been said that make-up sex is perhaps second only to conjugal-visit sex. I've even heard of couples who pick fights just to have make-up sex. They're disturbed, dysfunctional couples, but they exist nonetheless. Still, I understand. I tend to get as horny after a good fight as I do after a good soft-porn video. I can only imagine that there's some sort of scientific explanation. After an altercation, your hands are trembling, your adrenaline is pumping, and your heart is pounding like a native war drum—sound familiar? Perhaps your body tricks your brain into thinking that all that screaming and yelling was foreplay. Channeling all of your tension and anxiety about the relationship into a no-holds-barred sexual romp always seems to hit the spot. Women seem to be especially excited by this kind of activity, maybe because we're not accustomed to being physically aggressive in other aspects of our lives. An uninhibited bout between the sheets is one socially acceptable way for a gal to play out her WWF diva fantasies, dominate her partner, and show him who's boss now. And I've got a sneaking suspicion that he won't mind a bit. The best part of making up may be the make-up sex, but I am convinced that the best part of make-up sex isn't the sex at all. It's how you'll feel the next morning when you wake up together—energized, rejuvenated, clear-headed, and able to take on whatever challenges may arise. Together.

> THE BEST PART OF MAKING UP MAY BE THE MAKE-UP SEX, BUT I AM CONVINCED THAT THE BEST PART OF MAKE-UP SEX ISN'T THE SEX AT ALL. IT'S HOW YOU'LL FEEL THE NEXT MORNING WHEN YOU WAKE UP TOGETHER—ENERGIZED, REJUVENATED, CLEAR-HEADED, AND ABLE TO TAKE ON WHATEVER CHALLENGES MAY ARISE. TOGETHER.

phase IV

Commitment is the bomb. You know there will be at least one person in the world who will remember your birthday. You've got someone around to scratch that spot on your back that you can never quite get yourself. And there's always the prospect of breakfast in bed. You have a compliant partner for new sex positions, an instant audience for culinary experimentation, and an unconditional ally when the whole

CINA

world seems to be conspiring against you. It's hard to fathom why some people would trade all of this for a lifetime of meaningless one-nighters with strangers. Feeling loved is grand. Once you exchange vows, exchange rings, and exchange your one-butt kitchen for a two-butt kitchen with Italian marble countertops, you may be concerned that your picnicking experiences will be farther and farther apart, your steamy surprise dinners more rare, and your Nooky Hooky days and Reddi-wip nights numbered. But that's up to you. With a little effort and a whole lot of Booty Food, I guarantee you can keep your relationship Marathon of Lust hot for years to come.

CINA

16)

cooking with commitment: cozy foods and flannel pajamas

Where the early stage of a romance is like a frozen margarita with a beer chaser, commitment is the cognac—warm, inviting, and thoroughly intoxicating. The chase has ended, the heart is captured, and you two belong to each other.

Unfortunately, marital stereotypes lead us to believe that upon returning from the honeymoon, you will be greeted by a big sign on your front door welcoming you to the world of minivans and elastic-waisted pants. Nothing could be further from the truth. Marriage is fun! In fact, now I understand why those Hollywood types walk down the aisle six and seven times. Don't be afraid of this phase of your relationship; celebrate it. Revel in it. Make your home cozy. Make your food cozy.

Although there are some similarities, cozy foods are not the same as comfort foods. Comfort foods are a response to *my boss sucks/our relationship is in the toilet/the world is coming to an end*. They make you feel better when things are rough. Cozy foods, on the other hand, are the prelude to high-octane marital booty. They make you feel like purring. Think: big stacks of fluffy pancakes served in bed at 11 A.M., soul-stabilizing soups and stews, roasts and casseroles that slow-cook all day while you lie in your sweetie's arms on the overstuffed couch, listen to NPR, and take in the aromas from the kitchen.

Cozy foods say, "Ahh, I'm finally home." Not your parents' home, but the home you're creating together.

I PROMISE TO LOVE, CHERISH, AND NEVER SERVE MYSTERY MEAT

Whether you're a George who's found his Gracie, a Gracie who's found her George, or a George who's found his George, you may be ready to make your hot-monkey love official. Commemorate your colossal accomplishment with some pomp, some circumstance, and some worthy food and drink—heavy emphasis on worthy.

Wedding food is often indistinguishable from airplane food, with the notable exception that at weddings you're allowed to use real cutlery. Most wedding food is so nondescript you can't even remember it—sandy salads, Mojave-dry chicken, roast beef charred to the color of coal—and I've always been baffled as to why a couple would start their married lives together over the worst meal they've shared to date. Perhaps we need to start thinking of a wedding as the ultimate dinner party. Put your money into the food and drink instead of some of the more frivolous accoutrements (i.e. a $15,000 dress you'll only wear once) and you just

may end up with a Booty Food wedding. Who wouldn't love being invited to that?

The same way many people write their own wedding vows, incorporate your own personalities into the menu. Personal touches not only make the big night more meaningful for the two of you, it will make the event far more memorable, at least for those who go easy on the free champagne. You both work in foreign relations? Serve a multiethnic menu of all your favorite exotic foods. If you're avid gardeners, garnish all the dishes with edible flowers and send guests home with miniature pots of fresh herbs. Or, if a traditional matrimonial celebration doesn't feel like it suits the two of you at all, get creative and plan a party that's more your speed. Have a barbecue wedding, an afternoon-tea wedding, or get hitched on the beach, then celebrate with a big lobster feast. Or, do what my sweetie and I did and serve your friends and family "dinner by bite," a foodie term for a meal

made up of bite-sized entrées and appetizers. Don't be afraid to be daring or unexpected. Couples don't love the same way, and they certainly don't have to entertain the same way, particularly when wedded bliss is on the line. Of course this is coming from a woman who wore a red wedding gown, let her best friends pick their own dresses, and bucked custom entirely by walking down the aisle arm-in-arm with her beloved.

My wedding was a relatively small affair—eighty people—which allowed me to put my money where my guests' mouths were. We essentially threw an upscale cocktail party, and with what we saved on engraved place cards and a Cinderella carriage we were able to share all of our favorite foods with our closest family and friends. There were black and white truffle crème fraîche potato crisps, bite-sized entrées of lobster and lamb, a yummy raw bar, a chef customizing individual pasta plates, and an enormous cheese station (of course). Instead of offering a Viennese pastry extravaganza after our simple wedding cake, we served warm chocolate chip cookies and ice-cold shot glasses of milk. It was a way of saying good night to our guests in a fashion that truly reflected my honey and me—and our not-too-latent inner children. I can't wait for a big anniversary to come up so we can do it all over again.

There's only one teensy downside to serving fabulous food at your wedding—making the time to eat it. Anecdotal research suggests that 96 percent of all couples do not eat at their own weddings because they're either too stressed out, too busy flitting from table to table, or they somehow get stuck with chatty Aunt Eleanor between them and the buffet. The remaining 4 percent are just too drunk. Plan for these pitfalls in advance. Ask a trusted pal to pack you a goody basket for you to ravage when you get back to your room later that evening, comprised of all the dishes from that menu you worked your butt off to plan. Don't forget a chilled bottle of primo champagne, glasses optional.

With the fancy clothes back in the closet, the craziness behind you, and the love of your life by your side, this may end up being one of the greatest meals of your life.

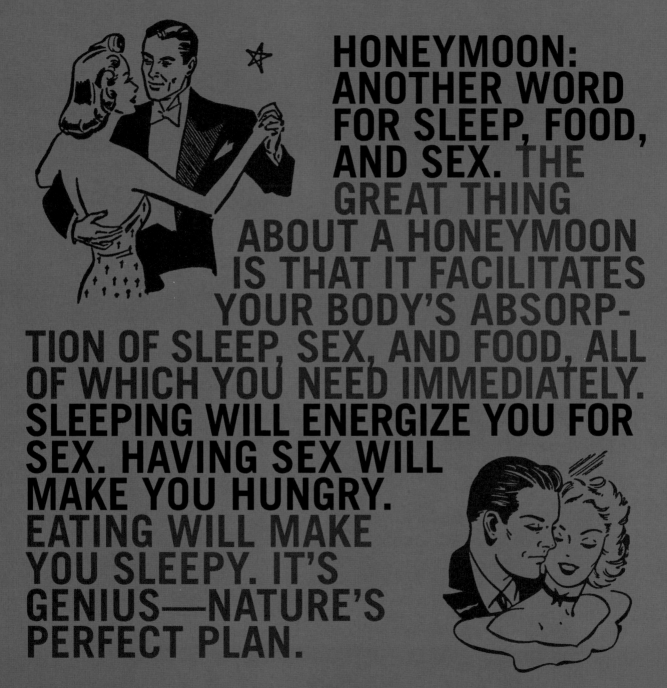

HONEYMOON: ANOTHER WORD FOR SLEEP, FOOD, AND SEX. THE GREAT THING ABOUT A HONEYMOON IS THAT IT FACILITATES YOUR BODY'S ABSORPTION OF SLEEP, SEX, AND FOOD, ALL OF WHICH YOU NEED IMMEDIATELY. SLEEPING WILL ENERGIZE YOU FOR SEX. HAVING SEX WILL MAKE YOU HUNGRY. EATING WILL MAKE YOU SLEEPY. IT'S GENIUS—NATURE'S PERFECT PLAN.

HAVING IT ALL

One of the perks of marriage (besides getting to buy the five-hundred-extra-sensitive condom pack at Costco) is that you can have it all. You've got access to both the sexual gymnastics and the cuddling. You can lose count of orgasms one night, and the next, lose track of time while you simply get cozy together. I know you're already an expert at the former, but how good are you at the latter?

Cozy is a sadly misunderstood word. Some people seem to equate it with *coma,* which is an entirely different concept. When you two are cozy, you're relaxed. You're at ease. You have awesome sex with your woolly socks on. When you're in a coma, it's best to stay away from sex altogether, or so I've been told. Cozy is not something you settle for when passion fades, it's something you aspire to. Just log onto one of those Internet dating sites and take a look at the personal ads. Easily 95 percent of them incorporate some version of "I like going out but I also like staying home with that special someone." And I'm not talking about creepy forty-five-year-old fast-food clerks who are looking for their first date. There are some hot prospects on the Web looking to get cozy! If I weren't already married . . .

I think people fear coziness because they somehow believe it portends the end of booty. Start reading the paper together at the breakfast table one morning and, *wham,* you're in a routine where you only do it once every other Tuesday. It's just not true. I recently found a survey from a condom manufacturer that determined married people have sex more frequently than singles. How cool is that? I only hope that they're doing it with their spouses.

If Nooky Hooky episodes are the yin of a relationship, Sunday mornings in flannel pajamas with the *Times* are the yang, both equally wonderful, both equally necessary. You can't expect to be Martha in the kitchen and Madonna (the slutty one) in the bedroom every day without breaking down completely. You need to take the time to enjoy the moments in between the carnal and culinary highs, which, by the way, are in no way lows. I adore lying on the couch with my head in my honey's lap while he watches the game. I love knowing that I look my worst in the morning and he's still there for me, stroking my hair while I read the paper, and often the snuggling is every bit as satisfying as our other activities. I'm aware that this all sounds unbelievably girlie (so sue me, I'm a girl), but I know my hubby really digs our quieter moments too. He would just never admit to it during *Monday Night Football* at Louie's house.

GRANNY UNDERWEAR: JUST SAY NO
Of course, getting cozy is definitely not the same as letting oneself go. Please understand the difference, or the depraved nights of "Let's do it on the fire escape" will start to wane before you know it.

COZY Not brushing your teeth before you make love in the morning
LETTING YOURSELF GO Not brushing your teeth at all

COZY Wearing your husband's pajama top to sleep
LETTING YOURSELF GO Wearing sweatpants to sleep

COZY Growing a vegetable garden
LETTING YOURSELF GO Growing leg hair

COZY The smell of cinnamon toast in the kitchen
LETTING YOURSELF GO The smell of your gym clothes in the bedroom

COZY Making love on a big, squishy couch
LETTING YOURSELF GO Becoming a couch potato

COZY Reading the paper at the table because you two don't need to talk
LETTING YOURSELF GO Reading the paper at the table because you've run out of things to talk about

COZY Weeping uncontrollably after an amazing orgasm
LETTING YOURSELF GO Rolling over after an amazing orgasm

Taking your spouse's undying affection for granted is not an ideal way to ensure you keep the fun flowing in the relationship. Your lawfully wedded husband may have promised to love and cherish you, but I sincerely doubt that he promised to love and cherish your granny underwear with the big yellow flowers and the elastic that's starting to separate from the cotton. Indeed, in response to the ever-growing divorce rate, I think there should be a national ban on giant cotton underwear altogether—for both sexes. I know things are getting rocky in my own relationship when those tight little CK briefs make only the rare appearance on my man. Big baggy knickers are a marital Berlin Wall, announcing, "You stay on your side of the bed and I'll stay on mine."

Married women wear thongs too. Or at least the ones in that survey who seem to be getting all the booty.

Cozy couples have cozy homes. Although, interestingly, the kitchen is one of the last rooms people think to make cozy. This doesn't mean replacing your linoleum floor with six-inch shag carpeting; it can be as easy as planting herbs on the windowsill above the sink or putting out a fresh vase of flowers every week. Cushion your kitchen chairs with plush, fuzzy pillows. Paint the walls a warm, inviting color. Install a set of speakers above the cabinets so you can move and groove while you slice and dice. Soon, mealtimes will start to feel far more fun than functional.

I know one couple who has a big, cushy couch in their kitchen. It's extremely cool. Granted, not everyone has a twenty-by-thirty-foot kitchen in which to set up a full-size sofa, but I love that they perceive their kitchen as a place for hanging out—and getting intimate when whatever is simmering on the stove inspires it.

COZY FOODS

I find couples' coziest foods are frequently family foods; perhaps a meal reflecting your cultural heritage that's been passed down to you from your great-great-great-grandfather, or simply a favorite recipe your mom swiped from an old Julia Child cookbook. These are the dishes that put you in a family state of mind, and sharing them can be a surprisingly intimate experience. Through food you are connecting to all those couples who came before you two, and somehow establishing your own place in the lineage. Of course no one likes to think of his own parents doing the nasty, but it's kind of cool to imagine your bootlegging great-granddaddy getting down with that so-called Vaudeville burlesque star. You can only hope that a century from now, your own descendants will be romanticizing you two in the same way.

Bringing your family recipes together is wonderfully homey. You whip up your dad's traditional Indonesian lamb recipe while your sexy wife simmers a pot of her grandmother's Greek chicken soup, and somehow all feels right with the world. But there's one thing that's even cooler than that: try adding your Indonesian spice mix to that Greek chicken soup and creating something entirely new, a dish uniquely sprung from the two of you. It's like giving birth to your epicurean offspring—"Awww, she's got her mommy's lemony base and her daddy's paprika." Experimentation, as you surely learned during the Marathon of Lust, is incredibly arousing and no less so in the kitchen. I guarantee that when you two bring a delicious new dish into the world, something that reflects a little bit of each of you, you will need to have a round of we're-married sex immediately—or after you've made quick work of your culinary creation. Cozy food and Booty Food are often one and the same.

As you can see from the following recipes, my sweetie and I like to play around in the kitchen. A lot. We now have a recipe repertoire that could keep us in cozy foods every meal for an entire month. Some of the results were accidental, some of them the product of a good deal of trial and error. But each of these dishes is the fruit of our collective culinary loins, and we happily share them with you.

Love means never having to say *TV dinner.*

BREAKFAST-IN-BED TIPS I pity those who think breakfast in bed is to be reserved for Mother's Day and bouts with the flu. It's both cozy and sexy—above the sheets you're indulging in omelets or chocolate chip pancakes, but below the sheets, your naked bottom serves as a reminder of the previous night's events (and perhaps a foreshadowing of those yet to come). Here's how to make your experience most delicious: While the omelet is setting or the bagels are toasting, bring out all the condiments you'll need (ketchup, cream, sugar, maple syrup). It stinks getting all snuggly in bed, then having to run back to the kitchen for the pepper mill. Put a little protein on that plate. Too many carbs and you'll crash, which doesn't bode well for after-breakfast activities—sexual or otherwise. If you want to keep the food out of the bed, serve everything on a breakfast tray that has legs that straddle your body and keep it upright. Pour coffee or tea into mugs, which are less likely to tip over than dainty little cups. For the same reason, serve juice in tumblers and not wineglasses. If you're treating your sweetie to breakfast in bed, don't let her get up to get anything herself. It's partly nurturing, partly sexy-dominant. Tailor the meal to her desires; if she loves movies, pop a favorite one into the bedroom VCR. If she does the Sunday crossword, bring it to her with a sharpened pencil (or a pen if she's a genius). Put on her favorite music, and don't forget a favorite flower in a bud vase on the tray. Details turn breakfast food into Booty Food.

Cozy Breakfast: Banana-Pecan-Chocolate-Chip Pancakes

My one and only brought his family recipe for waffles topped with sautéed bananas and crunchy pecans to the breakfast table. I contributed the philosophy that there is no bad day that starts with chocolate chip pancakes. The result is this glorious pancake recipe that can only be improved upon by serving it in bed.

2 tablespoons (¼ stick) salted butter
1 tablespoon brown sugar
2 ripe bananas, peeled and sliced
¾ cup all-purpose flour
¼ cup sugar
1 teaspoon baking powder
½ teaspoon baking soda
⅛ teaspoon salt
¾ cup milk
1 egg yolk
½ teaspoon vanilla
2 tablespoons (¼ stick) unsalted butter, melted
1 egg white, at room temperature
4 ounces toasted pecans, chopped
5 ounces high-quality semisweet chocolate chips

• Preheat the griddle.
• Melt the salted butter and brown sugar in a medium frying pan. Add the bananas and briefly cook on low heat. Remove the bananas from the heat and take them out of the sauce. Save the sauce for garnish.
• Whisk together the flour, sugar, baking powder, baking soda, and salt in a large bowl.
• Whisk together the milk, egg yolk, and vanilla in a separate bowl, and add this mixture to the dry ingredients. Mix well, then add the melted unsalted butter and mix again. Set aside.
• In a third bowl, beat the egg white until stiff (but not dry) peaks appear. Gently fold the egg white into the batter mixture. Fold in most of the pecan pieces, saving a few for garnish.
• Butter the griddle. Pour enough batter onto the hot griddle to form 6-inch pancakes. Drop some banana slices and chocolate chips into each pancake as you go, pushing them into the batter so they won't burn. (Save some banana slices and chips for garnish.) Cook the pancakes until golden brown on each side, flipping accordingly. Serve with real maple syrup and the brown-sugar sauce, and garnish with the reserved nuts, banana, and chocolate chips.

SERVES 2 / PREP TIME: 20 MINUTES / COOK TIME: ABOUT 15 MINUTES

Cozy Lunch: Scalloped Potatoes and St. Jean Cured Ham Pot

My grandma used to make me scalloped potatoes with leeks on snow days, and so it has always been the food that makes me feel most nurtured and loved. The food that has the same effect on my husband is his dad's Sunday supper roast ham. By putting them together, we created an easy, homey dish that practically demands throwing a log on the fire.

1 precooked ham (4 pounds), preferably St. Jean ham
½ cup brown sugar
1 can pineapple rings (drained, ½ cup juice reserved)
1 tablespoon butter, softened
2 pounds Idaho potatoes, peeled and very thinly sliced
1½ cups half-and-half
½ cup milk
8 ounces crème fraîche
1 teaspoon kosher salt
1 teaspoon freshly ground black pepper
Chives for garnish

FOR HAM:
- Preheat the oven to 350 degrees.
- Coat the ham with brown sugar and place in a small roasting pan. Top the ham with 2 or 3 pineapple slices and pour the pineapple juice around the ham. Bake for 40 minutes, or until the internal temperature reaches 130 degrees, basting occasionally. If you want your ham to have a smoky flavor, place loose black tea in a small oven-proof dish beside the ham while in the oven. When the ham is cool enough to handle, cut off a pound section, and cut it into rustic strips or chunks to use with the scalloped potatoes.

FOR SCALLOPED POTATOES:
- Preheat the oven to 350 degrees, and butter a medium-size casserole dish.
- Combine the potatoes, half-and-half, and the milk in a large saucepan. Bring to a gentle boil, and stir until the mixture begins to thicken, about 10 minutes. Lower the heat; add the crème fraîche and the ham, then season with salt and pepper. Stir to blend, and pour into the buttered casserole dish.
- Cover with foil and bake for about 40 minutes, then bake uncovered for an additional 10 minutes. Remove from the oven, and check that the potatoes are tender. Let the casserole sit, then serve garnished with chopped chives.

MAKES 8 SERVINGS / PREP TIME: 20 MINUTES / COOK TIME: 50 MINUTES TO 1 HOUR

Cozy Dinner: Grilled Lamb Chops with Shaved-Truffle Gnocchi

While my husband was growing up, his family made an amazing osso buco with a side of shaved-truffle risotto every Christmas and Easter. One night we prepared the dish on our own, substituting the veal with a succulent lamb-chop recipe that had been my great-grandfather's. We swapped the risotto for tender potato gnocchi, which is a little faster to make, and ended up with one of our favorite dishes in the world.

FOR LAMB CHOPS:
8 rib lamb chops (1 rack plus 1 extra chop), cut about 1 inch thick
¼ cup extra-virgin olive oil
Freshly ground black pepper
2 cloves garlic, minced
4 sprigs rosemary, 2 reserved for garnish

FOR GNOCCHI:
¼ cup red wine
8 ounces button mushrooms, sliced
12 ounces crème fraîche
1 ounce white-truffle oil
Kosher salt
1 pound fresh or frozen gnocchi
Freshly ground black pepper
1½ ounces black truffles, shaved

- Rub the lamb chops with 3 tablespoons of the olive oil, pepper, the garlic, and the leaves from 2 sprigs of rosemary. Cover and let sit for at least 1 hour, although overnight would be ideal.
- Bring a pot of salted water to a boil for the gnocchi, and preheat the broiler for the lamb chops.
- Meanwhile, put the red wine in a medium sauté pan over high heat, and reduce to a fine syrup. Drizzle in the remaining olive oil. Add the mushrooms, reduce the heat to low, and cook for 2 minutes. Add the crème fraîche and white-truffle oil, stir, turn off heat, and cover to keep warm.
- Season the lamp chops with salt, and broil them for about 4 minutes on each side. (I like them medium-rare.) They cook very quickly, so watch out. Remove the chops from the broiler.
- Boil the gnocchi until they rise to the top, then cook for about 1 minute. (Frozen may take longer; follow package directions.) Drain.
- Pour the sauce over the gnocchi, season with salt and pepper, and garnish with shaved black truffles. Garnish the lamb chops with the reserved rosemary, and serve.

SERVES 2 / PREP TIME: 15 MINUTES / COOK TIME: 15 TO 20 MINUTES

Cozy Dessert: Ginger Cake with Peaches and Maple Cream

The smell of gingerbread baking automatically says "home" to my honey. The smell of maple syrup does the same thing for me, Canuck that I am. This spicy, peachy, mapley dessert just begs to be eaten while snuggling under a hand-me-down afghan together on the comfiest couch in the house.

FOR MAPLE CREAM:

4-inch-piece ginger, skin on, smashed and cut into 4 pieces
1 cup water
¼ cup sugar
3 tablespoons dark rum
4 tablespoons maple syrup
16 ounces (1 pint) heavy cream, well chilled

• To make the syrup, combine the ginger, water, sugar, rum, and maple syrup in a saucepan, and cook over medium heat for 5 minutes. Lower the heat, and simmer for another 15 minutes. Strain the syrup, and chill completely before proceeding.

• Whip the cream in a metal bowl. Once it forms soft peaks, slowly whip in the cold syrup to taste. Refrigerate. (The whipped cream can be rewhipped a bit if necessary before serving the cake.)

FOR GINGER CAKE:

1 large egg, at room temperature
¼ cup maple syrup
¼ cup molasses
½ cup water, at room temperature
4 tablespoons (½ stick) unsalted butter, melted
½ cup peeled, minced ginger
¼ cup brown sugar
1½ cups all-purpose flour
1 teaspoon baking soda
Pinch salt
Cinnamon sugar (optional)

• Preheat the oven to 350 degrees.

• Combine the egg, syrup, molasses, water, and melted butter in a medium bowl. Then combine the ginger, brown sugar, flour, baking soda, and salt in a large bowl. Slowly add the wet mixture to the dry mixture, mixing until smooth.

• Grease a 9x5x3-inch loaf pan. Pour in the batter, and bake for 25 to 30 minutes, or until a toothpick inserted into the center comes out clean. Let cool, and sprinkle with cinnamon sugar if desired.

FOR PEACHES:

⅛ cup (1 ounce) orange liqueur, like Triple Sec
⅛ cup (1 ounce) apricot brandy
½ cup brown sugar
½ teaspoon lemon juice
Pinch nutmeg
Pinch cinnamon
5 fresh peaches or nectarines, peeled and cut into ¼-inch slices

• Combine all the ingredients, except the peaches, in a medium saucepan, stir, and simmer on low heat for 3 minutes. Add the fruit, and simmer for another 10 minutes. Remove from the heat and let sit until cool.

• To serve the cake, cut into ¼-inch slices. Arrange 2 slices on each plate, along with a dollop of maple cream, 6 or so peach slices, and a drizzle of peach syrup.

SHORTCUT: You can buy a cake or make one from a box. The lovingly homemade peaches and maple cream will more than compensate for your trip to Winn-Dixie.

MAKES ABOUT 10 SERVINGS / PREP TIME: ABOUT 50 MINUTES / COOK TIME: ABOUT 1 HOUR

AS ANY RELATIONSHIP PROGRESSES, THE SEX-SHOP HANDCUFFS WILL LOSE THEIR APPEAL AND OTHER PRIORITIES WILL TAKE PRECEDENT OVER PLAYING SAILOR BOY AND THE HOT DANCE-HALL GIRL. BUT COZINESS IS SOMETHING THAT CAN LAST FOREVER. WHETHER YOU'RE JUST BACK FROM YOUR HONEYMOON OR SHOPPING FOR A THIRTY-FIFTH WEDDING ANNIVERSARY GIFT, NEVER FORGET TO SNUGGLE UP FROM TIME TO TIME AND DIP INTO YOUR REPERTOIRE OF FAMILY RECIPES. INTIMACY CAN BE MORE DEEPLY FULFILLING THAN EVEN LUST. AND IF THAT SOUNDS LIKE GIRLIE DRIVEL TO YOU, IT'S ONLY BECAUSE YOU HAVEN'T EXPERIENCED IT YET.

17)

keeping it hot

I'm all for comfort foods. I'm vehemently against complacency foods. Boredom is a virus, and when it settles into your kitchen, you'll find it spreading to the other rooms of your house in no time.

If you want to keep things spicy in the relationship, maybe you need to turn up the fires in your recipes. No slight to Mexico, but chips and salsa are so ubiquitous these days, they're about as exotic as country-western music. Instead, expand your culinary repertoire to such hot spots as India, Morocco, Sri Lanka, Brazil, and the Caribbean, and I guarantee your relationship will heat up accordingly.

It's easy to fall into the salad-in-a-bag trap when you've been in a relationship a while. While I'm never one to malign quick-prep meals, pretorn leaves of iceberg lettuce are generally not going to put you in the mood for a little duka-duka. Nor will frozen dinners, canned fruit, or anything with the word *helper* in the name.

THE SPICE IS RIGHT

Whether you're two years or two decades into a relationship, you may start to feel . . . I don't want to call it a slump, but in the natural ebb and flow of a relationship, there's some serious ebbing happening. You're no less in love, but perhaps you're a bit less in lust? Here are a few signs that your relationship could use a little spicing up.

— The sexy lingerie has permanent creases in it from the back of the drawer.
— You've had an unopened bottle of champagne in the fridge for months.
— Your condoms are reaching their expiration date.
— You bring concealed weapons to bed: unshaved legs, super-sharp toenails, laser breath.
— No tongue trumps tongue three-to-one.
— Showering is a lonely business.
— The last voice you hear before falling asleep is Larry King's.
— You're saving the candles for company.
— You're saving the dessert toppings for dessert.
— Missionary position.

If more than a couple of these look familiar, I have three words for you: *exotic foods aisle.*

237

Feeding my man a crazy-hot vindaloo somehow makes me sweat every bit as much as he does. What is it about spicy food that gets me so turned on? I suppose it just conjures up all these erotic images: strong, brave matadors; crazy naked revelers in Rio; eager sailors on shore leave in Bangkok; sultry summer nights in Cuba with clothes sticking to bodies and bodies sticking to each other. *Oof.* But it's not just my one-track mind that makes the leap from spicy to steamy. There's physiological evidence that hot peppers lend themselves nicely to adult activities. Peppers actually trigger the release of endorphins, which make you feel *mmm-mmm good.* Spicy foods wake you up, get your heart racing, and increase blood flow to your entire body—and some parts more than others. Sounds to me like a gratifying scratch for that seven-year itch. Besides, when your lips are alive and tingling with hot-pepper heat, they're practically yearning for a long, wet, cooling kiss.

There are arguable parallels among the sexiest corners of the globe and the regions that serve the most amazingly spiced delicacies. Let's just say that the Queen Mum was not raised on spicy black beans and mojitos. India, the curry capital of the world, brought us (happily, gratefully) the *Kama Sutra* and Tantric sex. Thailand is the home of those infamous kinky sex shows. And Brazil is the land where anything goes—who else could have invented "the forbidden dance"? But I am most captivated by the customs of Morocco, where both booty and food come together on a regular basis.

Moroccans have truly got the art of the feast down. It's all about detail—a meal can take an entire week to prepare, and some chefs have been known to spend an entire day on a single pastry leaf. (Don't worry—I'm not implying that you should spend an entire day on a pastry leaf.) They also understand, perhaps better than anyone, the importance of appealing to all five senses. The music, the lighting, the colors on the table, are often no less important than the food itself. Smells in particular play a huge role in turning an ordinary meal into a gastro-erotic celebration: there's the aroma of pungent smoke wafting from the kitchen; allspice, cumin, and cinnamon rising up from the dishes; and rose incense filling the air. Even the lucky lovers at the table douse themselves in fragrant oils to help stimulate their appetites—and their appetites for each other. So after dinner, you can imagine that things can get a little crazy.

You would think that Moroccan men rule the roost, but actually the opposite is true. Women are believed to have a great deal of power, as they control both the food and the sex. Since Moroccan men (like all men) are hoping to get a lot of both, they absolutely revere their wives, making those seemingly docile women by day the dominant sex by night. I think I've even heard the term *worship* thrown around. How hot is that?

YOUR OWN LITTLE CASBAH

If you want all the carnal benefits of a faraway vacation with your mate, sometimes you simply have to take a trip to the world food market. I like the premise of mixing cuisine from the world's most exciting regions into one audacious meal. Try serving a Moroccan chicken with a side of spicy rice and beans instead of couscous. Make a curry-intensive Chicken Ramani, a Sri Lankan dish with a whole lot of attitude, and serve with a traditional Lebanese tabbouleh salad. Or, for a lighter but no less arousing dinner, serve a robust Brazilian black bean stew as your entrée and accompany with a side of raita and various Indian breads. The entrées are intended to bring the fire and the side dishes offer cooling relief, but mix and match regions as you please. The only rules are to have an adventurous palate and a sweet and icy beverage to quell the fire. Mojitos are my poison of choice, but a cosmo or even fresh lemonade would do the job just as well. Spread the sofa pillows on the floor and cover the coffee table with a brightly colored swath of fabric. You could even hire a belly dancer. Or do your own belly dancing—or lap dancing?

At the end, finish with a pot of steaming hot tea. Just make sure you pour it for your partner. In many parts of the globe, it's bad luck to allow someone to pour his or her own tea, and after tonight, you definitely want to get lucky.

THE WORLDLY SPICE RACK

If you're going to embark on a culinary tour of India, Morocco, and the Middle East, you will be well rewarded, but your first stop must be the spice rack. The following are some of the ingredients you may be lacking. By the way, if you can't handle blistering hot peppers at the top of the Scoville scale, the world of erotic exotic cuisine is not off limits to you. Few imported spices are actually spicy.

ALLSPICE: Often used in chutneys or desserts.

CARDAMOM: Available ground or in whole pods, this slightly lemony spice is one of the key flavors in curry powder.

CHILI: The base of all spicy cooking. There are green and red chilies, fresh, dried, or powdered.

CORIANDER: Fresh coriander leaves (also called cilantro or Chinese parsley) are often available in decent supermarkets.

GARAM MASALA: An Indian blend of spices also known as curry powder. There are also very specific curry blends, such as sambhar, madras, and muchi.

SAFFRON THREADS: Saffron is the dried stigma (a.k.a. woman-organ) of the crocus flower. It's used in rice dishes, stews and pasta to add delicious flavor and a golden color. Saffron costs about $100 an ounce—it's a good thing you never need more than a tablespoon or two at a time.

TURMERIC: Also called Indian saffron or yellow ginger, it's used in curries and Asian cooking.

TAMARIND: Actually a fruit, generally called for in chutneys and sauces.

None of these items is particularly hard to find. Any good gourmet store or ethnic-food market should carry them, or there's always the Internet, source of all things hot and spicy. If you don't have the particular ingredient a recipe calls for, move on to another recipe or beware the results. Spices are the heart of world cooking, and the right one can be the difference between a tikka masala and a marinara.

Chicken Ramani

A dear friend of mine comes from Sri Lanka, and she has a most enviable, passionate marriage. I credit her chicken, among other things. It's not only unbelievably mouth-watering but I can personally attest that it leads to heavy petting. Since the first Sri Lankans were nomads, the women probably served this to keep the men from wandering!

2 tablespoons olive oil
½ yellow onion, julienned
3 small green chilies, cut lengthwise into 3 pieces each
3 cloves garlic, minced
6 chicken thighs, cleaned and skins removed
¼ teaspoon turmeric
¾ teaspoon muchi curry powder
2 teaspoons madras curry powder
⅛ teaspoon sambhar curry powder
1½ teaspoons kosher salt
2 cardamom seeds
2 cloves
½ cinnamon stick
1½ teaspoons white vinegar
½ cup water
1 plum tomato, cut into semicircles

• Heat the oil over medium heat in a large saucepan. Add the onion, chilies, and garlic, stirring until you achieve slight color. Add the chicken thighs, and cook on medium heat for 10 minutes, stirring occasionally. Stir in the turmeric, all the curry powders, the salt, cardamom seeds, cloves, and cinnamon stick. Add the vinegar and cook for 2 minutes. Add the water and the tomato; cook for 20 more minutes. Reduce the flame to low and cook for 10 more minutes, or until the chicken is cooked through.

SERVES 2 / PREP TIME: 30 TO 45 MINUTES / COOK TIME: 45 MINUTES

exotic shortcuts

If you don't have time to scour ethnic markets for unusual spices and rare curries, you can still make terrific international entrées and sides. Just start with a mix from the international-foods aisle, which will generally provide all the arcane ingredients you need. Buy a box of rice pilaf and stir in sautéed wild mushrooms and slivered almonds. For a side dish less on the starchy side, start with a package of couscous, then add your own fresh onions, bell peppers, dates, and raisins. Or go for my favorite—tabbouleh. I buy the tabbouleh starter kit at the store, then add my own scallions, parsley, cucumber, radishes, mint leaves, and lemon juice. Although it may be blasphemy to my Lebanese grandfather, I'd rather put my effort into booty than into straining bulgur wheat through a sieve.

Cucumber Raita

In the lustier parts of the planet, both yogurt and cucumber are renowned for relieving scorched palates. This creamy raita recipe combines both. It's delicious alongside hot curries and basmati rice, and it could cool any kiss—in a good way.

3 cloves garlic, passed through a press, or smashed and finely minced with salt
1 small to medium cucumber, peeled, seeded, and finely chopped
3 tablespoons mint, finely chopped
16 ounces plain yogurt (natural is the best kind)
½ teaspoon kosher salt
¼ teaspoon ground black pepper

• Gently fold all the ingredients together. Serve alongside your favorite spicy treats with pita bread, flatbread, or nan. Eat when your mouth needs a quick break from chili powder.

MAKES ABOUT 3 CUPS / PREP TIME: 10 MINUTES

Thai Jasmine Rice with Toasted Cashews and Sun-Dried Cherries

This stunning side dish could be made with any fragrant rice, but I like jasmine rice from Thailand. Toss in a handful of tart, sweet dried cherries (cranberries would do too), add the nutty crunch of whole cashews, and you've got a delicious accompaniment to any highly spiced entrée. Be forewarned: Rice is a symbol of fertility on every continent on earth!

1¾ cups water
2 teaspoons salt
1 cup jasmine rice, rinsed
¾ cup cashew pieces
¾ cup dried cherries

• Preheat the oven to 350 degrees.
• Bring the water to a boil in a medium saucepan. Add the salt and rice. Cover the pan when the water returns to a boil, reduce the heat to the lowest setting, and cook for 15 to 20 minutes, until all the water is absorbed by the rice. Remove from the heat and fluff the rice using a fork.
• Put the cashews in a pan, and toast them in the oven for about 5 minutes, watching carefully. Gently fold the cashews and the cherries into the rice.

SERVES 2 / PREP TIME: 5 MINUTES / COOK TIME: ABOUT 25 MINUTES

Minty Cuban Mojitos

A combination of sugar and water has been said to soothe pepper-scalded puckers better than water alone, and apparently the Cubans agree. This refreshing mixture of rum, lime, sugar, and fresh crushed spearmint leaves was born in Havana's hottest nightclubs during the city's heyday. If you have a mortar and pestle to grind the mint, the result will be well worth the elbow grease.

    2 large bunches mint
    Juice of 6 limes
    3 tablespoons sugar
    Ice
    3 ounces white rum
    Splash soda water or seltzer
    1 lime, for garnish

• Grind up most of the mint with a mortar and pestle (or in a blender), saving some for garnish. To aid grinding, add a dash of lime juice and sugar, and make a paste. Transfer the paste to a cocktail shaker and add ice, rum, remainder of lime and sugar, and a splash of soda water. Shake, pour into glasses, garnish with mint and lime, and serve.

SERVES 2 / PREP TIME: 10 MINUTES

Marinated Pineapple with Rum and Toasted Coconut

After all those peppers and onions, this dessert is a refreshing finish and has a lot more allure than a boring fruit salad. It smells like Piña Coladas and tastes like the Caribbean. Serve with a dollop of coconut ice cream and transform your dining room into your very own adults-only resort.

1 small ripe pineapple
4 ounces light rum
$\frac{1}{8}$ cup sugar
4 ounces pineapple juice
$\frac{1}{4}$ cup brown sugar
Coconut ice cream (optional)
Toasted coconut shavings for garnish

• Cut the pineapple into quarters with a sharp knife, keeping the top leaves attached to each piece. Cut the core away from each section, and discard. Cut the pineapple flesh off the skin, saving the skin for presentation. Cut the pineapple into slices 1 inch thick, and place them in a large flat dish.

• Combine the rum, sugar, and pineapple juice in a small saucepan, and reduce the mixture down a bit into a syrup. Pour the syrup over the pineapple, cover, and refrigerate for at least 2 hours.

• Roll the pineapple in brown sugar, and begin cooking in batches on a hot grill pan. Grill for 3 minutes, or until the pineapple achieves color. Reserve syrup. Reassemble the slices back in the skins so that each quarter appears to be whole. Top with some of the remaining syrup. Garnish with toasted coconut and serve with coconut ice cream if desired.

SERVES 2 / PREP TIME: 15 MINUTES, PLUS $\frac{1}{2}$ HOUR TO MARINATE PINEAPPLE / COOK TIME: ABOUT 15 MINUTES

TRYING NEW THINGS IN THE KITCHEN IS EXCEEDINGLY SEXY, AND NOT HARD TO DO AT ALL. INJECT YOUR MEALS WITH MORE EXOTIC FLAVORS, AND I ASSURE YOU THAT YOUR LATE-NIGHT ACTIVITIES WILL SOON MATCH.

18)

everything old is new again

Food has the remarkable ability to take you back months or decades in time to those early phases of your courtship when nothing came between you and your libido.

If you want to feel the way you felt in the beginning of your relationship, there's only one way to do it: Go back to the beginning of your relationship. Re-create the flavors, the smells, the sweaty-palmed excitement of those early days. It's like clicking your ruby slippers three times and repeating "There's no place like home . . . in bed with you." Before you know it that's exactly where you'll be.

It just goes to prove once again that food is more than mere sustenance; it's the ultimate marital aid.

Ask even the most stoic, crusty dinosaur of a couple about the first meal they fell in love over and they get completely gooney. Their eyes glaze over, furtive grins creep across their faces, and you realize they've absolutely been transported back to that baked penne, that shared pupu platter, or that hot dog in the park by which all subsequent meals were judged.

THE PASSION PANTRY

We all have a sensory memory. Familiar smells, tastes, sounds, touches, and visuals are triggers that can allow you to access profound emotions instantly. Think about hearing a song you danced to at your senior prom—I'll bet even now it brings up all those amazing feelings of first love. Aromas can be even more powerful; to this day I can't smell a wet slicker without flashing back to rainy recesses in second grade and the cute boy I had my first crush on.

Food is an especially powerful sensory trigger because it flirts with all five of your senses at once. The sound of a spoon cracking the crust of a crème brûlée can be every bit as potent as its faint caramel aroma or the sensation of a cold spoon depositing a slippery mouthful onto your tongue. Together—triple threat. Suddenly you two are right back in the coatroom of that French bistro with your pants around your ankles. Certain foods can take you on a magic-carpet ride back to those feverish moments of infatuation, and once you're aware of the magnificent power that those dishes hold for you, you can tap into it and mine it for all it's worth.

LUSTY WINE PAIRINGS
Instead of deciding what goes best with steak, try a wine pairing with your wife. Determine which vintage best complements a navel, a nipple, the small of her back, or the strip of skin just behind her ear. Just please don't do it in a restaurant.

Picture an imaginary cabinet filled with all the nibbles and munchies and gourmet delights with which you two formed your most special memories—sort of a greatest-hits compilation. I like to think of it as the Passion Pantry. Go there from time to time, dig into your arsenal of Booty Foods and re-create the flavors and aromas that got you two here in the first place. By now you've got plenty to choose from: the foods that are aphrodisiacs to you, the foods you've shared on special occasions, and your first-date meal. Make use of the first two as often as possible. If you prepare an outrageous pork tenderloin with figs and port wine sauce (a veritable orgy of aphrodisia), your sweetie will get the idea that it's time to turn off must-see TV and put on the groovy sex music. Similarly, if you break out the linguine-with-clams recipe that reminds you of your summer on the Amalfi coast, soon you'll be frolicking through trouble spots as if your biggest problem were converting lira to dollars without a calculator.

Your first-date meal, however, is not something to be toyed with lightly. It is the glass one breaks in case of emergency, the once-in-a-very-long-while meal that you bring into play only when those frightening "Good God, what did I ever see in him?" thoughts start to creep into your brain.

My own marital regression therapy is the Bistecca alla Fiorentina meal from chapter 5. The Hope diamond wouldn't have the same restorative effect on me as that dinner. If my honey and I are having a rough week and I come home to him searing a fat T-bone on the grill while the homemade pasta boils and the smell of his tomato-butter sauce permeates the house, it's like a fresh start. Whatever (probably) stupid issue we've been squabbling over evaporates as we're somehow transported back to that night we were tipsy on Bordeaux and punch-drunk on each other. It's as if some nearly forgotten memory has been jarred, and at once I see him with all the hope and passion that I did before we had car payments and a mortgage to worry about. I get giggly, he gets sentimental, and sometimes we don't even make it to the meal. (We have, upon occasion, vulcanized a couple of prime four-inch steaks while swept up in a lusty whirlwind of Booty Food moments past.) Of course this dinner wouldn't have the same effect if we made it every Sunday night. If you're going to re-create your first-date experience, do save it for a time when you really need it.

There will be plenty of occasions when your spouse, and life in general, makes your blood boil, and your Booty Food repertoire can certainly be a remedy. However, you shouldn't wait until there are issues in your relationships to make a trip to the Passion Pantry. Employ its contents to celebrate a special occasion, to celebrate an ordinary occasion, to mark a milestone, or simply to keep the embers glowing. I know of one foodie couple who's been married twenty years. They finally saved up enough to build their dream kitchen, complete with marble countertops and a restaurant-quality stove. To christen their new kitchen, they went right to the Passion Pantry and made a pot of chili—*their* chili—the same recipe he made the first night he cooked for her nearly two decades before. I guarantee it's not the only way they christened the kitchen that evening.

IT'S THE LITTLE THINGS

BIG THINGS IN THE BEDROOM ARE OFTEN THE RESULT OF LITTLE THINGS DONE OUTSIDE THE BEDROOM. HERE ARE A FEW EASY WAYS TO KEEP YOUR LUST ALIVE:

PAT YOUR HONEY ON THE BOTTOM

GASP WITH PLEASURE THE NEXT TIME YOU CATCH A GLIMPSE OF YOUR HUSBAND NAKED

MOAN AT YOUR SPOUSE'S COOKING

THROW A FLIRTATIOUS GLANCE ACROSS THE THANKSGIVING TABLE WHEN THE IN-LAWS AREN'T LOOKING

LIGHT A FEW CANDLES, EVEN IF YOU'RE EATING NOTHING MORE GOURMET THAN SOUP FROM A CAN

HAVE A QUICKIE IN A COMPLETELY INAPPROPRIATE PLACE

GO TO A MOVIE AND LET YOUR HANDS WANDER

FLASH A BIT OF LINGERIE BEFORE DINNER, SOMETHING RED AND RACY THAT YOUR HUSBAND'S NEVER SEEN BEFORE

GIVE A MASSAGE BEFORE YOUR HONEY ASKS

LIPSTICK WORDS OF LOVE AND LUST ON THE BATHROOM MIRROR

The Passion Pantry is a powerful thing. But I'm sure that in your capable hands it will be used for good and not evil.

THE MARRIED QUICKIE

I read somewhere that the average lovemaking session is fifteen minutes long, although my personal and very disappointing record was a scant thirty seconds. Despite the fact that society spends a lot of energy extolling the virtues of length (of time) in the bedroom, quickies can be quite satisfying in their own right; a rapid romp isn't always the result of a premature ending. Just think back to the days when you first started getting biblical with your honey. A quickie wasn't disappointing. It was a hot way of expressing "I don't have a lot of time right now, but, good lord, I just cannot keep my hands off you."

Unfortunately, a married quickie is rarely as satisfying. It's often no more than a release of pressure, like some valve that you turn to let the steam out of the boiler so the house doesn't blow up. Not too sexy.

When couples don't have hours to get lost in lust, they need to find ways to get back to that whole *I want you, I need you, I have to have you now* kind of rushed experience. I know that even that's not easy. Coordinating schedules can be maddening, let alone that when you do find the time, the sound of your kids (if you have them) in the next room and an endless stream of cereal commercials doesn't exactly put you in the mood. But if you can somehow find thirty minutes—just thirty little minutes to yourselves—you have fifteen minutes apiece for both a quickie dinner and a bit of the old you-know-what. Try sending your kids to the store for milk, or out for an extended game of running bases. Skip your favorite sitcom just for a night. Or forget the car wash this week; I'm sure you can live with a dirty car for a few days if you've got a smile on your face to match.

The dinner part is easy. Here are two mouth-watering pasta dishes that you can prep and savor (well, quickly savor) in fewer than fifteen minutes. The carbs will give you the quick burst of energy you need for some express-lane love afterward. If even fifteen minutes seems too long, use fresh pasta. It will boil faster. Or if you'd really rather tip the eating/carnal-pleasure ratio in favor of the latter, prepare the pasta the night before. Both of these recipes are utterly delicious right out of the fridge.

Fresh Fettuccine with Mozzarella, Basil, and Heirloom Tomatoes

When you need to eat and run (or eat and . . . *ahem*), this pasta dish is perfection. It's so delightful, you might even be tempted to slow down and savor every melted mozzarella-drenched drop.

4 to 6 large heirloom tomatoes, or 8 to 10 plum tomatoes, seeded and cut into 1-inch cubes
4 cloves garlic, minced
5 large basil leaves, chiffonade or torn
5 tablespoons extra-virgin olive oil
½ teaspoon kosher salt
1½ teaspoons freshly ground black pepper
½ pound fresh mozzarella, cubed
1 pound fresh fettuccine

- Put salted water on to boil.
- Combine all the ingredients except the pasta in a large bowl, and toss together. Drop the pasta into the boiling water and watch carefully: Fresh pasta can cook quickly, so check after 2 minutes.
- Drain the fettuccine, add the mozzarella-tomato-basil mixture to the hot pasta, and fold together with tongs.

SERVES 2 / PREP TIME: 8 MINUTES / COOK TIME: 2 MINUTES

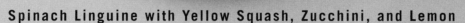

Spinach Linguine with Yellow Squash, Zucchini, and Lemon

When my honey sees four lemons sitting on the kitchen counter, he knows he'll be getting lucky (and this light, tangy pasta dish) before the night is through. This is one of my favorite quickie dishes, so easy to make that you won't feel guilty if you have to race through dinner.

    4 tablespoons extra-virgin olive oil, plus 1 teaspoon for the pasta water
    3 cloves garlic, minced
    1 medium zucchini, sliced into ¼-inch rounds
    1 medium yellow squash, sliced into ¼-inch rounds
    Kosher salt
    Freshly ground black pepper
    Juice of 4 lemons, strained
    1 pound fresh spinach linguine
    ¾ cup finely grated Parmesan (about ⅛ pound)

- Put oiled and salted water on to boil.
- Pour the rest of the olive oil into a large sauté pan over medium-high heat. Sauté the garlic until it just starts to get color, then add the zucchini and the squash to the pan, being sure to coat well with the garlic and oil. Add salt and pepper. Cook for about 3 minutes: Be careful not to overcook; you want the veggies to retain a bit of their crunch.
- Pour lemon juice over the mixture, and stir. Let the juice simmer and reduce for 2 minutes.
- While the lemon juice is reducing, drop the pasta into the boiling water. Fresh pasta cooks quickly, so check after 2 minutes. Drain the linguine when it's al dente.
- Pour the veggie sauce over the pasta, add the grated Parmesan, and fold together with tongs.

SERVES 2 / PREP TIME: 2 MINUTES / COOK TIME: 8 MINUTES

BACK TO SQUARE ONE, IN A GOOD WAY

The same way you can go to the Passion Pantry for the foods that got you two here in the first place, you can also return to your favorite Booty Food activities.

The picnic chapter of this book isn't just for third dates, and the Marathon of Lust phase isn't limited to hormonal twenty-five-year-olds with no responsibilities in the world besides satisfying their primal urges. In fact, getting it on in a bathtub full of pudding is probably a whole lot sexier with your wife than it was when she was just your girlfriend. How many men get to say, "That's my wife under all that chocolate, and, man, she's hot!" This is the stuff legendary marriages are made of.

If you're experiencing any kind of minipostmarital meltdown, just flip through these pages. They're overflowing with antidotes for some of the obstacles that may be coming between you and wedded bliss. An ounce of Booty Food prevention can indeed be worth sixteen pounds of marital self-help books.

➤ **PROBLEM: THE POSTHONEYMOON BLUES**
The thank-you notes have been sent, the bad gifts returned, and now it's just . . . life. The transition from fantasyland to reality can be like running into a brick wall. Nose first. At 479 miles an hour.

➤ **REMEDY: CHAPTER 17, KEEPING IT HOT** Make a meal of exotic foods from the spicier parts of the planet; hot peppers can literally pluck you from a tsunami of depression and make you feel rejuvenated. Make a spicy meal, put on some lambada music, and get forbidden on your honey's ass.

➤ **PROBLEM: THE EIGHTY-HOUR WORK WEEK** Some people hoard vacation days as if it were some badge of honor. These vacation anorexics may be rock stars at the office, but I guarantee you their relationships suffer.

➤ **REMEDY: CHAPTER 12, GET OUT OF THE HOUSE, FOR GOD'S SAKE** If you don't take the time to recharge, your honey is only privy to stressed-out, crispy, tired you, not happy, relaxed, sexy you, and that doesn't bode well for your future together. So grab your sweetie, open the atlas, and pick the spot that will most make you forget the tribulations of everyday life. Bali, Cancún, Pittsburgh—just pack a bag and go!

➤ **PROBLEM: ESCROW HELL** Purchasing a home together can comprise forty-five of the most stressful days of any marriage.

➤ **REMEDY: CHAPTER 6, WHEN COOKING'S THE LAST THING ON YOUR MIND** Do not contribute to the stress by taking on dinner duties as well. Bring home a big cheesy pizza or a truckload of Chinese, pair it with a great bottle of wine, and work off your real-estate tensions with a little adult gymnastics. Better make it two bottles if this is your first experience with escrow.

➤ **PROBLEM: THE NIGHTMARE OF RENOVATION**
The contractor is over budget, the electricity has gone out again, and the prospect of unclenching your teeth long enough to make out is far-fetched, to say the least.

➤ **REMEDY: CHAPTER 9, AFTERNOON DELIGHTS** You need to get out of the house immediately and leave it all behind, at least for several hours. Cut out of work, check yourselves into a nearby hotel, and jump right into bed. Don't even worry about disturbing the other guests. If they've ever tried to turn a bedroom alcove into a sauna, they'll give you a free pass.

➤ **PROBLEM: TRYING TO GET PREGNANT** Knowing you've got a window of twenty-four to forty-eight hours to get busy is the bane of booty—the pressure will definitely get to you and sex will be no fun at all, let alone reproductive.

➤ **REMEDY: CHAPTER 7, FOODS THAT PROMOTE ROUND TWO** Turn a baby-making marathon of work into a Marathon of Lust. Put aside those ovulation kits, just for a moment, and share a couple of cheesy omelets for stamina, or a dozen oysters which are reputed to raise the sperm count. You two will be fruitful and multiplying in no time.

➤ **PROBLEM: WISHING YOU HAD NEVER GOTTEN PREGNANT** The kids are making you nuts and, for whatever reason, boarding school isn't an option. Lust has taken a backseat to carpooling and PTA meetings.

➤ **REMEDY: CHAPTER 8, DESSERT'S ON ME** Ship the kids off to Grandma and Grandpa's for the night, and plan a hot home-cooked meal, with your sweetie as the dessert. That naughty girl who enjoyed having her belly turned into an ice-cream-sundae dish is not MIA, she's alive, well, and living inside your wife.

➤ **PROBLEM: EMPTY NEST SYNDROME** The kids are gone, off to college—or kindergarten. You're happy for them but a little sad for you. You're going to miss those rascals.

➤ **REMEDY: CHAPTER 10, SAY AHHH: GET-WELL FOOD** You need a big helping of TLC and a pot of chicken soup to nurse your soul back to health. When you get there, you'll be so excited to have the run of the house again, you'll start working your way through the other Marathon of Lust chapters too.

I'M NOT IMPLYING THAT TAKE-OUT FOOD CAN SAVE A MARRIAGE OR THAT A NIGHT OF CHEESE FONDUE CAN MAKE ALL THE PROBLEMS OF THE WORLD DISAPPEAR, BUT RECONNECTING WITH THE LOVE AND PASSION THAT BROUGHT YOU TWO TOGETHER IN THE FIRST PLACE WILL CERTAINLY HELP. BOOTY FOOD IS ABOUT MAKING YOUR RELATIONSHIP A PRIORITY. AND WHEN YOU KNOW YOU COME FIRST IN THE EYES OF THE ONE YOU LOVE, THERE'S NO BIGGER TURN-ON IN THE WORLD.

INDEX

JACQUI MALOUF is best known as cohost of the Food Network's Emmy-nominated *Hot off the Grill with Bobby Flay* and regularly appears on several Food Network programs, including Sara Moulton's *Cooking Live* and Emeril's *Viva Lagasse*. She also hosts Metro Channel's multiple Emmy Award–winning reality show, *Subway Q & A*, and Cablevision's Women's Entertainment's *Full Frontal Fashion*. An accomplished self-taught chef, Jacqui has lived and cooked all over the world. She currently lives with her husband in Los Angeles and New York.

LIZ GUMBINNER is a freelance writer living in New York. This is her first book.

THANKS, KUDOS, AND CREDITS
MY DEEPEST GRATITUDE GOES TO:

Jim McCauley for being a great partner, friend, and the sexy dude that inspired this book. Love to all my friends and family for their support, especially Mum (Katy) and Billy, Dad (David) and Ceci, and the whole Malouf/Morand/McCauley clan. To Kate, Janice, and Rachel for being my best friends. To the pals in NYC we miss so much. To Nita and the Group and Master Lu and the Center for much needed guidance. To Liz for being a wonderful collaborator. To Janis Donnaud for being a great agent and guide. To my passionate and fabulous publisher Karen Rinaldi, my tireless editor and friend Lara Carrigan, my ever-patient production manager Greg Villepique, and the rest of the Bloomsbury staff: Sara, Colin, Alan, Amanda, Alona, as well as the whole sales, marketing, and press team. To Jen for checking and rechecking. To Julie for checking and rechecking. To the world's best designer, Elizabeth Van Itallie. To Ronnda Hamilton and her assistant Christine for the awesome food styling. To Alayne Berman and to her assistants Mike, Nan, and Eleanor for making recipe testing such a joy. To Bill and Jason for graciously letting us shoot at their house. To Dan and Wendy from The Village Gourmet in L.A. and À la Vie for letting us use dishes and props and gourmet goodies. To Mary Pat for being the go-to woman on all things production: you rock, woman! To Phil and everyone at the Chateau Marmont (the sexiest hotel ever) for letting us shoot there. To Nadine Johnson and company for setting it up. To Ben and his assistant Simon for the rockin' photos. To Jason for driving the getaway car. To Alan Kaufman, legal genius. To the Dutch (Sirene). To Ciro and the gang at Murray's Cheese Shop, Frank and the guys at Ottomanelli's, and the Haley's Comet fish guys at Fulton Street Fish Market. To my friends and loved ones who appear in the book: Rachel, Kimberly, Tamara, Julie, Joe, Lori, Jamie, MP, Moo Shoo Pork #45, and Puddin'. To Naissance on Melrose for the clothes. To Carla and Vanessa for the hair. To Adam and Tonya for the makeup. To Tina for the hands and feet. To the *Hot off the Grill* team past and present for putting me on the map. Love to the Food Network fans for being so loyal and encouraging. —JM

Professional thanks to Bill Tsapalas, Nate Gerloff, and David Angelo. Personal thanks to Paul and Amy's chicken satay, Jeff and Maggie's Pork Wellington, and Chris and Nancy's Dead Squirrel Soup. —LG

Jacqui and Liz would like to thank all the boys they have loved and cooked for before (a husband or two, three live-ins, numerous boyfriends, and an undisclosed number of one-night stands).